Crisis of the Strauss Divided

Crisis of the Strauss Divided

Essays on Leo Strauss and Straussianism, East and West

Harry V. Jaffa
With Thomas L. Pangle, John A. Wettergreen, Robert P. Kraynak, Michael P. Zuckert, and Leo Strauss

ROWMAN & LITTLEFIELD PUBLISHERS, INC.
Lanham • Boulder • New York • Toronto • Plymouth, UK

Published by Rowman & Littlefield Publishers, Inc.
A wholly owned subsidiary of The Rowman & Littlefield Publishing Group, Inc.
4501 Forbes Boulevard, Suite 200, Lanham, Maryland 20706
www.rowman.com

10 Thornbury Road, Plymouth PL6 7PP, United Kingdom

British Library Cataloguing in Publication Information Available

Library of Congress Cataloging-in-Publication Data

Jaffa, Harry V.
Crisis of the Strauss divided : essays on Leo Strauss and Straussianiasm, East and West / Harry V. Jaffa.
p. cm.
ISBN 978-1-4422-1711-9 (cloth : alk. paper) -- ISBN 978-1-4422-1713-3 (electronic)
1. Strauss, Leo--Political and social views. I. Title.
JC251.S8J34 2012
320.01'1--dc23
2012013616

™ The paper used in this publication meets the minimum requirements of American National Standard for Information Sciences Permanence of Paper for Printed Library Materials, ANSI/NISO Z39.48-1992.

Printed in the United States of America

For Marjorie
The girl in the canoe
"I took one look at you,
That's all I had to do,
And my heart stood still."
Forever

Table of Contents

Foreword

> We have no higher duty, and no more pressing duty, than to remind ourselves and our students, of political greatness, human greatness, of the peaks of human excellence. We are supposed to train ourselves and others in seeing things as they are, and this means above all in seeing their greatness and their misery, their excellence and their vileness, their nobility and their triumphs, and therefore never to mistake mediocrity, however brilliant, for true greatness.
>
> —Leo Strauss, eulogy of Winston Churchill, January 25, 1965

Harry Jaffa has written and said many beautiful things in a long lifetime of scholarship and teaching. Among the most beautiful have been his expressions of reverence and gratitude for his teacher, Leo Strauss. He credits Strauss with giving him a gift dearer than life itself. Strauss taught him what to do with his life—he brought Jaffa to reason. When the young Jaffa's mind, unbeknownst to itself, was in the grips of the historicism and relativism that remain the conventional wisdom of our time, Strauss's teaching "struck off [his] shackles," turned him from his illusions, and dragged him up from the cave of nihilism to the light of natural right.

Jaffa's reverence for his teacher is made possible by the greater reverence his teacher taught him to have for truth. In the service of this greater reverence, Jaffa has spent a fair portion of his life arguing with those intellectually closest to him—not least among them, himself. A friend recently gave me a copy of *Crisis of the House Divided*, on the cover page of which Jaffa had written in pencil half a century ago, "For Willmoore Kendall who knows that amicus quidem Socrates amicior veritas." Jaffa used to argue to the knife with Kendall about the character of the American founding and the significance of Abraham Lincoln, late into the night on long distance telephone from Claremont to Dallas. When he later disagreed with himself on these questions, as he did most notably in his two great works—*Crisis of the House Divided* and *A New Birth of Freedom*—he might be forgiven for thinking the pursuit of truth had brought him up against an even more formidable opponent. It is that wide ranging pursuit that gave rise to the disputations collected in this volume.

One of the common criticisms of Jaffa is that he takes politics and morality more seriously than philosophic minds would do; that he shows a regard for America in particular that no philosophic mind would show for any earthly regime; that he shows more regard for America than

Strauss ever did or more than Strauss's thought could ever justify. If I understand Jaffa's response to such criticisms, it is, in part, that these critics fail to understand political philosophy because they have lost sight of the "experience that is antecedent to books." They do not pay sufficient attention to the natural prephilosophic world of political life and the real questions raised there and always abiding there, which make political philosophy necessary and possible. Because of this, they fail to understand the relationship between political philosophy and statesmanship—between natural right and political right. He argues that admiration of the good and detestation of evil are grounded in nature and are inherently disinterested, that the moral and political phenomena are the "theoretical, no less than the practical, ground of philosophic wisdom." Jaffa admonishes these critics, then, in the name of politics and morality, but as he would say, mainly and ultimately in the interest of philosophy itself. It is his duty, he thinks, to try to teach philosophers—or those who think of themselves as serving the cause of philosophy—to act responsibly. In doing this, he understands himself to be defending political philosophy, Western civilization, political freedom, America, and the legacy of Leo Strauss.

Strauss was concerned with "the crisis of our time, the crisis of the West," as he put it in *The City and Man*. Jaffa made the judgment that the decisive crisis of the West was the crisis of America, the Crisis of the House Divided. At the heart of each crisis was the repudiation of natural right. Strauss spoke of the loss of the sense of purpose, the loss of confidence in the West. Jaffa wondered about the loss of confidence in America, whose essential principle is that "Almighty God hath created the mind free." His life and the life of his teacher taken together are great monuments to the freedom of the mind. The essays collected here compellingly express that freedom and the purpose of that freedom—which is to be determined by the truth. Harry Jaffa's students have for many years been fondly calling him The Old Man. He has by now richly earned the moniker. Let The Old Man speak for himself, as he does in the stirring, thought-provoking exchanges gathered in these pages.

Christopher Flannery

Preface

What follows is the introductory chapter to a collection of essays entitled *Crisis of the Strauss Divided: Essays on Leo Strauss and Straussianism, East and West*.

The essays do not form chapters in a unified treatise or book. They span almost forty years, and are presented chronologically, each representing an insight or point of view that seemed important at the time. Whatever "Leo Strauss for the Ages" the reader may distill from these pages will be his or her responsibility.

ONE

Straussian Geography

A Memoir and Commentary

I

Professors Catherine and Michael Zuckert, in a remarkable example of connubial collaboration, have coauthored a remarkable book, entitled *The Truth About Leo Strauss: Political Philosophy and American Democracy*. This title would have been misleading, if they had said "the whole truth about Leo Strauss" which no one is likely to possess in our lifetime, if ever, but they have undoubtedly made a major contribution to the pursuit of that truth. The sudden and explosive notoriety of this little known political science professor, more than thirty years after his death, is an extraordinary phenomenon. It is perhaps even more striking to me than to the Zuckerts. They knew him as graduate students at the University of Chicago, where he enjoyed the eminence of a major chair at a major university. At the Graduate Faculty of Political and Social Science of the New School for Social Research (to give it its full name) he was a little known figure in a little known institution. The Graduate Faculty had been added in the thirties to the original New School, which had been founded in the twenties by some of the leading lights of the Progressive era as a progressive enterprise in adult education. The Graduate Faculty had been originally called the University in Exile, to provide a haven for distinguished scholars who were refugees from Hitler's Europe. Prestigious or not, that faculty in the forties, may have been, for a decade or more, the greatest faculty of its kind ever assembled under one roof, courtesy of Adolf Hitler. But it received little or no notice in the world of the elite universities. In the finest act of his glorious but ill-starred career, Robert Hutchins snatched Strauss out of obscurity and brought him to Chicago. In time, Strauss became the Robert M. Hutchins Distinguished Service Professor. I doubt that I myself would have had an academic career had Strauss remained where I had found him. He wrote to me in the summer of 1948, when I was visiting at my wife's family farm in Missouri, that he had been offered the position at Chicago. He wrote that he would have made it a condition of his acceptance that they find a position for me, who then had none. But he was sure that it would be a simple matter once he was there. And so, when he made his courtesy visit to Hutchins, and Hutchins made his courtesy request, many doors were opened to me. David Riesman, who was then at the height of his fame as the author of *The Lonely Crowd* came to interview me in our New York apartment, and I was flown to Chicago for further interviews. I was offered a choice between the College and the Basic Program of Liberal Education for Adults, in the downtown campus. I chose the latter, as it offered me a greater opportunity for my own work. My dissertation—on Thomas Aquinas's *Commentary on the Nicomachean Ethics*—was accepted by the University of Chicago Press in 1950 when it arrived there, with Strauss's commendation. In 1951 I accepted a tenure track appointment at Ohio State University, one that would never have been offered to me had Strauss remained in New York. But I can never forget his generosity in 1948, in linking his career with mine, when my prospects were at their bleakest.

In 1939–1940 I had been a graduate student in Political Science at Yale (where I had been an undergraduate major in English). As far as the Socratic tradition was concerned, Yale was a land of dead souls. I could have stayed there in a mindless stupor, and earned a doctorate with all of Yale's prestige. All a graduate student needed to pass the exam in theory was to memorize passages in Sabine's *History of Political Theory,* a book which announced in its preface (inaccurately) that Hume's discovery of the fact-value distinction had made all previous political theory obsolete. And the fact-value distinction had pronounced reason (i.e., political philosophy) impotent to determine all questions of value! (See chapter 2 of *Natural Right and History*.) A course in political philosophy was like a tour through a wax work museum. The figures may have been brilliant, but they were all dead. Hence there was literally no reason, other than the unburied presences, to study political philosophy. The foregoing were received opinions in pre–World War II political science, as unchallengeable as the doctrine of the Trinity was presumed to be in thirteenth-century Paris. While at that time I had no intellectual equipment to challenge the reigning assumptions, I had an instinct that told me that a career lived under their authority would not be a life worth living.

II

I would not like to leave the impression that this judgment of the graduate program in political science applied to my Yale education altogether. As an undergraduate English major I read nothing but good books. The greater part of my reading in those years was poetry, and many of my assignments I read to myself out loud. I did this out of mere intuition, but unbeknownst to myself, I was pursuing one of the best methods for improving as a writer. I had no knowledge then that Lincoln did much of his reading aloud. Immersed in politics and public speaking early in life, he always wanted to know how something sounded as well as what it meant. I remember being very self-consciously dissatisfied with my own writing at an early age. I have (fortunately) never overcome that dissatisfaction. But I did learn from my undergraduate habit that good prose has many resemblances to good poetry. Without rhyme, a good sentence, and even a good paragraph, may nonetheless have (or may need) a muted rhythm, as well as a harmony of sound that enhances a harmony of meaning.

My favorite English professor was Alex Witherspoon, with whom I had sophomore English and, later, as a senior, "The Age of Milton." While I always enjoyed every second of every class with him, I cannot today say exactly why. I believe he represented the literary scholarship of the day at its best. But Witherspoon also had a Bible reading group that met every Thursday evening in his rooms at Berkeley College. He made no announcement of this, and he issued no formal invitations. But if you came you were welcome. I never missed a single meeting in four years. Witherspoon's Bible readings constituted what was by far the greatest of my many profits from my Yale education. We used as our text Ernest Sutherland Bates's *The Bible: Designed to be Read as Living Literature.* Witherspoon had a soft Kentucky accent which, I suspect, was not far from Lincoln's. Listening to him read that glorious Elizabethan prose was for me not very different from listening to Heifetz play Beethoven. After *Crisis of the House Divided* was published in 1959, I sent a copy to Witherspoon, with an inscription that said that it was his Bible reading that made me aware of many of Lincoln's biblical allusions and resonances, and that without this *Crisis* could not have been written. Shortly thereafter I drove up to New Haven to have dinner with him at Mory's. We had a glorious evening together. We both, I think, had a sense of belonging together in that immortal company, into which he had helped to initiate me, of those who would gladly learn and gladly teach. It was little more than six months later that I learned of his passing. Witherspoon had been on the editorial board of Columbia University Press's critical edition of the works of John Milton. I discovered that *Thomism and Aristotelianism* had been incorporated into one of the bibliographies. Alex had been following my career before *Crisis.* I recalled however that Satan's speech to Eve, before the Fall, was pure Aristotle.

Another course in my senior year was a seminar on twentieth-century poetry and critical writing. The instructor was Andrews Wanning, still I believe in his twenties, then fresh from Oxford, and a wonderful classroom presence, along with I.A. Richards. Almost everything good and bad in the avant garde poetry and critical writing of that time may be found in the life and works of T. S. Eliot. At the time I saw only the good. *The Wasteland* was Eliot's summary judgment on Western civilization. It was a kind of apotheosis of contemporary philosophic pessimism. His popularity in the thirties undoubtedly owed much—apart from his phenomenal genius—to the prevailing disillusionment with World War I and its sequel in the Great Depression. The spirit of the time was dominated by enthusiasts for high culture, as most contemporary poets and critics fancied themselves (and as I fancied myself) and most were on the political Left. Many of them looked forward to Socialism for cultural salvation, Eliot looked backwards to the Christian culture that had preceded the Enlightenment and the American Founding. The first edition of Russell Kirk's *The Conservative Mind*, published in 1952, had as its subtitle "From Burke to Santayana." The second edition was "From Burke to Eliot." Restoring Christianity, if not as an established religion, but as some kind of political authority, became one of the goals of the paleo-conservatism that radiated from *National Review.* I would admit however that Eliot's essay on "Tradition and the Individual Talent" has permanent insights into the nature of literature that transcend all partisan differences. All such thoughts came long after my undergraduate days. It is however worth noting that my first book, on Aristotle and Aquinas, was published the same year (1952) as Kirk's *Conservative Mind.* Mine passed virtually unnoticed, while his was celebrated as a kind of Second Coming of Edmund Burke. But Kirk's Burke was not the real one, but rather the invention of the Holy Alliance in its war against the French Revolution and Napoleon. European conservatism throughout the nineteenth century—and beyond—was an attempt to restore the *ancien régime.* When it crossed the Atlantic before the Civil War, it substituted the defense of slavery for the defense of the *ancien régime.* The real Burke not only attacked the French Revolution, but defended the American. Churchill's essay on "Consistency in Politics" sets out the two Burkes, of liberalism and of conservatism. Kirk saw only one.

At the time I was infatuated by Eliot's poetry and his literary criticism, and paid little attention to his politics. In particular I hardly noticed "Burbank with a Baedeker, Bleistein with a Cigar." This 1919 poem sounds the theme of the Third Reich more powerfully than anything that would later come from Berlin, since the Nazis had no one at their disposal with Eliot's poetic genius. In *Bleistein* the decline of the West is represented as Venice, sinking into the Adriatic, the crumbling piles supporting the great buildings and great works of art being gnawed by rats. But underneath the rats, we are told, is "the Jew." No greater attempt to justify the extermination of Jews can be imagined. All of this however passed me by at the time. Later, I wrote a full analysis of the poem but have never found anyone who would publish it.

One high consequence of that seminar was that I dragged Dick Ellmann into it, and thereby (I believe) helped to launch his great career as a literary scholar, particularly on Yeats and Joyce and (at the end of his life) on Wilde. The critical writer who fascinated me most in those days of pristine political innocence was William Empson, author of *Seven Types of Ambiguity* and *Some Versions of Pastoral*. I had never encountered microanalysis as micro as Empson's. It fascinated me, and I devoted many long hours trying (unsuccessfully) to translate it into something I could understand. It profited me as a kind of preparation for Leo Strauss, although with Strauss the microanalysis was always linked to a macroanalysis. With Strauss, one never forgot the trees when looking at the forest, and one never forgot the forest when looking at the trees. It would be some years before I discovered the devastation of forest and trees by modern nihilism. Then I came to realize that the quest for meaning in contemporary literature (as for example Eliot's and Joyce's) was a quest in which, without knowing it, they had been assured beforehand by modern philosophy that the universe was meaningless, and that poetry was not an interpretation of nature (as it was for Shakespeare) but a substitute for it.[1] Until Leo Strauss came along, no one had questioned this premise of modernity.

My one meeting with Empson was a comic masterpiece. During the year I was in graduate school at Yale, Andrews Wanning invited me to a dinner party at which Empson was a guest. It was a pleasant social occasion, but if there was any flashing brilliance at the dinner table, I do not remember it. What I do remember is that at one point Wanning's wife, who was a medical student (or perhaps an intern), had to leave for the hospital. After a polite farewell, she returned to say that her car would not move out of the garage. Three brilliant intellects, including Empson and Wanning, plus myself, stationed ourselves at the four corners of the automobile, and with a heroic heave moved it several feet. Then someone at one of the corners called out, "There's no wheel here." Then the other three corners also shouted the missing of a wheel. By sheer misapplication of our virtues we had moved a vehicle that had no wheels. Why no one of the assembled geniuses had noted the absence of wheels, like the secrets of *Seven Types of Ambiguity*, I never found out. At the time we trooped back into the house, and the lady sent for a taxi. That was the last contact I had with Wanning, something I have always regretted. I believe his career was mainly at Bard College. I tried to look him up years later, after the publication of *A New Birth of Freedom*, and found that he had died the year before.

Another course in my senior year was an independent study with Eugene O'Neill Jr., a member of the classics department. He was friendly as an old shoe, but he gave me no direction whatever. He turned me loose to do whatever reading took my interest. I chose some books on the sociology of the ancient city, books whose titles I cannot now remember. Several years later, after I had been studying with Strauss more than a year, O'Neill published a review (I believe in the *New York Times*) of a book on Plato's *Republic*. I remember it as a more or less academically correct (in the style of Karl Popper) denunciation of the tyrannical character of Plato's alleged authoritarianism. I wrote a long letter to O'Neill giving some of the features of Leo Strauss's interpretation of the *Republic* (having recently studied it with him). According to Strauss, one of the purposes of the dialogue was to teach the difference between the desirable and the possible, and to prevent the best from becoming the enemy of the good. In short, it was to teach the importance of moderation in action, by understanding the distance of thought from action. It also taught that the perfection of thought did not depend upon the perfection of action. It taught that in some sense—the most important one—the dialogue on the best regime *was* the best regime. The great enemy of Plato (and of philosophy) was the belief that historical circumstances determined thought no less than action, and that we were all prisoners in thought no less than in action, of our particular time and place.

O'Neill did not answer my letter, but I ran into him outside the dean's office at the New School, sometime in early 1949, before I had taken the position at Chicago. I discovered that we were both there for the same reason, to book courses at the New School for the next academic year. (As far as I knew he was still on the faculty at Yale.) He greeted me with the warmth of an old friend. I asked him why he had not answered my letter. He said it was because he had no answer. The occasion did not permit me to pursue the matter further. There would not however be another occasion, since it was not long after that I read of his suicide. At some point (I cannot remember exactly when) I looked up his doctoral dissertation. It was a statistical analysis of the metrical characteristics of five hundred lines of the *Iliad* and five hundred lines of the *Odyssey*. It was an embodiment of the contemporary classical scholarship that Strauss inveighed against: great technical competence unconnected to any purpose of understanding. O'Neill's suicide had a Roman (or anti-Christian) model. It has often occurred to me that had O'Neill attended a single lecture or seminar of Leo Strauss, he would have found in the classics a reason to live, no less than a way to die.

I did not at first attempt to continue my graduate studies, nor did I know where that would be. After leaving Yale, I was under a dire necessity to find paid employment, and in New York in 1940–1941 the Depression had not ended, and I could not find anything in the private sector. My hopes turned to the Federal Civil Service in New Deal Washington,

DC, which had an entry level program for recent college grads called "Junior Professional Assistants." The only option open to me was public administration, a subject I loathed, but I had earned the necessary course credits at Yale. During my one year as a graduate student I nearly dropped out because of my dissatisfaction with my courses, above all with public administration, which I found infinitely boring. But the department chairman, old Frank Coker, a wonderful gentleman in the Southern tradition, but a terrible classroom teacher, persuaded me to finish my courses and get credit for the year's work. This turned out not only to be good advice, but the foundation of every good thing that has happened to me in all the years that have followed. I remain grateful to Coker, but even more alert to the mystery of the ways of Providence, which often proceeds by the most inauspicious indirection to accomplish its ends.

I knew from the experience of some of my fellow graduate students at Yale, who had flunked it, that the Civil Service exam in public administration was difficult, so I buckled down to study. I discovered that there was a two-semester course in public administration being given by one Arnold Brecht at the New School (conveniently located near my father's restaurant off Washington Square), and signed up for it. Brecht had been a judge in Weimar Germany. He was a great gentleman, a great scholar, and a fine teacher—just then completing a book on relative and absolute justice—and I learned more political theory in his first class than I had learned in the year long theory course I had taken with Coker. Much later I had a wonderful course with Brecht on the End of the Weimar Republic. In April of 1941 I passed the public administration exam with a good grade, and on July 14, 1941—Bastille Day—I reported for salaried employment for the first time in my life. The day is memorable not for that fact, nor is it what we celebrate each year. But on that morning at breakfast in the boardinghouse in which I had become an inmate the night before, I found myself looking into the eyes of the most beautiful and wonderful girl I had ever seen. I made a date for that evening, and never looked back. In April of 2010 we celebrated our 68th anniversary. Three years ago the Senate of the California legislature presented us with a "certificate of recognition" in honor of our 65th anniversary. Never had any alchemist, believing he could turn lead into gold, envisaged anything so miraculous as the rewards awaiting me from those detested public administration courses. They led in due time, not only to my bride, but to my teacher Leo Strauss, the Socrates of our millennium.

I spent most of the war years in the federal service in Washington, having failed the service's eye exam several times. When I returned to graduate study in 1944—now with a working wife in support—I thought at first only of Brecht, with whom I had established a good relationship, and who generously secured a scholarship for me. But nothing had prepared me for Leo Strauss. Unlike his students at Chicago, I encountered him unadorned by any distinction of position or place. Unlike Brecht, who was a tall, stately presence (he might have been a model for Aristotle's great-souled man), Strauss was a physically insignificant little man with a weak voice. His presence was as unimpressive as the dilapidated classrooms provided by the New School. But he was pure overwhelming intellectual force. After a few minutes into one of his seminars, the little man became a giant. Every great book was a kind of Treasure Island, or more particularly a map of an island holding a treasure. But you had to decipher the map, and do the work of discovery, overcoming the obstacles by which great art, imitating nature, trains the mind to be worthy of its gifts. One of Strauss's secrets was that he made you feel not a passive receptacle of his insights, but as his partner in a voyage of discovery. He was the captain of the ship. But you were part of the crew. And you sailed together. Saul on the road to Damascus was not more stunned, nor more transformed than I, by my encounter with Strauss. Over the next seven years (five in New York and two in Chicago), I attended some nineteen of his courses, and on many Saturday afternoons (before Chicago) I traveled to his home in Riverdale, in the Bronx, where we spent several hours alone together. In Chicago, I had the outer office to his inner office and we met nearly every day. I never spent five minutes in his company without learning something that seemed at the time to be a discovery of a lifetime. Strauss seldom or ever presented his wisdom as his own. But you felt that you had Plato or Aristotle or Cicero or Hobbes as your personal tutor. Of course the great books differed within themselves and among themselves. But a book was great—or was thought to be great—precisely because the author was thought to be seriously concerned with the ultimate meaning of the universe. However mistaken the author of a great book might be, one could learn more from his mistakes than one could learn from a less heterodox author of a lesser book. But the contradictions of even the greatest books forced you to face the problem of truth for yourself. Reading great books with Strauss was never an end in itself, but part of the larger quest—the unfinished and unfinishable quest, for the crucial truth about the highest things. No one had ever awakened in me as he did the meaning of the Socratic axiom that the unexamined life is not worth living. I had heretofore lived, as a Yale student, within the historicist dogma that we were all prisoners of our own time and place, and that we had no access to any truth outside of it. Strauss freed one from this prison, or at least pointed one to the upward path, by which one could make his escape. It was one of Strauss's familiar sayings, that Socrates had more in common with any intelligent American than with any stupid Athenian! There was a way out of the Cave—and a community beyond the Cave. But first you had to discover that you were in a cave, and that there was a world beyond. The cave dwellers, as always, hated anyone who brought this message. Strauss gained no popularity beyond the circle he created around himself.

III

In chapter 6 of *The Truth About Leo Strauss*, "The Emergence of the Straussian Study of America," I am the first mentioned in the Zuckerts' opening paragraph, together with Robert Goldwin. Later, Walter Berns, Herbert Storing, Joseph Cropsey, William Galston, and Allan Bloom are brought into the picture. The Zuckerts write:

> On reflection, it is not surprising that Strauss's students have made systematic study of America one of their chief foci, even though Strauss himself did not do so. He was not an American, but they are, and concern for one's own is a powerful force. Strauss had observed that in the quest for scholarly knowledge of politics, the "center of reference is the given political situation." Both the "given political situation" and the natural concern with their own led Strauss's American students to study their own country. . . . Strauss had set down as one of the guiding principles of an adequate political science that it "view political things in the perspective of the citizen" and the statesman. . . . [T]he turn by Strauss's students to the study of the United States was in accord with his mandates for political studies.[2]

The foregoing is entirely plausible. It describes what might have happened, but not what did happen. A Straussian concern with America began when I discovered the Lincoln-Douglas debates in 1946, a year after beginning work on my dissertation, and three years before Strauss went to Chicago. I had also made the stunning discovery that this central event in American history had not been seriously studied by anyone. I thereupon added the study of political speech to the study of great books, as a dimension of Straussianism. But the fundamental Straussian principle of understanding the authors of the past as they understood themselves, before attempting to understand them better or differently, applied to all authors, and not only to the authors of great books. This principle was certainly vindicated when the author of the speeches possessed the genius of Abraham Lincoln. Whenever I reread Strauss's great essay on "Classical Political Philosophy," I see *Crisis of the House Divided* springing from its pages. Never was the continuity of the perspectives of the citizen, the statesman, and the political philosopher more visible than in Lincoln's performance in the 1850s. Never was the understanding of this continuity more evidently indispensable for the understanding of political reality. In opening up this area of study—which American historians had entirely ignored—I had from the outset the enthusiastic encouragement of Strauss. Lincoln took center stage in my academic concerns after I completed the dissertation in Chicago in late 1949.

Before I took the position at Chicago, I was scheduled to give a course on the debates at the New School in the following academic year, and Joseph Cropsey (still in New York) gave it after I had left. But I did give a course on the debates in the Political Science Department of the University of Chicago, in the spring quarter of 1950. In the fall of 1951 (after moving to Columbus), I gave a lecture at St. John's (Annapolis) on "Expediency and Morality in the Lincoln-Douglas Debates." It was published (at long last) in 1957 in the first issue of the *Anchor Review* (together with excerpts from *Lolita*!), but in unpublished form it was certainly available to Strauss's students (as well as to those who had taken my course). In the academic year 1956–1957 I had a Rockefeller Fellowship which I spent in Chicago, researching and writing on Lincoln and Douglas, giving three public lectures in the summer of 1957. The text of these lectures became the basis of *Crisis of the House Divided*, which was finished in the spring of 1958 and published by Doubleday the following year. Throughout the year in Chicago I profited greatly from conversations with Martin Diamond, Allan Bloom, and Robert Goldwin—and, at the end of the year, with Joseph Cropsey,[3] as well as with Strauss.

All the Staussians mentioned by the Zuckerts were, I believe, exposed to my Lincoln as soon as, if not before, they had completed a course with Strauss. It was a characteristic witticism of Martin Diamond that at St. John's the students were taught that political philosophy had its origins in Socrates' critique of the opinions of the Athenians. But it was I, he said, who discovered that political philosophy might equally be grounded in a Socratic critique of the opinions of the Americans. That the critiques in question were at bottom not two but one is shown by the fact that the opposition between Lincoln and Douglas was identical in principle with the opposition in Book I of the *Republic* of Socrates and Thrasymachus. Thrasymachus had said that justice was the interest of the stronger. Douglas's "popular sovereignty" meant that in a democracy, the majority was the stronger, and that justice was (as Thrasymachus said) whatever they considered to be in their interest. Dividing up the wealth of the rich was of course something the poor frequently thought to be in their interest. Like Socrates, Lincoln believed however that there were moral boundaries to what majorities or minorities might rightfully do. A vote for slavery could not justify slavery, any more than a vote of the poor could justify plundering the wealthy.

The foregoing does not mean that it was I and not Strauss that turned his students towards American themes. But I believe it was the excitement (and it was very great) generated by my discovery of a Socratic Lincoln who had been invisible to mainstream historians that propelled Strauss's Chicago students on the American path.

My conception of Lincoln was influenced from the outset by Strauss's exposition—especially in the long afternoons at Riverdale—of the meaning of prophecy in Maimonides, and of the relationship of prophecy to philosophic kingship. The epigraph for Strauss's *The Argument and Action of Plato's* Laws was from Avicenna, and was as follows: "[T]he treatment of prophecy and the Divine law is contained in . . . the *Laws*." The cross-fertilization of inspiration, between Plato, Avicenna, and Strauss, which implies the mutual influence (or confluence) of Reason and Revelation, is mind-boggling, but it is not improbable, once one grants that the conversation of great minds is not confined by place or time. And, like the proverbial fly on the wall, one need not be a great mind to profit greatly from such conversations.

Lincoln combined the perspective of citizen and statesman, but he shared the dispensation that combined them with the perspective of a political philosopher. His eulogy of Henry Clay tells even more about Lincoln than it does about Clay: "He loved his country partly because it was his own country, but mostly because it was a free country, and he burned with a zeal for its advancement, prosperity, and glory, because he saw in such the advancement, prosperity, and glory of human liberty, human right, and human nature."

Love of human liberty, human right, and human nature encompasses love of one's own with love of the good. It was a feature of the American Founding that the rights to which the Americans appealed to justify their independence were rights which they shared with all human beings everywhere. This is the true meaning of American exceptionalism, and it is one that can never be shared with any other nation. The American Founding comes to sight as unique in identifying itself with a universal humanity. The Athenian myth of autochthony is preserved in Plato's *Republic* in the noble lie that the Guardians have had their life and education underground, implying a right against the world to occupy their particular land. This parallels the Promised Land of ancient Israel, God's promise canceling anyone else's right to that land. The God of Israel gave the land of Israel to Israel. It is not correct to say however, as the Zuckerts do, that Strauss was not an American. He was born a German, but became American. Here is Lincoln in Chicago, July 10, 1858—explaining the unique meaning of Americanization.

> We have besides these men—descended by blood from our ancestors—among us perhaps half our people who are not descendants at all of these men, they are men who have come from Europe—German, Irish, French and Scandinavian—men that have come from Europe themselves, or whose ancestors have come hither and settled here, finding themselves our equals in all things. If they look back through this history to trace their connection with those days [e.g., of the Fourth of July] by blood, they find that they have none, they cannot carry themselves back into that glorious epoch and make themselves feel that they are part of us, but when they look through that old Declaration of Independence they find that those old men say that "We hold these truths to be self-evident, that all men are created equal," and then they feel that that moral sentiment taught in that day evidences their relation to those men, that it is the father of all moral principle in them, and that they have a right to claim it as though they were blood of the blood, and

flesh of the flesh of the men who wrote that Declaration, and so they are.

This is reminiscent of the Gospels, when Jesus is speaking to his disciples, and a messenger comes to him, and tells him that his mother and his brothers are waiting to see him. "Who are my mother and my brothers?" Jesus asks. Then, pointing to the disciples, says "There are my mother and my brothers." This is the teaching of the Declaration of Independence no less than of the Gospels.

In the first year that I knew Leo Strauss we had many private conversations. One in particular stands out in my memory. When he first came to this country, in the 1930s, he said he found (whether rightly or not) that, in polite society, the word "atheist" might not be pronounced. According to his account, it was what the "N" word has become today. When he discovered this, he told me, he realized that he had "come home." The "coming home" of Leo Strauss was no different than the Americanization of the European immigrants celebrated by Lincoln. It was also not different from the coming home celebrated in the great Negro spirituals.

Nothing is more important for understanding Strauss than the place of the Declaration of Independence in the beginning of *Natural Right and History*, where Strauss quotes: "We hold these truths to be self-evident, that all men are created equal, that they are endowed by their Creator with certain unalienable Rights, that among these are Life, Liberty, and the pursuit of Happiness." He then goes on to say "The nation dedicated to this proposition has now become, no doubt partly as a consequence of this dedication, the most powerful and prosperous of the nations of the earth." Then he asked, "Does this nation in its maturity still cherish the faith in which it was conceived and raised? Does it still hold those 'truths to be self-evident'?" Strauss never returned to these questions, or answered them directly. Rather his book as a whole is an attempt to explain, on the deepest level, how in Western civilization Nature was replaced by History as the ground of morality. The uncritical partisans of modern philosophy have assumed that the replacement of Nature by History—the heart of Progressivism—was made on the basis of a rational argument. According to Strauss however such an argument has never existed. Belief that there has been such an argument equals any willing suspension of unbelief in any dogma of revealed religion.[4] It is of some interest that the original Walgreen Lecture (at which I was present), delivered in the fall of 1949, had a different beginning from the first chapter of *Natural Right and History*, published in 1953. In 1949 Strauss began by quoting a medieval aphorism, *Solet Aristoteles quaerere pugnam*, Aristotle is accustomed to seeking a fight. Strauss then promptly reenacted the role of Aristotle, in plunging into his war against historicism, and its misbegotten offspring, relativism, positivism, and nihilism. But in 1949 he made no reference to the Declaration.

Between 1949 and 1953 Strauss apparently decided that the fate of the Declaration of Independence was an authentic representation of the fate of Natural Right. Whether "Expediency and Morality in the Lincoln-Douglas Debates" (1951) had anything to do with this decision, I cannot say. It is notable, however, that although Strauss in 1953 gives the words of the Declaration in direct quotation, he uses Lincoln's words at Gettysburg as his own, without quotation marks. In speaking of the nation's dedication to a proposition, and of the faith in which it was conceived and raised, he speaks with Lincoln's voice as if it were his own.

He thus makes himself a partisan in the most controversial of all issues in American history. How partisan may be only faintly grasped by the fact that that old Confederate Willmoore Kendall called the Gettysburg Address a "giant swindle."[5] Garry Wills received a Pulitzer Prize for his book on the Gettysburg Address while repeating the "giant swindle" charge of his old Yale professor.[6] Wills, however, in deference to his latter day left-wing constituency, called it a good swindle! But he nonetheless repeated that it was a swindle. Wills accepted as true Kendall's baseless assertion that Lincoln at Gettysburg had given the idea of equality a character and prominence it had not hitherto possessed.[7] Strauss knew that Calhoun, who was Kendall's and Wills's hero, had called the idea of racial equality "the most false and dangerous of all political errors." And Calhoun was the archenemy within the American political tradition of everything Lincoln believed and fought for. Strauss's beginning *Natural Right and History* by invoking the Declaration of Independence and then identifying himself with Lincoln's understanding of it could not have made clearer his intention.

In the same opening paragraph of *Natural Right and History* Strauss wrote that a generation ago (that is, a generation before 1953) German thought, by "abandoning the idea of natural right and through abandoning it . . . [had] 'created the historical sense,' and thus was led eventually to unqualified relativism." The aforesaid earlier generation in America was that of the Progressives, whose great star was Woodrow Wilson, but which included such eminences as John Dewey, Charles Beard, Herbert Croly, J. Allen Smith, Walter Lippmann, and many others. Not least among them was Justice Oliver Wendell Holmes Jr., the hero of the late Chief Justice Rehnquist, as well as of the great majority of the legal profession in the twentieth century, both liberal and conservative.

Concerning the unqualified relativism which by 1953 had traveled from Germany to America, Strauss wrote that "It would not be the first time that a nation, defeated on the battlefield and, as it were, annihilated as a political being, has deprived its conquerors of the most sublime fruit of victory by imposing on them the yoke of its own thought." The defeated nation Strauss then had in mind was the Third Reich. But among its predecessors, none was more conspicuous than the Confederacy, defeated on the battlefield in 1865 and also annihilated as a political being. Although the Union cause had prevailed, and chattel slavery was brought to an end, the principles of the Declaration of Independence, celebrated in the Gettysburg Address, were eclipsed almost immediately. Certainly from the end of Reconstruction (1878) political thought in this country has been overwhelmed by a combination of Darwinism and Hegelianism. Pragmatism, the supposedly American philosophy, was little more than Hegelianism without the dialectic. The case for democracy was, in effect, that it had proved its "fitness" by its "survival," especially by victory in the Civil War. There is no better representative of the professoriate of our elite universities in the twentieth century than Carl Becker. His 1922 book on the Declaration of Independence is, apart from the beauty of its language, still the most authoritative work on its subject. Yet in it he says that "To ask whether the natural rights philosophy of the Declaration of Independence is true or false is essentially a meaningless question." This means that to ask whether slavery was just or unjust is a meaningless question. It would accordingly be meaningless to ask whether the cause of the Union was worthy of those who gave it their last full measure of devotion. It would also render meaningless the question of whether the defeat of the Third Reich was a good thing or a bad thing. Strauss at the outset of *Natural Right and History*, by affirming America's birthright in the principles of the Declaration of Independence, has pointed to the moral chaos that follows their abandonment. Before the publication of *Crisis of the House Divided* in 1959 there was no one in the academic historical establishment who asked whether that question, which alone gave meaning to Lincoln's life, was truly meaningless.

It is of some note that in the 1930s, Hitler, Mussolini, and Stalin were almost invariably referred to as "dictators," although originally dictatorship was a constitutional office in the ancient Roman constitution. The more appropriate name for these men would have been "tyrants." The condemnation of tyranny in the Declaration of Independence was in perfect harmony with its classical antecedents. When, before World War II, Winston Churchill called Hitler "that bad man," the sophisticates in the universities fell out of their chairs laughing at him for failing to realize that he had, without knowing it, committed a "value judgment." But they did not laugh when the bombs were dropping on London, and Churchill rallied them to fight.

IV

According to the Zuckerts, the Straussian study of America was complicated from the outset by three propositions that they attribute to Strauss:

1. America is modern.
2. Modernity is bad.
3. America is good.

Clearly, the third proposition is in conflict with the first two. It is in the light of this alleged conflict that the Zuckerts subject *Crisis of the House Divided* to a minute and detailed analysis. Their analysis is so detailed that it would require a separate monograph to do it justice. We here beg indulgence however to introduce once again something merely anecdotal. When Strauss was teaching in Claremont (as he did from December 1967 until June 1970) he was being driven locally by one of our then more prominent graduate students. The subject of *Crisis* came up. "That," said Strauss, in the most emphatic mode of his rhetorical arsenal, "is a *book*." Then he complicated this most wonderful of compliments by adding, "and Professor Jaffa and I are the only ones who understand it."[8] The complication however indicates that he meant to include *Crisis* among those books that required and justified Straussian hermeneutics. Here however is the Zuckerts's summary judgment of *Crisis* (or at least a major part of it):

> [I]n his effort to enlist Lincoln in a Strauss-inspired reformulation or refounding of America, Jaffa unwittingly fell into a serious self-contradiction. A central part of Lincoln's "refounding" or reformation of the regime is the effort to instill reverence for the laws and the source of the laws, "the fathers," and the principles on which they based their legislation. One cannot carry out the Lincolnian project by, in effect, discrediting the founders, as Jaffa does. *Crisis of the House Divided* is itself a book divided, a book caught up in a self-contradiction. It tells us: follow Lincoln, the higher path, because the founding was modern and therefore imperfect and inadequate. Yet Lincoln tells us: follow the founders. We are to follow the imperfect founders as a solution to the imperfection of the founders. That self-contradiction led Jaffa to modify his position over time; these modifications led to the creation of West Coast Straussianism.[9]

If there is any justification for Strauss's praise of *Crisis*, it is at least improbable that it would have fallen "unwittingly" into such a contradiction. The question is however moot, because the contradiction does not exist. The Zuckerts here speak of Lincoln's "refounding" as an "effort to instill reverence for the laws and the source of laws." The most notable instance I can recall of Lincoln speaking of "reverence for the laws" is in the Lyceum speech of 1838. That speech is a sequel to the "Protest" by Lincoln and Dan Stone, the representatives from Sangamon County, to a Resolution recently passed by both houses of the Illinois legislature, a Resolution condemning abolitionism—but not slavery. The Lincoln and Stone Protest expressed their opposition to slavery, but added that abolitionism tended to "increase rather than abate the evil." The occasion for the legislature's denunciation of abolitionism was the recent lynching at Alton of the abolitionist editor Elijah Lovejoy, and the destruction of his printing press. It is remarkable that the Illinois legislature was moved to condemn, not lynching, but the victims of lynching. This tells us much about the virulent racism in Illinois in the 1830s, and of the fragility of the consent of the governed to the principles of the Declaration of Independence. Lincoln and Stone were courageous in taking their cautious stand against popular opinion, anticipating the caution in Lincoln's stand against slavery in his debates with Douglas a decade later.

In the Lyceum speech "reverence for the laws" meant respect for the rule of law, apart from majority rule. There is no question of a defective founding remedying a defective founding. Lincoln's concern in the Lyceum speech is for security from arbitrary violence. The rule of law is independent of the form of any non-tyrannical government. We are reminded that the very purpose of removing mankind from the state of nature into the state of civil society is to have a government in which the power of all can defend the security of each. This security—against being deprived of life, liberty, or property without due process of law—is in principle independent of the particular form that the people may legitimately choose for their government. It belongs to minorities no less than to majorities. Lincoln does not here, or anywhere, assume perfection in the political system as a condition for the rule of law. Thus:

> When I so pressingly urge a strict obedience of all the laws let me not be understood as saying there are no bad laws, nor that grievances may not arise, for the redress of which no legal provisions have been made. I mean no such thing. But I do mean to say, that, although bad laws, if they exist, should be repealed as soon as possible, still while they continue in force, for the sake of example, they should be religiously observed. So also in unprovided cases. If such arise let proper legal provision be made for them with the least possible delay, but, till then, let them if not too intolerable, be borne with.

The Preamble of the Constitution speaks of forming "a more perfect Union," implying a movement from less perfect to more perfect, but not to absolute unqualified perfection. Today, most of us would agree that many of the amendments to the Constitution, among them the first ten—the Bill of Rights—the Civil War amendments, and the amendment guaranteeing women's right to vote, were improvements of the 1787 Constitution. These did not imply however that obedience to the law of the earlier Constitution had been dependent upon these improvements. The earlier Constitution had made these improvements possible. Here is the answer of ordinary prudence to the charge of contradiction in making a defective Constitution the cure for its own defects. Obedience to the defective Constitution made improvement of that Constitution possible. Lincoln's defense in 1850 and in the following decade of the obligation, however abhorrent, to obey the fugitive slave clause of the Constitution, is a notable example of the doctrine set forth in the Lyceum speech of 1837. But Lincoln's critique of the fugitive slave law of 1850 in his 1861 inaugural address is a model of how to try to improve a bad law required by an imperfect Constitution. This can lessen its bad effects, without weakening respect for law in general. We should however take note of the qualification at the end of the foregoing passage from the Lyceum speech. Lincoln recognizes that there may be evils unprovided for by present law, for which better laws are necessary. Let these, he says, be borne with, "if not too intolerable." But what if some *are* "too intolerable"? We may ask what recourse was available to the abolitionists lynched in 1837, with the government on the side of the lynchers? Or what recourse was there for the civil rights workers of the 1950s and '60s, when the state governments of the deep South were on the side of a virulent and murderous racism? The campaigns of non-violent civil disobedience led by Martin Luther King, Jr., wisely and effectively inculcated respect for law even in the supposed acts of disobedience. Their decisive effect was to change public opinion in the country from either indifference or hostility to one of favor to the cause of civil rights. When that happened a government of the people itself changed sides. This was precisely the way in which Lincoln believed a government founded, however imperfectly, upon the principles of the Declaration of Independence might proceed without contradiction towards its proper end. The strategy of Lincoln's rhetoric was to teach the people that the security of their own rights was dependent upon recognizing the equal rights of others. But this strategy also cautioned prudential patience. The alternative—the use of arbitrary or despotic power favored by many abolitionists—he resolutely rejected.

Lincoln's whole Lyceum speech can be seen nonetheless as a defense of abolitionists. He cannot defend them as abolitionists because they are too unpopular, but he can include them, along with everyone else, as entitled to the protection of a lawful government. In this speech Lincoln warns not only against mob violence, but against the danger of men of overweening ambition and overpowering ability. Alexander, Caesar, and Napoleon are the great destroyers of republics. The end pieces of Lincoln's warnings in the Lyceum speech are lynch mobs and tyrants. Mobs and tyrants are reciprocals, the former easily becoming the armies of the latter. The mobs of the French Revolution became the armies of Napoleon. "All honor to Jefferson—to the man who, in the concrete pressure of a struggle for national independence by a single people, had the coolness, forecast and capacity to introduce into a merely revolutionary document, an abstract truth, applicable to all men and all times."

In a response to Stephen Douglas in 1858 Lincoln said:

> It is said in one of the admonitions of the Lord, "As your father in Heaven is perfect, be ye also perfect." The Savior, I suppose, did not

> expect any human creature could be perfect as the father in Heaven, but he said 'As your Father in Heaven is perfect be ye also perfect.' He set that up as a standard, and he who did most towards reaching that standard attained the highest degree of moral perfection. So I say in relation to the principle that all men are created equal, let it be as nearly reached as we can.[10]

There is in Lincoln's words here a convergence with Aristotle's assertion that "there is only one form of government that is everywhere by nature best." The best form of government is not possible everywhere and may not at any given time be possible anywhere. As an abstract truth it may nonetheless supply a direction to policy, and to the improvement of the laws. But there is a danger of tyranny in the attempt to treat the desirable as if it were always possible, when in fact it is not. This teaching against utopianism is certainly one of the great lessons of classical political philosophy. It is manifest in the Lyceum speech when Lincoln warns against freeing the slaves by enslaving the free. He almost surely had in mind the Declaration's invocation of the dictates of prudence, and mankind's disposition to suffer while evils are sufferable, than to right themselves by abolishing the forms of government to which they are accustomed.

Whether or not the unwitting contradiction that the Zuckerts think they have discovered in *Crisis* actually exists, depends finally upon whether there was such a crisis of the divided house as the one addressed by Lincoln in the House Divided speech. None of the notable and influential mainstream academic writers before *Crisis* believed that there actually was such a crisis as Lincoln proclaimed. The aforesaid scholars did not believe that there was any possibility of slavery becoming lawful in the free states. They believed that, while Lincoln was praiseworthy for being on the side of Progress, it was Progress, understood as historical necessity, not Lincoln, or any abstract truth, that was destined to bring about the end of slavery. Hence they showed no real interest in the facts and arguments brought forth by Lincoln in support of his views, since they did not believe that these facts and arguments would have any decisive role in determining the fate of slavery—or of freedom. The dominant opinion among American historians in the 1940s and '50s (during the genesis of my Lincoln scholarship) was that the major cause of the Civil War was the shameless exploitation of the slavery question by politicians North and South. Taking morality seriously became the most serious offense against morality. The slavery question, against all reason, excited the voters on both sides, helping to elect antislavery politicians in the North, and proslavery politicians in the South, while making impossible any reasonable political compromise. Lincoln was of course the most egregious example of a politician successfully exploiting slavery to gain office, while Douglas was the most salutary example of someone attempting to defuse the sectional crisis by making popular sovereignty, which appeared to be both democratic and racist, a sufficiently principled alternative. This was the conventional wisdom of the historical establishment before *Crisis*. It was greatly fortified by the rise of the fact-value distinction in the social sciences, and the accompanying conviction that moral questions could not be resolved by reason. To be reasonable, according to the ruling academic dispensation, meant to recognize the impotence of reason in moral discourse, and to label every moral judgment a non-rational "value judgment." To denounce the Holocaust as evil, or to call the USSR an "evil empire" had to be recognized as value judgments emanating from the passions with no intrinsic rational justification. In the court of reason, the passions of Nazis or Communists, or of anti-Nazis or anti-Communists, had the same standing, which was none at all. However, the idea that the slavery question, and moral questions generally, could be resolved by reason, was implicit in the "laws of nature and of nature's God." But the Declaration of Independence, with its foundations in a rationalist tradition that included Aristotle and Locke, was not taken seriously in the academic community. Hence they did not take Abraham Lincoln seriously, a supreme rationalist who would have gladdened the heart of Socrates. *Crisis* was the first work by an academic to examine the moral reasoning implicit in the Declaration and in the speeches and writings of Abraham Lincoln. It was also perhaps the first to import into the study of the American political tradition Leo Strauss's revival of classical political philosophy. But the academic community was not merely blind to Lincoln's rationalism. It was friendly towards Douglas's "popular sovereignty" precisely because it attempted to find a way that was all the more principled precisely because it did not attempt to decide on the basis of reason whether slavery was good or bad.

The theoretical deficiencies in Douglas's popular sovereignty doctrine were exploited to the full by Lincoln: it was an attempt to find a middle ground between right and wrong, vain as the attempt to find a man who should be neither living nor dead. This rationalist judgment did not however find much resonance among academics. In the political world, Douglas had the advantage in offering a solution that, like the American people of that time, was equally racist and democratic.

To a problem that seemed not otherwise soluble, *Crisis of the House Divided* was notable in that "The Case for Douglas" held nothing back in presenting the advantages of popular sovereignty as a practical solution to the sectional crisis. The main advantage of "The Case for Douglas" was of course that it made no moral judgment as to whether slavery was right or wrong. In this Douglas was undoubtedly closer to the average voter in 1858 than Lincoln. Douglas could exploit existing opinion which was overwhelmingly racist. One reviewer said that the case for Lincoln in *Crisis* was all the more impressive because it had done full and complete justice to Douglas. In doing so, however, it had to argue that with civil war threatening there had to be a subordination of theoretical truth to practical ends. In the end, however, Lincoln proved that such subordination was impossible. Douglas's "solution" could only postpone the crisis, not solve it. Unless the United States set its face, once and for all, against the extension of slavery, the appetite for more land in which to plant slavery would prove insatiable. The important lesson to draw here is that of *e pluribus unum,* that prudence is singular, however many the circumstances in which it may be called on to supply moral and rational guidance. In short, there can be no ancient or modern prudence, distinct from each other. In the *Nicomachean Ethics* Aristotle says of natural right, that it is all changeable. I believe that natural right and practical wisdom are virtually synonymous.

V

The crisis as seen by Lincoln in June of 1858 arose from the conjunction of the 1854 Kansas-Nebraska Act and the decision and opinion of the Supreme Court in the 1857 case of *Dred Scott.*[11] The former had declared that the Missouri Compromise exclusion of slavery from the Nebraska territory was "inoperative and void" and that the people of the territory would by the Act be left "perfectly free under the Constitution" to decide whether to accept or reject slavery. However, Taney's opinion in *Dred Scott* had said that the right to own slaves was expressly affirmed in the Constitution. This "express affirmation" which Lincoln proved had no foundation in the text of the Constitution, was then conjoined in Taney's opinion with the supremacy clause of Article IV, which declared that "This Constitution, and the laws . . . which shall be made in pursuance thereof . . . shall be the supreme law of the land, and the judges in every state shall be bound thereby, anything in the constitution or laws of any state to the contrary notwithstanding." This meant that no state constitution or law could deny an expressly affirmed constitutional right. Thus the perfect freedom of the people of a territory under the Constitution to decide for or against slavery proved to be exactly no freedom at all. In *Dred Scott* the Court drew the conclusion that neither Congress nor a territorial legislature could deny the right of slave ownership in a territory. It did not say anything explicit about a right of slave ownership in a free state. But the supremacy clause was unambiguous: no state constitution, any more than Congress or a territorial legislature, could deny an expressly affirmed constitutional right. The Court in *Dred Scott* did not expressly draw the conclusion that slavery was now lawful in every state, even if the state's constitution prohibited it. But the premises leading to this conclusion were in place in Taney's opinion, as Lincoln demonstrated, awaiting only a propitious political moment to be declared the law of the land. But the danger of slavery becoming lawful in the free states was very real, Progressive historians to the contrary notwithstanding. Lincoln was determined to prevent this from happening. In the Ottawa debate

Lincoln read from a recent speech of Douglas, in which Douglas denounced the *Washington Union* (President Buchanan's mouthpiece) for asserting that under *Dred Scott* slavery was already lawful in all the free states. The *Washington Union* quoted the proslavery Lecompton Constitution—which Buchanan was resolutely supporting—to this effect. Douglas was, without realizing it, giving the heart of Lincoln's House Divided speech months before Lincoln!

In December of 1860 Lincoln wrote to Alexander Stephens, "You think slavery is *right* and ought to be extended, while we think it is *wrong* and ought to be restricted. That I suppose is the rub. It certainly is the only substantial difference between us." These words were repeated almost exactly in Lincoln's first inaugural. All other differences could have been assimilated to the political process. Had there been no differences concerning the rights and wrongs of slavery, there would have been no Civil War. There is however nothing in *Crisis of the House Divided* that asserts or implies any division among those opposed to the extension of slavery, that might justify saying that *Crisis* was a book divided against itself. This is not to say that there were not important political divisions among free-soilers. Lincoln at the end of the House Divided speech refers to the movement as composed of "strange, discordant and even hostile elements." Moreover the Free Soil movement was not in itself uniformly antislavery. It was against blacks in the territories, whether free or slave. Among the first laws passed by the Free Soil government in Topeka, Kansas, was one excluding free blacks from the territory. Ending the extension of slavery was only the first step on the long road to complete equality of the races, but there could be no doubt as to the direction of the road Lincoln wished to take.

We may say, as I do, that in 1959 I regarded the founders as condemning slavery from the perspective of a prudent form of modern natural rights. This, I then held, was transformed by Lincoln into a prudent form of classical Aristotelianism. Now I believe that the prudent form of classical Aristotelianism was already present in the founding, and that Lincoln found it there. That is because I do not now think that prudence, rightly understood, admits within itself any division between ancients and moderns. I have come to believe that it is of the essence of the pristinely modern persuasion to eliminate prudence, along with morality, from statesmanship and political philosophy. Wise constitutions would replace any need for wise statesmen—or wise people.

The prudence of the Declaration is the prudence of Aristotle and Lincoln because there are not two kinds of prudence. While the manifestations of prudence are as many as the circumstances in which prudent action is possible, the virtue itself remains one and the same. This is why regarding Aristotle and Locke as representing opposing and contradictory philosophic doctrines is mistaken. The assumption that there is such a difference is the nerve of the difference between Eastern and Western Straussians.

To repeat, I do not believe that in political philosophy, rightly understood, there can be more than one prudence. Aristotle remarks that natural right is all changeable. Its changeability does not affect its identity, or its critical role in relating prudent action to morality. It does not weaken or compromise the integrity of the opposition to slavery extension in the 1850s. When Lincoln, in the joint debates, denied any intention to make voters or jurors of Negroes, he was not telling the whole truth. He certainly had no present or immediate intention to make voters or jurors of Negroes. The racism of Illinois voters in 1858 would not consent to it. But Lincoln did say that in the right of a black man or black woman to put into their own mouths the bread that their own hands had earned, they were his equal and the equal of every man. And Lincoln knew perfectly well that that right which the black had equally with the white could not be defended unless the blacks had the vote. But he kept that truth within himself in 1858, because it was a truth that would have destroyed him as a free soil leader. It would have made impossible the day, which did come, when he could successfully advocate Negro voting. Hence it would have been imprudent.

VI

If there was no contradiction in *Crisis* to explain the necessity for "West Coast Straussianism," what is this alleged Straussian phenomenon, and what explains it? At this point we take exception to the three propositions the Zuckerts attribute to Strauss. If by "America is modern," we mean that our mortal existence is within the time frame of the calendar, based upon the motions of our solar system, then it is a mere truism. If it means that the principles of our regime—those set forth in the Declaration of Independence, the Virginia Statute of Religious Freedom, and in the Gettysburg Address—are determined by this time frame, and only have such transient validity as may be attributed to a transient time frame, then we disagree. The principles of the American regime, being abstract truths, have their existence both in time and out of time. That is to say, they have an existence that is both chronological and ontological. According to Lincoln the truth that all men are created equal has no dependence upon the events of the day that sent it forth to the world, or upon the events of the days that led up to it, or of the events of the days that followed from it. Truth as abstract exists out of time, and independence of time is what gives it the rightful influence it ought to have upon events in time-bound reality. History may be the theater or stage upon which the uncertain fate of truth in our world is played out, but it is not the source or determinant of that truth, or of its success or failure in our world of time and change.

Winston Churchill in *The Second World War* remarks that in war it is impossible to guarantee success. It is possible only to deserve it. We believe that this is true of life as a whole, and not of war only. A world in which noble failure is impossible, is also a world in which noble success is impossible. It would be a world that knows neither success nor failure, a world without heroes—or villains. It would in fact not be a world inhabited by humans. It would be a world either of gods or of beasts, but not of humans. In permitting evil, God was not intending evil, but only the good that human freedom made possible. This good is not possible if men are protected by God from suffering the consequences of their own failings.

Prudence is the ability to influence events in the particular circumstances of particular times and particular places, so as to bring about a desired result or end. It is also a virtue that may on occasion tell us that success is impossible, and that noble failure is the only rational alternative. In our world men or women are celebrated as prudent if they show a marked ability to bring about the ends that they and their followers most admire. "Why are the wise at the doors of the rich?" is the ancient conundrum. And the answer is always the same: It is because "the one know what they need and the other do not." The wise know (or may know) that they need money, but the rich do not often know that they need wisdom. One reason for their ignorance is that they are praised for wisdom merely because they are rich, or are thought to know how to become rich. True prudence is hard to understand because it is so often identified with mere worldly success, which is often only the outcome of sordid means. Prudence is thus thought to imply an absence of moral virtue, while Aristotle tells the exact opposite: that it always implies the presence of moral virtue. According to the *Nicomachean Ethics,* an action cannot be moral if it is not prudent, and it cannot be prudent if it is not moral. George Washington reflected this when, in his first inaugural as president, he declared that "[T]he foundation of our national policy will be laid in the pure and immutable principles of private morality . . . since there is no truth more thoroughly established than that there exists in the economy and course of nature, an indissoluble union between virtue and happiness."

It is impossible to imagine anything more Aristotelian than the assertion of the union of virtue and happiness. Thus the mention of the pursuit of happiness in the Declaration of Independence as among the supreme natural rights of mankind, can only be understood as the pursuit of virtue. According to those characterized by the Zuckerts as "East coast Straussians" it is commonplace to regard the pursuit of happiness as Hobbesian, or idiosyncratic. To them it means "doing your own thing," without regard to reason, or to those immutable moral principles which ought to guide men and nations when they are governed by the dictates of prudence. This is also the virtue that forges the rational bond between the different moral virtues, on the one hand, and happiness, on the other.

This view of prudence, with its distinct difference from the pursuit of the merely self-serving, marks the American Founding as classical in principle. No one since 1789 has had greater authority with the American people than George Washington. Hence nothing can be more authoritative for the American political tradition than this assertion that public policy would have "a foundation in the pure and immutable principles of private morality."

The prudence invoked in the Declaration of Independence is the same virtue whose classic formulation is in the *Nicomachean Ethics*. It is the virtue that mediates between unchanging principles and the changing circumstances in which they are to take effect. It may seem sometimes that circumstances are all, and that principles, so called, are mere emanations from the penumbra of circumstance. Let us consider however the crisis which divided Europe in the centuries that preceded the American Revolution. The slaughter of Catholics by Protestants, and of Protestants by Catholics, was the melancholic historical backdrop to the American Founding. It was clear that unless sectarian religious differences were kept out of the political process, no form of self-government, incorporating majority rule, would be possible. It is necessary that we today understand how unprecedented was the idea of majority rule, in a government in which rival parties, or factions, could settle their differences by the ballot box, how ballots could replace bullets. There was at that time in the old world no place in which sectarian religious differences did not dominate the political scene, and in which therefore republican government was not possible. For the American people to demonstrate the ability of a people to govern itself, it was necessary that they incorporate in their political constitutions the idea of the free exercise of religion as a natural right, immune to political interference. This was therefore a supreme dictate of prudence. It was irrelevant whether it be called Aristotelian or Lockean. It was a dictate of impartial reason, and a dictate of natural law, which is the law of reason.

To establish government without a king or priesthood or hereditary aristocracy ran against the grain of the experience of mankind. But what would have been utopian at any other time and place suddenly became prudent, as a result of the particular circumstances of the American Revolution. When the Pilgrims landed at Plymouth Rock in 1620, they sought freedom to practice their own religion unmolested. But they did not then consider that the right they sought for themselves did not belong to them because they were Christians, or Christians of a certain persuasion. It belonged to them only because it belonged to all men everywhere. It was a natural right, and it belonged to those they regarded as infidels or heretics no less than to other Christians, or to non-Christians. The Pilgrims, and other refugees from religious persecution who peopled the colonies, evolved over time into disciples of the philosophy of natural rights incorporated into the Declaration of Independence, and into the

Virginia Statute of Religious Freedom, as well as into the Bills of Rights in the state constitutions.

In England in the seventeenth century, the regime changed four times between Catholic and Protestant in thirty years, leading to this famous celebration:

> And this is law that I'll maintain
> Unto my dying day, sir,
> That whatsoever king shall reign
> Still I'll be Vicar of Bray, sir.

Governments changed from Catholic to Protestant, and back again, many times. Whatever the regime, persecution of dissenters almost always followed. The idea of disestablishment accompanied by the natural right to free exercise was a political idea whose time did not come in the political world (as distinct from the world of ideas) until the Virginia Statute of Religious Freedom, penned by Thomas Jefferson, in the wake of the movement led by James Madison. The inspiration of the Americans was John Locke's *Letter Concerning Toleration*. The doctrine of religious freedom, which privately guided the leaders of the English Revolution of 1689, did not guide their public policy, which made prudent concessions to public opinion, which was still dominated by religious prejudice. The private opinions of the Whig leaders in 1689 became the public doctrine of the Virginians of 1787 who supported the Statute of Religious Freedom. It was a change of circumstance not change of opinion that distinguished the private opinions of the English Whigs of 1689 from the public opinions of the Virginians of 1787. There is much in what the Zuckerts say about the contradictions inherent in antebellum politics. But the contradiction to which they refer is not in the place to which they refer. I would also remind the Zuckerts what Strauss says about the "unwitting" contradictions of careful writers. The contradiction they identify is not present in the Lyceum speech of 1838, in which Lincoln is explicit in calling for reverence and obedience to the laws. It is worth noting, moreover, that whereas in 1838 he would speak of reverence for the laws and the Constitution, after 1854 he gave priority to the Declaration of Independence. In his meditation on the Book of Proverbs 25:11, "A word fitly spoken is like apples of gold in pictures of silver," Lincoln said that the apple of gold ("that all men are created equal") was at the center, and that the Constitution was subsequently framed around it. The picture, he said, was for the sake of the apple, the Constitution was for the sake of the principle of equality, and the Constitution had no ultimate justification apart from that principle. For Lincoln, reverence for the Constitution and the laws meant reverence for them as embodiments of that apple of gold.

In 1838 Lincoln said, "When I so pressingly urge a strict observance of all the laws, let me not be understood as saying there are no bad laws. . . . If such arise, let proper legal provision be made for them . . . but till then let them *if not too intolerable* be borne with." The words I have italicized show that the tradition of civil disobedience—immortalized in our time by Dr. Martin Luther King, Jr.—was alive and well in Lincoln. How could it not be? Slavery was a gigantic anomaly in a regime dedicated to that apple of gold. In the Lyceum speech Lincoln warned against men of the greatest ambition, men like the three great historic destroyers of republics, Alexander, Caesar, and Napoleon. Napoleon was a recent memory, and Napoleon had used tyranny to advance the goals of equality. The abolitionists, or some of them (e.g., John Brown), had urged direct methods of dealing with slavery, methods inconsistent with the rule of law embodied in the Constitution. Lincoln made clear that he opposed willingness to abandon the Constitution. He did not, he said, believe in freeing the slave by enslaving the free. Lincoln was committed, from first to last, to working out the problem of slavery within the political methods sanctioned by the Constitution. Taking the side of the principle of equality, while accepting the constitutional protections of slavery, involved Lincoln (like the founders) in what might be thought to be contradictions, but in *Crisis* I proved that these were strategic and prudential adaptations to inexorable practical political realities.

The Lyceum speech as a whole was a polemic against the mob violence being directed against abolitionism. Lincoln cautiously defended the lawful liberties of antislavery agitators from the unlawful actions of proslavery mobs. His call for strict observance of the law was in effect a defense of what was then a most unpopular minority. The problem Lincoln was struggling with was that of a government based upon consent of the governed in which the people did not recognize that the ground of consent—of their own authority—was human equality. The possibility of laws that were intolerable meant laws, or actions, by the people arising from that equality which, at once, enfranchises them and condemns certain of their actions. Lincoln had to show respect for the authority arising from equality while condemning the race prejudice which was at war with that same equality. This is a problem inherent in the Declaration of Independence itself, in which equality is the basis of legitimate authority, which may nonetheless be exercised illegitimately. Nothing in *Crisis* on this theme needs any apology or emendation.

Securing consent to wise decisions is a theme of classical political philosophy upon which Leo Strauss had much to say. It is clear that the solution of that problem, whether ancient or modern, lies in the influence of an elite which can educate the people in the principles which justify their regime. As History came to replace Nature, in Western society as a whole, and especially in the United States, the possibility of such education has become ever more remote, and it is more remote today than it was in Lincoln's lifetime. Indeed, the professoriate which is the elite from whom that education ought to emanate is the main source of the attack upon it. Strauss's career is a paradigm of the possibility of an education that can rescue Western civilization from the "cave beneath the cave" in which it is presently trapped.

The achievement of *Crisis,* I believe, was the demonstration that Lincoln had, throughout the period of the debates, acted prudently upon principles of classical natural right. From the Lincolnian perspective rights were correlated with duties, and the fulfillment of duty was as essential to man's perfection as the defense of his rights. This would seem to depart from the most commonly held view of the Enlightenment, by which rights were everything, and duties, if they existed at all, were merely derivative and contingent. Lincoln had of course to adapt those classical principles to circumstances very different from those in which they had their origin. Lincoln had made his appeal to an "ancient faith," although the fourscore years since the founding did not make the government notably ancient. But the principles of the Declaration, he made clear, were the principles of nature, and nature is more ancient than history. My articulation of Lincoln's principles in *Crisis* was proof that classical natural right could succeed within the framework of American history and politics. But the crisis of our time is essentially the same as the rejection of Lincoln by American historians and, *a fortiori,* by the academic world as a whole.

There had been a tendency, even among Straussians, to think that classical political philosophy dwelt only in the ancient *polis,* and that modern regimes displayed only modern principles. But it had been Strauss's project from the outset to bring classical political philosophy to the support of decent modern regimes. He would not have thought this was possible, if he did not think that the application of these principles was independent of time and place. Lincoln, in his eulogy of Jefferson, had said that Jefferson had incorporated in the Declaration, "an abstract truth, applicable to all times and places." I do not think that before *Crisis* any twentieth-century scholar who had written about Lincoln or the Civil War era seriously believed in the existence of such truths.

The Zuckerts's finding that *Crisis* advised us to "follow the imperfect founders as a solution to the imperfection of the founders," is a caricature, but it is not without merit. When I wrote *Crisis* I believed then—and believe now—that Lincoln represented the classical principles in the highest degree, and with the greatest purity. But I did not then think, as I now do, that the founding to which he turned as a source of authority, represented these same classical principles. I thought that the American Founding was a decent modern regime, because it represented what Strauss called the First Wave of Modernity, or modern natural right, particularly as set forth in the teaching of John Locke. But Strauss's chapter on Locke, in *Natural Right and History,* was a scathing indictment, and hardly calculated to inspire respect for any regime whose founders looked to the authority of the *Second Treatise.* Any depreciation of the Founding Fathers in *Crisis* was a response to this chapter. Gradually, however, I came to doubt the authority I had ascribed to it. I did so, in part, because I believed Strauss himself had another point of view on this entire subject. In his essay on "Liberal Education and Responsibility" in *Liberalism: Ancient and Modern* (1968), he cites Locke repeatedly and with unvarying favor. In "What Is Liberal Education?" Strauss speaks of liberal education as the "ladder by which we ascend from mass democracy to democracy as originally meant." What democracy originally meant, that is to say, what the founders intended it to mean, and what Strauss understood it to mean to the founders, is set forth with magisterial authority in a letter by Jefferson to John Adams in 1813:

> For I agree with you that there is a natural aristocracy among men. The grounds of this are virtue and talents. . . . There is also an artificial aristocracy, founded on wealth and birth, without either virtue or talents. . . . The natural aristocracy I consider as the most precious gift of nature, for the instruction, the trusts, and government of society. And indeed it would have been inconsistent in Creation to have formed man for the social state and not to have provided virtue and wisdom enough to manage the concerns of society. May we not even say that that form of government is the best, which provides the most effectually for a pure selection of these natural *aristoi* into the offices of government? The artificial aristocracy is a mischievous ingredient in government, and provision should be made to prevent its ascendancy.

It is impossible to imagine a more lucid summary of Aristotelian political philosophy. Democracy as originally meant by Jefferson, and as understood by Strauss, clearly meant a democracy in which the influence of a liberally educated elite would go far to erasing the difference between democracy and aristocracy. From the author of the Declaration of Independence, this Aristotelianism is at the same time the Lockeanism of the founding. In "On Classical Political Philosophy" (1945), Strauss's discussion of the question of the best regime, the central question of classical political philosophy, culminates (in the mathematical center of the essay)[12] in the quotation from Jefferson, about the pure selection of the natural *aristoi* into the offices of government. The decisive fact that unites Jefferson and Strauss—and Locke and Aristotle—is the belief in a natural *aristoi*. Finding them, providing for their education, and discovering the ways and means in particular circumstances to maximize their influence, is the task of political philosophy, whether in the ancient or modern world.

But how in fact do we reconcile the belief in natural *aristoi* with the natural equality of the Declaration of Independence? This is the stumbling block that divides Eastern and Western Straussianism. It ceases to be a stumbling block when we distinguish those respects in which all human beings are equal from those in which they are not equal. In chapter 2 of the *Second Treatise*, "Of the State of Nature," Locke asserts that it is a

> state also of equality, wherein all power and jurisdiction is reciprocal, no one having more than another, there being nothing more evident than that creatures of the same species and rank, promiscuously born to all the same advantages of nature, and the use of the same faculties, should also be equal one amongst another without subordination or subjection.[13]

Locke is saying, and Jefferson understood him to say, that there is no difference between one human being and another, such as to make one by nature the ruler of the other. This does not mean that there are not very important differences among human beings, or that some of these differences are not very important in deciding who should hold office. In the case of the relationship of man to dog, or of man to horse, the question of who should rule and who should be ruled, is decided by nature, by the difference of species. No such natural difference within the human species decides the question of who should rule. We are reminded of Aristotle's discussion of natural slavery. A natural slave is one who differs from a normal human being as much as if he were of an inferior species. All others held as slaves are held by force and held unjustly. Later Aristotle says that all slaves should have freedom set before them as a goal. That means that no slaves are natural slaves. Aristotle also says that if there is someone who is as much above the human species, as the human species is above the lower species, that person should rule without the consent of the governed. But of course, no such person can be found, even though some men have fraudulently claimed to be gods, or descended from gods. In the literature of the founding, God is said to be the only one with the "infinite wisdom, goodness, and rectitude" that entitles Him to govern without the consent of the governed. But since God has not condescended to perform the office of rule, and humans who claim to rule by the right that belongs only to God are frauds, human governments ought to be based upon the consent of the governed. God has left us the distinction of species in nature, as it is in Locke and in Aristotle, in locating the natural right of human freedom.

Locke knows that most of the human race, through all time, has been governed on the basis of assertions of superiority in some individuals and in some families that amount to claims of intrinsic differences equal to differences of species. These are the artificial aristocracies denounced by Jefferson. The Enlightenment was first and foremost the debunking of the myths that supported these artificial aristocracies.

The foregoing relates to the state of nature, and the law of reason that governs that state. We must however understand how those who are equal by nature can become members of civil society, in which distinctions of ruling and being ruled arise legitimately among them. We must also see how the law of nature, which is the law of reason, continues to furnish guidance to those in civil society. The law of nature does not rule only in the state of nature.

VII

In the Introduction to *The City and Man* (1964) Strauss wrote:

> Only we living today can possibly find a solution to the problems of today. But an adequate understanding of the principles as elaborated by the classics may be the indispensable starting point for an adequate analysis, to be achieved by us of present day society in its peculiar character, and for the wise application to be achieved by us, of these principles to our tasks.[14]

The more I pondered these injunctions, the more convinced I became that this was precisely what the Founding Fathers had done some two centuries before. And to recapture what they had done—and what Lincoln had done in pursuit of their goals—was what our task was today. I was even more convinced that no advantage to public policy from the founders' achievement was possible until we had grasped that achievement. And for that we had to recapture the founders's Locke, which most certainly was not the Locke of *Natural Right and History*. I believe that in doing so, I was more faithful to Strauss's intention than those guardians of a Straussian orthodoxy who can "learn nothing and forget nothing" in their insistence that modernity is bad and that America is modern.

Let us consider once more the place of religion in the founding. Sectarian religious warfare of incredible ferocity had dominated Europe in the sixteenth and seventeenth centuries, and most of the original colonists were refugees from religious persecution. While the colonists sought religious freedom for themselves, the idea of religious freedom as a human right belonging to them, not in virtue of their particular modes of worshiping God, but in virtue of their common humanity, was slow in developing. Practical reason, uncluttered by religious fanaticism, played an important role over time, as the advantages for the colonists and the colonies of cooperation in meeting common dangers—from Indians, the French, pirates, and later, the British—commended itself. Protection against the alleged impurities of the other man's faith receded gradually in importance. The idea of a common citizenship, based upon the laws of nature and of nature's God, which transcended sectarian differences, gradually replaced revealed religion as the paramount ground of citizenship. A decisive influence however—to repeat—was Locke's *Letter Concerning Toleration*. This seminal work inspired Madison's "Memorial and Remonstrance," the principal source of the arguments deployed in the party struggle for disestablishment in Virginia. It was also the principle resource for Jefferson in drafting the Virginia Statute for Religious Freedom. The latter was the second of the three things that Jefferson wanted most to be remembered by, and which he had inscribed on his tombstone. The first of those three things was, of course, the Declaration of

Independence. The two together I believe are the greatest documents of human freedom in all human history.

The Virginia Statute states "that our civil rights have no dependence on our religious opinions any more than our opinions in physics or geometry." No government in the history of the world had ever admitted or acknowledged such a proposition. The ancient city understood itself as a creation of its gods (or God).[15] The Israelite polity celebrated in the Old Testament, whatever may be distinctive in its monotheism, is typical of other ancient cities in its proclaimed dependence upon a divine lawgiver. However universal the Hebrew Deity was believed to be, the Mosaic legislation was particular. In the ancient city, citizenship, or membership in a polity, is identical in principle with obedience to the god or gods of that polity. No distinction was possible between civil and religious liberty. When the Constitution of the United States in 1787 declared that there should never be a religious test for office it effected the greatest change ever in the relationship of man to government.

The proximate source of the ideas that brought about this change was, to repeat, Locke's *Letter Concerning Toleration*. A more remote, but not less powerful cause, is to be found in the response of Jesus to the Pharisees, when he said to render to Caesar the things that were Caesar's, and to God the things that were God's. This was the first authoritative assertion of a relationship of man to God independent of civil authority. Locke's *Letter* represented the fulfillment of the doctrine set in motion by Jesus. It is instructive however that Jesus spoke not as an Israelite under the government of David or Solomon—in an ancient city—but in a conquered province of the Roman Empire, a way station to the modern state.

That a man's relationship to his God was a private matter, and that it had nothing to do with civil government, contradicted everything that men had hitherto believed about the relationship of man to God and to government. Each ancient Israelite inherited God's promise to Abraham. The transmission of this promise was through the patriarchal family. The obligations it entailed formed the core of the civic life of ancient Israel. The most intensely personal relationship—of man and God—was also the most public and political relationship. The idea of a realm of privacy immune to this relationship was unintelligible. Yet such immunity came to form the core of American constitutionalism. Can one imagine Moses coming down from the mountain, and finding the children of Israel worshiping the golden calf, shrugging his shoulders, and muttering something about "free exercise of religion"? If God is regarded as the source of law, then obedience to God and to law (and to one's father) form an unbreakable unity.

In Shakespeare's dialogue between King Henry V (disguised) with Bates and Williams in the camp the night before Agincourt, the soldiers question whether they can die well in a battle for an unjust cause. Their conclusion is that their duty to God is to obey the king. It is the king's duty to God that his cause be just. We see that the line of authority is from above and that the "Nuremburg plea" of superior orders would be valid by their lights. We can see, as undoubtedly Shakespeare saw, that this is unsatisfactory. Only if the king's authority came from the people, and the people's authority came from God, would moral responsibility and political responsibility be in harmony with each other. It is this harmony that is brought about by the Declaration of Independence.

In the establishment of Christianity in the Roman Empire, the Christian God, as the God of all mankind, was not the lawgiver of a particular people, in the way that the God of Israel was the author of the laws of Israel. Whatever further claims might be made in behalf of Israel's God as the Creator of the world, He remained the God of one people among many, and as an ancient city Israel remained one people among many. According to Dante, however, behind the Christian worldview was Julius Caesar, and Rome's conquest of the ancient world. At the end of this conquest, there were no independent cities, and hence no independent gods. (Ancient Israel became a province of the Roman Empire. See the New Testament.) By the logic of the ancient city, if there was but one city there could be but one God. But that God would not be the author of the laws of individual cities or countries. Nevertheless, for more than a millennium Western political thought continued to see political authority descending from above, whether from popes, emperors, or divine-right monarchs. Since Lincoln identified the divine right of kings with slavery, and with the justification of all forms of unjust inequality, I have given a more extensive account of divine right monarchy in the second chapter of *A New Birth of Freedom*. The heart of the problem of divine right monarchy is presented by Shakespeare (from whom Lincoln probably learned it), especially in the English histories. Two propositions emerge from Shakespeare: first, that legitimate authority requires the sanction of divine right; second, that to be legitimate is not enough, that without competence in governance it will fail. We see Richard II as legitimate but incompetent, and Henry IV as competent but illegitimate. Henry V is somewhere in between! He asks God to forget his father's usurpation of the crown and tries to gain legitimacy for the usurped crown by ascribing the victory at Agincourt to God alone. We know however that God did not grant his wish, that his rule was brief, and that it was followed by renewed and prolonged civil war. It is clear from Shakespeare that divine right monarchy, notwithstanding all its spectacular grandeur, can never join legitimacy to competence in a constitution that will satisfy the purposes inherent in the nature of political governance.

In *Julius Caesar*, the conspirators, over the dead body of Caesar, having cried "Peace, Freedom, and Liberty," say:

> How many ages hence
> Shall this our lofty scene be acted over

In states unborn and accents yet unknown

This could be, if it is not, a prophecy of the American Revolution. For in the American Revolution are elements which were lacking in the Roman republic, and which made that republic a prey to Caesarism. What Caesarism is we can find in Antony's speech over Caesar's dead body, together with the reading of Caesar's will. Caesar we are told loved the people of Rome, and left all his property to them. The resemblance of Caesar's love of the common people, and Jesus' love of the poor, is striking. The Christianity which in time followed is the joint product of Caesar's conquests and Jesus' gospel. Without the former, the latter could not have been preached throughout the Roman world. But those called poor in spirit, who Jesus said would inherit the world did, in an illusory sense, inherit it when popes and emperors came to rule in their name. But this illusion could become a reality, only when popular sovereignty enshrined the rule of the people into constitutional reality. This was finally accomplished by the American Founding, rightly understood.

Harry V. Jaffa
Claremont, California
May 12, 2011

NOTES

1. See 'Macbeth and the Moral Universe,' *Claremont Review of Books*, Volume VIII, No. 1 (Winter 2007).
2. Catherine and Michael Zuckert, *The Truth About Leo Strauss: Political Philosophy and American Democracy* (Chicago: University of Chicago Press, 2006), p. 198.
3. Cropsey had a Rockefeller Fellowship for 1957–58. He had been a member of the Economics Department at City College, New York. His degree was in Economics and from Columbia. He began attending Strauss's seminars with me in New York in 1946, after his return from the battlefields of the North African, Sicilian, and Italian campaigns of World War II. At the end of his fellowship year he joined Strauss in the Political Science Department at Chicago, where he remained for the balance of his career, which included, among many great distinctions, the joint editorship of the Strauss-Cropsey *History of Political Philosophy*.
4. As far as I can recollect, Sabine's acceptance on faith of the fact-value distinction was never even discussed at Yale when I was a graduate student there.
5. Willmoore Kendall and George W. Carey, *The Basic Symbols of the American Political Tradition* (Baton Rouge: Louisiana State University Press, 1970).
6. Garry Wills, *Lincoln at Gettysburg: The Words That Remade America* (New York: Simon and Schuster, 1992), p. 38.
7. In the Peoria speech (1854), denouncing the repeal of the Missouri Compromise, Lincoln listed among its evils, that it "forces so many really good men amongst ourselves into an open war with the very fundamental principles of civil liberty—criticizing the Declaration of Independence, and insisting that there is no right principle of action but *self interest*." [Lincoln's italics.]
8. I am reminded of someone who said that, when he wrote a certain poem, only he and God knew what it meant. Now, he said, only God knew.
9. Zuckerts, p. 227.

10. Abraham Lincoln, 'Speech at Chicago, Illinois,' 10 July 1858, *The Collected Works*, ed. Roy P. Basler (New Brunswick, NJ: Rutgers University Press, 1953), Vol II, p. 501.

11. *Dred Scott v. Sandford*, 60 U.S. 393 (1857).

12. A calculation made by Professor Colleen Sheehan of Villanova. It was she who invented "Crisis of the Strauss Divided." That the ultimate characterization of classical political philosophy by Strauss is provided by the author of the Declaration of Independence, and that it was placed by Strauss at the very center of this essay, conveys the intimacy in which Strauss came to hold the relationship of the American Founding to classical political philosophy.

13. John Locke, ed. Peter Laslett, *Two Treatises of Government* (New York: Cambridge University Press, 1960), p. 269.

14. Leo Strauss, *The City and Man* (Chicago: University of Chicago Press, 1962), p. 11.

15. Fustel de Coulanges, frwd. Arnaldo Momigliano and S.C. Humphreys, *The Ancient City* (Baltimore: Johns Hopkins University Press, 1980).

Harry and Marjorie Jaffa on their wedding day, April 25, 1942.

Harry and Marjorie Jaffa on their 60th weddding anniversary in Claremont, California.

Harry and Marjorie on the Potomac in 1941.

TWO

Leo Strauss Remembered

Our purpose here is to honor the memory of Leo Strauss.[1] It is fitting that we should do so. But honor depends upon the competence—if not the virtue—of those who give it, as well as upon the excellence of him who is to receive it. A great man once said of his teacher that he was such a one as bad men had no right even to praise. We cannot admit a doubt of our own wisdom without casting one as well upon him whom we would honor. Still, no one would have insisted more rigorously upon the necessity of both doubts than Leo Strauss.

Willmoore Kendall called Strauss the greatest teacher of politics since Machiavelli. I do not think that we—or at least I—know enough about politics to know who was its greatest teacher, either before or after Machiavelli. But I think I know what Kendall meant by that assertion, and why it is eminently plausible. For it was Strauss who, in a long series of works, culminating in *Thoughts on Machiavelli,* laid bare the Machiavellian roots of modernity and of the specific teachings of the great moderns. With very few even apparent exceptions, Strauss proved beyond a reasonable doubt that the great political philosophers after Machiavelli—for example Spinoza, Hobbes, Locke, Montesquieu, Rousseau, Hegel, and Marx—were all, in the decisive respects, disciples of Machiavelli. All of them attempted in their doctrines to guarantee the actualization of a certain kind of just or legitimate regime, by taking their bearings, not by that regime which is everywhere best, but by what all men actually everywhere are. They tried to assure the fulfillment of the goal of political life by lowering that goal.

Kendall rightly observed that Strauss would not have been able to penetrate the Machiavellian origins of modernity, had he not himself transcended those origins. Machiavelli had denied that political life can be understood best or guided by what is highest. Yet Strauss, notwithstanding his respect, or even awe, of Machiavelli's greatness, quietly denied that denial. No brief quotation can epitomize the vast sweep of Strauss's work, but I commend to you the following, for the concise simplicity—indeed for the classic grandeur—with which it denies Machiavelli's most fundamental denial. It is taken from the Preface to the 1965 translation of *Spinoza's Critique of Religion.* "It is safer," wrote Strauss, "to try to understand the low in the light of the high than the high in the light of the low. In doing the latter one necessarily distorts the high, whereas in doing the former one does not deprive the low of the freedom to reveal itself fully as what it is." Clearly, all the state of nature theorists, and all the historical schools, tried to understand decent civil society—the high—in the light of the most indecent and powerful passions. Kant's doctrine of Categorical Imperative would seem to be that point in modern philosophical thought furthest removed from Machiavellianism. In it, every consideration of personal advantage, every element of expedience, would seem to be removed. But what is the "good will" celebrated by Kant? Is it not an abstraction from that view of morality that is drawn from the distinction between mere interestedness and disinterestedness? And is not this view blind to the differences between noble and base interests? Is not Kant's attempt to "democratize" morality, by getting rid of the wise man as the judge of the moral man, an attempt to present the high in the light of the low? There are other and even stronger proofs that in the decisive respects, Kant too was a Machiavellian.

PERMANENT QUESTIONS

Strauss never thought that Machiavelli or his greatest disciples themselves understood the high simply in the light of the low. Had they done so, they could not have created works of such complex beauty, and Strauss thought that Machiavelli's works were very beautiful. The distinction between the wise few and the unwise many was as fundamental to Machiavellianism as to the classics. Political philosophy, Strauss often said—and wrote—was constituted essentially by permanent questions, to which there were no final answers. The great moderns agreed with the great ancients, both as to the permanence of these questions and as to the loftiness of life devoted to their consideration. But they did not think that the kind of man devoted to this life—the man of utmost refinement—could be the prototype of the political man. They placed more confidence in institutions, institutions whose dark foundations would be laid by unrefined men, institutions which incorporated their refined understanding of political reality, but whose success would not require such understanding for their operation. Still, only theoretical men could have denied so comprehensively to theory its sovereign role, or have constructed such theoretical books to enshrine that denial. The contemplation of the modern—or the Machiavellian—alternative is that it points toward the annihilation of that horizon within which alone its greatness is visible.

On what we may call the practical level, Strauss's career was constituted by the articulation of the difference between ancients and moderns. For it was with this difference that he provided us the bearings for understanding "where we are, and wither we are tending." On the purely theoretical level, it turned rather upon the difference between reason and revelation. These two principles represented the most fundamental alternatives to the most permanent of questions, concerning how man ought to live. Modernity itself was seen by Strauss as the most determined and comprehensive of human efforts to escape from the dilemma arising from the conflicts engendered in political life by these rival and ambiguous principles. Within the Jewish community, Spinoza was the greatest authority for that new conception both of reason and revelation in which all hitherto insoluble differences were to be reconciled. Spinoza as the philosophical founder of the critical-history study of the Bible, was a founder—if not the founder—of both liberal Judaism and liberal Christianity. He was moreover the first great political philosopher who may be said to have been a proponent of liberal democracy, of that regime which, among its other advantages, transcends the age-old differences of race and religion and allows men to become fellow citizens under a rule of law on a ground supplied by natural rights.

When Strauss wrote that first book on Spinoza he was, as he tells us in that same Preface, "a young Jew born and raised in Germany who found himself in the grip of the theologico-political predicament." What was that predicament? The Weimar Republic was a liberal democracy, says Strauss, which "proclaimed its moderate, nonradical character: its resolve to keep a balance between the dedication to the principles of 1789 and the dedication to the highest German tradition." In short, the Weimar regime represented, in a high degree, that resolution of the human problem that modernity at its best had promised. Strauss never failed to see the weakness of the Weimar regime as a paradigm of the weakness not merely of German liberal democracy, but of modernity. While he never failed to appreciate all the particular reasons for the tragedy of German liberalism, he never thought that the deepest and longest run, the strongest reason for tragedy was merely German. No one appreciated better than he—nor was anyone more grateful than he for—the strength no less than the decency of Anglo-American democracy. But he began his Walgreen lectures in 1949 with a prophecy, that what was happening here would be the first time that a nation, Germany in this case, defeated on the field of battle, had imposed the yoke of its thought on its conqueror. Still, that thought was radically modern, rather than radically German.

THE HUMAN PROBLEM

The young Strauss knew the weakness of the Weimar Republic. He knew the vulnerability of the German Jewish community—also the most liberal in Europe—should Weimar fail. But neither he nor anyone else could guess that the regime that would replace it would have no other clear principle, as he says, than murderous hatred of the Jews. Strauss was certainly attracted then by political Zionism. But political Zionism was an attempt to provide a political solution to a problem originated by religious differences, the very differences that liberalism was designed to transcend. But it was itself essentially a liberal solution, since it was based upon an idea of nationality—of humanity and culture—divorced from Jewish orthodoxy. But there was no idea of Jewish nationality or culture that was possible that did not point to Jewish orthodoxy as its core. Merely political Zionism proved to be a self-contradiction. In this context, Strauss's Jewish studies led him, not merely to a profounder understanding than Spinoza, but beyond Spinoza, to that greatest Jewish thinker, Maimonides. And it was Maimonides who pointed the way for him to Al Farabi, the tenth century Muslim philosopher, and ultimately to Socrates. Henceforth his Jewishness would not take the form of any political commitment as such, but of a quiet pride in a tradition that he now knew incorporated the highest as well as the most sacred wisdom.

The establishment of the state of Israel, Strauss thought, "procured a blessing for all Jews everywhere regardless of whether they admit it or not." But it did not solve the Jewish problem. That problem was at bottom the problem arising from the challenge of the revelation itself, which science had not refuted, and for which the ethics of humanity was no substitute. The Jews, whose heritage made them the highest symbols of the demand of God Himself that men live on the highest level, had become symbols of that cosmopolitanism which represented the lowering of goals of political life, ultimately in the interest of the universal and homogenous state. The Nazis had singled out the Jews as representatives of international banking and international Communism, the ostensibly degenerate symbols of the lowered goals of modern cosmopolitanism. But the Nazis were not Christians. Their hatred of the Jews was a hatred of the entire tradition of the West. Hitler's romantic longing for the Middle Ages was an irrational longing for a past purged of the reality of its struggle with reason and revelation. The Jewish problem was, in the end, the human problem.

Strauss did not believe that the principles of reason and revelation could ever be reduced one to the other. Hence he did not believe in the possibility of a synthesis, since any synthesis would imply a higher principle than either, a principle which regulated the combination. Catholic Christianity, which found its highest expression in Thomas Aquinas, attempted such a synthesis. Strauss admired the magnificence of Thomas' efforts, and saw in them a great humanizing and moderating of Catholic theology. Perhaps the greatest gain from the Thomistic synthesis was that Aristotle, from being a forbidden author, became eventually a recommended one. But only in traditional Judaism did the idea of revelation, and of tradition undivided and uncompromised by syncretism, find its full expression. And Western civilization at its highest expressed the tension between Greek rationalism and Jewish revelation.

Strauss may in the end be best remembered for his works on Socrates, the preoccupation of his last years. For Socrates was the man who seemed to have discovered, or to have invented, political philosophy. For he was the man who either first asked the questions which formed its core, or at least asked them in such a way as to make their asking itself a way of life. The Socratic way of life was a continual demonstration that the rulers of Athens—and of course every actual regime anywhere—did not really know the things they thought they knew, knowledge of which was implied in every action they took. By implying that statesmen should know what they needed to know, Socrates implied that every existing regime was defective, and that it had a duty to transform itself into something better—ultimately into the best regime. That of course, implied a disloyalty to Athens sufficient to justify Socrates' execution. Yet Strauss did not think Socrates' teaching was utopian, in the sense that everyone should strive to introduce the best regime. Socrates confessed that he knew nothing, and that knowledge of ignorance is, or should be, moderating, if not humbling. Statesmanship informed by the awareness of ignorance is not likely to aim at final, much less at universal solutions, solutions which imply that we actually do know what we do not know. The best regime is not a political regime: it lives in speech and not in deed. But it *is* the best, and we need not transform the world in order to live there—we need only to transform ourselves. No one who has experienced the magic of Leo Strauss's teaching can doubt that whatever amelioration of our condition is possible will come about by the influence upon those who exercise political power of its spirit.

I have been asked to say a word on my own studies of Lincoln, and the American regime, in their relationship to Strauss. The most obvious connection is between Strauss's many expositions of Locke and Locke's massive influence upon America. Locke certainly represented modernity in its soberest form, although Strauss was careful to emphasize Locke's ultimate, if concealed, insobriety. But Strauss also thought that American politics at its best showed a practical wisdom that owed much to a tradition older than Locke. Indeed Locke's esoteric teaching, which emphasized that older tradition, was taken with the greatest seriousness here. But the American regime was not formed only by Locke. Many a frontier log cabin, which had in it no philosophical works whatever, had the King James Bible—and Shakespeare. And Shakespeare was the greatest vehicle within the Anglo-American world for the transmission of an essentially Socratic understanding of the civilization of the West.

CLASSICAL PHILOSOPHY

Most Americans' studies begin, and properly begin, with the Constitution. The Constitution does not define the regime, but it is the most public and visible expression of it. It is part of the defect of modern politics that it looks to the character of the law, more than the character of the men who make and enforce the law, however intimate the connection between them necessarily is. However admirable the character of the American Constitution, it was not, I thought, the most admirable expression of the regime. The Constitution is the highest American thing, only if one tries to understand the high in the light of the low. It is high because men are not angels, and because we do not have angels to govern us. Its strength lies in its ability to connect the interest of the man with the duty of the place. But the Constitution, in deference to man's non-angelic nature, made certain compromises with slavery. And partly because of those compromises, it dissolved in the presence of a greater crisis. The man—or the character of the man—who bore the nation through that crisis, seemed to me—and Strauss gave me every encouragement to believe it—the highest thing in the American regime. The character of Lincoln became intelligible, not on the basis of *The Federalist*—profound as that work is—but on that of the *Nicomachean Ethics*. In the final analysis, not only American politics, but all modern politics, must be clarified on the basis of classical political philosophy. That is because, "It is safer to try to understand the low in the light of the high than the high in the light of the low. In doing the latter, one necessarily distorts the high, whereas in doing the former one does not deprive the low of the freedom to reveal itself fully as what it is."[2]

We leave to others—more detached and more objective—the judgment of Strauss's place among the political philosophers. For us who have had the privilege of knowing him as a teacher and as a friend, we can only say that of the men we have known, he was the best, and the wisest, and the most just.

NOTES

Originally published in *National Review*, Vol. XXV, Issue 49, 1973.

1. These remarks prepared especially for *National Review* were delivered orally at a memorial service for Leo Strauss at the Claremont Colleges on November 3, 1973.
2. Leo Strauss, *Liberalism Ancient and Modern* (New York: Basic Books, 1968), p. 225.

THREE

Political Philosophy and Honor

The Leo Strauss Dissertation Award

> In what way shall we bury you? However you wish, if you can catch me, and I do not escape from you. Then he laughed gently, and turned and looked at us, and said: I do not, men, persuade Crito, that I am that Socrates who has been discussing and conducting argument; but he thinks I am that other one, whom he will see a little later as a dead body, and asks, how will he bury me.
>
> —*Phaedo*, 115C

Nothing perhaps better illustrates the enduring character of political philosophy than the enduring presence of its body servants, whose piety would inter the soul of the teaching with the body of the teacher.

At its annual meeting in 1974 the American Political Science Foundation established the Leo Strauss Annual Dissertation Award in political philosophy. This action followed a petition addressed to the Council of the Association, signed by some forty-four distinguished teachers and scholars. Of these, it appeared, more than half were former students of Leo Strauss. The petition declared, among other things, that:

> There is at present no such award in the field of political philosophy. We believe the establishment of one to be particularly important and timely. It is important that the association signalize to the profession in general, and to graduate students in this field, its recognition of political philosophy as one of the important traditions within the discipline.

In 1959 Leo Strauss published a book with the title essay, "What is Political Philosophy?" In that essay, Strauss wrote that: "Today, political philosophy is in a state of decay and perhaps putrefaction, if it has not vanished altogether. Not only is there complete disagreement regarding its subject matter, its methods, and its function; its very possibility in any form has become questionable."

Familiar as I am with this and many similar passages in Strauss's writings, I was compelled to wonder at this "important and timely . . . recognition of political philosophy." Had the corpse suddenly sprung to life since 1959? Or had Strauss been utterly wrong then (and indeed to the last moment of his life) concerning the state of political philosophy? Certainly the latter seemed more likely than the former. But if so, so much the more inappropriate such an award to honor a man who was so mistaken. In any event, the logical disjunction seemed to me to be complete, between Strauss's assertion of "complete disagreement" concerning what political philosophy was, and an award by those in complete disagreement, in honor of Leo Strauss.

On February 4, 1975, I addressed the following letter to the editor of the *American Political Science Review.* Needless to say, I was refused publication both in the *Review*, and its sister journal, *PS*:

> When I arrived in Chicago for the meeting of A.P.S.A. last August, I learned—after the fact—of the establishment of a Leo Strauss Annual Dissertation Award. At the time, I was too surprised to react in any way other than by astonishment. Since then I have given it much thought, and the more I have thought of it, the less I have liked it.
>
> In my own eulogy of Strauss, I observed with no little diffidence that to honor a man implies confidence in the one honoring, no less than excellence in him who is honored. To doubt the former necessarily involves doubting the latter as well. While there is no escape from this dilemma, one may nevertheless approach it with a certain prudence. This I fear the promoters of the award have not done . . .
>
> Leo Strauss was at odds with the mainstream—or perhaps one should say the various mainstreams—of the political science profession throughout his career. His best known statement about the majority of his colleagues concluded by declaring that, like Nero, they were fiddling while Rome burned. They were saved from the reproach of being Neronian, he said, only by the fact that they did not know they were fiddling, and that they did not know that Rome was burning.
>
> Strauss's contempt was warmly reciprocated within the profession. This was shown by the attack, not only on Strauss, but on his school, by Schaar and Wolin, in the pages of the *American Political Science Review* in an extended review (followed by rebuttals and replies) of *Essays on the Scientific Study of Politics*. This volume, by Strauss's former students, concluded with his famous epilogue. On the whole, Strauss enjoyed this adversarial relationship. *Solet Aristotles quaerere pugnam* was the epigraph for his Walgreen Lectures in 1949. And Aristotle himself did not join the battle more assiduously than did Leo Strauss. How then is an Association consisting overwhelmingly of those whom Strauss attacked, and who attacked him, during his life, to agree on the standards of excellence to be honored in his name?

The motion in favor of the Strauss Award speaks of 'the universal recognition of Strauss's exemplary devotion to the philosophic study of politics.' In truth, however, there has been no such recognition of Strauss, nor did he ever wish for it. If there can be no universal recognition of the philosophic study of politics, how can there be universal recognition of Strauss's devotion to it? If Strauss ever taught anything, it is the impossibility, not to mention the undesirability, of such universal opinions. Indeed he was particularly averse to any alleged universal opinion in favor of a philosophic study of politics. Could there be such an opinion, he thought, it might lead to the establishment of the universal tyranny of the universal homogenous state. That was his contention in his debate with Kojève in *On Tyranny*.

The proposal to honor Strauss with an annual dissertation award bears a resemblance to a similar proposal made by the first political scientist, Hippodamus, as reported in the second book of the *Politics*. How will the field of 'political philosophy' be defined for the purpose of the award? The profession generally speaks of 'political theory.' And political theory is usually divided into 'normative' and 'empirical.' But this latter distinction is founded on that between 'facts' and 'values,' a distinction that Strauss attacked again and again. I cannot imagine anyone, familiar with Strauss's work, who would impute validity to the distinction between normative and empirical theory. Yet most dissertations in "theory" will probably be based upon it. Will they be eligible for the award or not?

The distinction between the 'normative' and the 'empirical' is paralleled by certain others, e.g., that between theory and practice. Is the field of 'political philosophy' to consist in the study of the books of those called political philosophers, or is it equally the philosophic study of political things, e.g., the words and deeds of politicians, legislators, judges, and generals, and including the study of constitutions, wars, elections, and trials. Although Strauss's own work consisted mainly in the reading and interpreting of philosophic books, the books he read—and praised—frequently encouraged a much more inclusive conception of the field of political philosophy. This was certainly true of Aristotle's *Politics*. But if the scope of the award is to be so broad how will the selection process deal with it?

But this brings us to the central problem, that of the judges themselves. Are they to be so called "Straussians"? If they are, I can assure my professional colleagues that it will not be long before differences as acute as any others will show themselves in any group so denominated. But surely, it would be as foolish as it would be impracticable, to try to appoint judges with such a bias. The American Political Science Association is, within limits, and in a manner appropriate to a professional association, a constitutional democracy. A prize committee of the Association *ought* therefore to reflect and to represent the standards of the majority.

And, I think, it inevitably will do so. As we all know, constitutional majorities are themselves almost invariably coalitions of differing groups, who have agreed to disagree on some things, in order to act together on others. It is not difficult to anticipate how this process will affect an awards committee. There will be logrolling between factions, so that a work reflecting one persuasion will win one year, to be followed by one of another the next. In neither case will the best work be chosen on its own merits. Any work that attempts to make peace among the factions by appealing to some common denominator among them will succeed only by calculated mediocrity. Works of genuine brilliance or distinction will seldom if ever have a chance, because they will antagonize by their uncompromising superiority. It is virtually inconceivable that any of Strauss's books, had they been submitted as dissertations, could have won such an award. The prize will, therefore, discourage, rather than encourage the emulation of Leo Strauss. I should add that among the minor features that I find objectionable, is making an *annual* award, without regard to whether there is, in any year, a dissertation of sufficient merit. Nor should there, I think ever be such an award, without an assurance of publication. Not only is publication a much better incentive than money, but it allows the work of the prize committee, as well as that of the prize winner, to be judged by a more impartial public.

> Leo Strauss was not a political man. He sought wisdom rather than honor. He certainly wanted recognition, in part to reassure himself in the critical and skeptical attitude he maintained even towards his own work. But he also felt that recognition of his work should form part of a learning process, that benefited the recognizers, and made them thereby more competent judges. Political honors are produced mainly by agreement; and, as Strauss taught, agreement leads to peace, but not truth. The truth seeker, on the contrary, is accustomed to seeking a fight. We honor Strauss best by carrying on the fight for truth, even if that may mean opposing so unwise an enterprise as an annual dissertation award in the name of Leo Strauss.

Copies of this letter were sent to many members of the profession, including most of those who had signed the petition for the award. Many I knew to be keen students of the problem of knowledge, so central to the problem of political knowledge, and hence to the question of what is political philosophy. They knew that I had asked, in effect, how one could offer a prize for the best drawing of a horse, to those who had never seen a horse. Or alternatively, how a panel of judges could award a prize for a drawing of a horse, if the judges themselves had never seen a horse, or did not know that they had ever seen a horse. Suppose that one judge thought a horse very much like a bear, another that it was much more like a lion, while a third was convinced it closely resembled a camel, but that all would instantly agree that anyone who pointed to a real horse, must be an ass!

The response to my letter may be characterized on the whole as a sullen silence, punctuated by muttered imprecations. I received altogether three written replies. Only one respondent was candid in agreement, saying that he doubted anyone would ever receive the Strauss Award to whom Strauss himself would have given a grade higher than a "C." The others, while not venturing to contradict either my premises or my reasoning, rejected the conclusion. Of course, I did not need this exercise to persuade myself of the very limited possibilities of persuasion in such a case. It was thirty years since I had last sat at the feet of Leo Strauss, and heard him discourse upon Polemarchus' refusal to hear why it might be good for Socrates and Glaucon to return to Athens from Piraeus. Still, it was more than merely ironical that such a refusal should come from those who have undertaken to honor Leo Strauss, and to promote the good of political philosophy.

In the murmured discontent that sometimes broke the sullen silence, I detected the objection that my argument, although perhaps correct in "theory," was nonetheless wrong in "practice." I was familiar with Aristotle's conception of prudence (*phronesis*), in accordance with which political speeches—or documents belonging to the genus of political speech—may be considered not merely as words but as deeds. Strauss often quoted Lord Macaulay's famous formulation, that "If they effect that which they are intended to effect, they are rational though they may be contradictory. If they fail of obtaining their end, they are absurd." But what end was the Leo Strauss award intended to effect? Let us suppose it was the end announced by the supporters, *viz.*, the "recognition of political philosophy as one of the important traditions within the discipline." We need not further labor the point that one does not promote the recognition of something that one has not recognized by pretending to recognize it. But we observe that the promoters call political philosophy "one of the most important traditions *within* the discipline." Who that knows anything of Strauss's work, does not know of his relentless denial that political philosophy, properly so called, was *one* among *many*? To provide only one of the many possible illustrations, we submit this passage from "What is Political Philosophy?"

> The goal of the general is victory, whereas the goal of the statesman is the common good. What victory means is not essentially controversial, but the meaning of the common good is essentially controversial. The ambiguity of the political goal is due to its controversial character. Thus the temptation arises to deny, or to evade the comprehensive character of politics and to treat politics as one compartment among many. But this temptation must be resisted if it is necessary to face our situation as human beings, i.e., the whole situation.[1]

One of the least invidious things one can say of the Strauss Award is that it exhibits a kind of amnesia in regard to what Strauss himself had insisted was the necessary condition for the possibility of political philosophy. Perhaps it also reflected a weariness with the controversy that always surrounded Strauss. But that controversy did not arise from any idiosyncrasy of Leo Strauss; it was instrinsic to the nature of his vocation.

If it seemed to be idiosyncratic, that stemmed from the fact that he took that vocation with greater seriousness than any other man of his time. The desire to make one's peace with the world is understandable. But it is the task of political philosophy to ask, what is that world with which one would make one's peace? To call that political philosophy, which asks that question in anything less than a perfectly comprehensive manner, is to abandon the possibility of a genuine answer. Yet upon the possibility of a genuine answer rests the fate of everything that is—or ought to be—dear to us. Such at any rate was Strauss's conviction.

We also observe that the promoters of the award—in the interest, no doubt, of the professional harmony and democratic consensus—not only dethrone political philosophy from its monarchical estate, but describe it as a "tradition." Without demeaning or impugning the traditions, and the many traditional things that are very dear to us, we must nonetheless ask, why in the world should political philosophy—a discipline of the mind—be commended as a "tradition"? Aristotle tells us that the remains of the ancient laws are "altogether foolish," and that what men seek is not the ancestral but the good [*Politics,* 1269a1–5]. Political philosophy comes to light with the discovery of the distinction between the ancestral (the old which is one's own) and the good. If there were but a single tradition in the world, such a discovery would not have taken place, and indeed would be unnecessary. But there are in fact many traditions of mankind, and they proclaim many contradictory things about the right way of life. If then political philosophy is itself nothing more than a tradition, it is utterly powerless to guide us in the face of conflicting traditions. For that which is itself but one among many, cannot tell us what the whole—the one compound of many—ought to be.

According to Strauss, "the character of classical political philosophy appears with the greatest clarity from Plato's *Laws,* which is his political work par excellence." The *Laws* is a dialogue between three old men which takes place on the island of Crete, by tradition the home of the oldest of Greek laws. One's first impression, says Strauss, is that the Athenian, the principal interlocutor, has come to Crete to discover the best laws. But one soon discovers that on the contrary he has come "to introduce into Crete new laws and institutions, truly good laws and institutions." The Cretans, Strauss reminds us, were famous not only for their laws, but for their mendacity; and the two, it appears, are not unrelated. For the authority of their laws was derived from the assurance that they had been given by Minos, son of Zeus. Have not the promoters of the Strauss Award, ignoring the distinction between the one and the many, and between the traditional and the good, promoted something much less akin to Strauss's own Socratic rationalism, than to Cretan traditionalism?

Another correspondent had pronounced my letter to the editor of the *American Political Science Review* to be "overly sectarian." This objection—

made without further explanation—struck me as having a peculiar irony. To be sectarian usually means to be unduly narrow. Yet I was defending political philosophy from a narrowing of its scope, and from its "domestication" within the "tradition" of current American political science. Still, the paradox of philosophy—the attempt to replace opinions of the whole with knowledge of the whole—appearing as a sectarian cause, is as old as philosophy itself. Hence I took this objection with some seriousness and responded as follows:

> I agree as far as the adjective which makes it impossible to agree to the adverb. Strauss himself was the Great Sectarian of our time, in much the same sense that Doctor Johnson meant when he said that the Devil was the First Whig. ["Philosophy, as distinct from wisdom, necessarily appears in the form of philosophic schools or sects" Strauss, in *On Tyranny*, p. 208.]
>
> Francis Bacon said of the Greek philosophy . . . that it was "like the boyhood of knowledge, and has the characteristic property of boys: it can talk but cannot generate; for it is fruitful of controversy but barren of works." Elsewhere Bacon speaks of the "contentious and thorny philosophy of Aristotle." Modern philosophy . . . seeks to put an end to the contentiousness of Socratic philosophy by finding a method that will at once produce agreement and truth. As far as I know, Strauss was the first, or at least the most radical, of those who have challenged this entire enterprise—in perhaps 400 years. Those who have heretofore challenged modernity—for example Rousseau, Nietzsche, and Heidegger—have done so, whether originally or in the end, on the basis of a more radical modernity. Strauss alone, so far as I know, has challenged modernity . . . from a point of view absolutely detached from its [modernity's] roots and its branches.

This provoked—or elicited—one further reply. I was told that I was "certainly right in saying that Leo Strauss is the most radical challenger of the entire modern enterprise." With this challenge, my correspondent declared, he had "considerable sympathy." However, he said,

"we live in modernity, not elsewhere, and I think it is a simple matter of prudence to 'work within the system,' to the degree that we can. One of the reasons I feel that way is that all the rebellions against modernity in our century seemed destined to assume monstrous shapes. Besides, I am essentially a reformist and meliorist by temperament."

To this I accordingly responded as follows:

> There is certainly no difference between us on the proposition that we must "live in modernity, not elsewhere," and that it is "a simple matter of prudence to 'work within the system.'" I agree emphatically that the typical "rebellions against modernity in our century . . . have assumed monstrous shapes." Like you, I think of myself as "essentially a reformist and a meliorist by temperament." Where then do we differ?

> One must, I think, be a meliorist and reformist, not only by temperament, but by conviction. Reformism and meliorism have their proper home only within a decent system, which offers reasonable modes of redress and of change. What place is there for reformism and meliorism in a Nazi concentration camp, or in the Gulag of Archipelago? The ultimate indictment of American slavery was not the brutal treatment—real or alleged—of the slaves. No matter what material rewards were offered within the system, the fact remains that no matter how talented, industrious, and ambitious a slave might be, he could never look forward to freedom. In the generation before the Civil War, nearly all roads leading towards emancipation were systematically cut off. In the end reform was not possible, and war became necessary.
>
> Strauss's indictment of the "new political science" was above all that it abstracted from the difference between a decent and humane constitutionalism, and the vilest of tyrannies. The reductionism of such a science led to the characterization of the political phenomena in terms of the sub-rational, in terms of impulses, urges, drives, and desires. In the urge and drive to quantify, qualities disappeared, and the differences of regimes disappeared from the characterization of regimes.
>
> The rebellions against modernity that have taken such shapes have done so because they have taken the forms of radicalizations of modernity. Because his detachment from modernity was so much greater than all previous critics of modernity, Strauss alone could supply us with a theoretical foundation for a moderate politics within modernity. For Strauss did have a practical teaching, and it took the form of a celebration of the virtues, above all, of Anglo-American constitutionalism at its best. The preoccupation, among his students, with the American Founders, with Lincoln, with Churchill, is a direct reflection of this teaching.
>
> But liberal democracy, Strauss taught, although it may treat many things unequal in themselves, as being politically equal, cannot treat the principles of liberal democracy as being no better or worse than their denial. Yet it was neutrality upon this life and death issue that constituted the heart of the 'new political science.' This is what Strauss meant when he said the fiddlers did not even know that Rome was burning. Is it not absurd then, for the sake of meliorism and reformism, to have a fiddler's award in the name of Leo Strauss?

A further objection to my letter to the editor of the *American Political Science Review* took the form of a query, whether this was the proper time to remind the profession of Strauss's opinion of it. What made "this time" improper, I gathered, was the willingness of so many with whom Strauss had differed to join in expressing pious regard for his memory. Surely such piety is commendable, and one should let the dead past bury its dead. But what of the living future of political philosophy? Strauss's life was a struggle against its grave diggers. In such a case, what has piety, any more than tradition, to do with right action? Strauss frequently pointed to the absence of piety from the lists of the virtues in the *Nicoma-*

chean Ethics. And he just as frequently pointed to the one passage in the book where piety is mentioned. It is where Aristotle, differing with the school of Plato, declares that, although both are dear to us, piety requires that we honor truth even before our friends. Certainly Socrates' piety consisted in nothing so much as his philosophizing, or in his refusal to cease philosophizing, in the face of any threat, or any temptation whatever. Strauss's quarrel with contemporary political science resembled Socrates' quarrel with the disciples of the ancient poets. For the myths of modern science upon which the academic discipline of political science today so largely rests are the pre-Socratic poetry of modernity. To obscure, much less to forget, this quarrel, is to obscure or to forget the purpose of Strauss's life, however one may piously intend to remember his name.

A final objection to my argument was that the Strauss Award was unlikely to have any grave consequences, either good or bad. This is perhaps the most difficult of all objections to deal with. Surely none of us who teach political philosophy—and that certainly included Strauss—expect anything we do or say (or write) to have "grave consequences," as the world usually understands these matters. All of Strauss's work took place within the setting of what he calls the crisis of the West. A diagnosis or prognosis of that crisis was the expressed or implied preface to nearly all of his reading of the great books. And the deepening of his understanding of that crisis was almost invariably part of the conclusion of such reading. Yet he never seems to have thought that his works would alter the course of that crisis—except as that crisis was also a crisis within the souls of those whom he taught. Like Churchill—whom I think he admired more than any other man in his time—Strauss seemed to think there are struggles which one has a duty to carry on, without regard to the prospect of success. But—again, like Churchill—he was no determinist, and did not believe that any cause is doomed to failure, simply because the odds against it are great.

Strauss was primarily concerned with the quality of human life. 'How does one live well?' 'What is virtue?' and 'What is the best regime?' were alternative forms of fundamentally the same question. But good action is its own end, and the gravity of an action is to be understood primarily with respect to its excellence, and not with respect to its consequences. So it seems to me that whether or not the Strauss Award has grave consequences is less important than whether its establishment is in itself a good or bad action. My argument was directed primarily towards demonstrating that it was a bad action, whose consequences—if there were any—were also bound to be bad.

Political philosophy is concerned to know the principles of political action, which in their true or comprehensive meaning are the principles of human action. The teachers of political philosophy, like all other human beings, reveal the quality of their principles by deed no less than by speech. They carry a greater responsibility for their actions than other human beings, to know what is the human good, and hence how to act well. If they do not act well, within whatever sphere is theirs, however small, and especially if they undermine thoughtful speech by thoughtless action, they inevitably corrupt the young. Can there be any graver consequence than that?

In the tenth book of the *Nicomachean Ethics*, Aristotle says that in matters of passions and actions, words (*logoi*) are less persuasive than deeds (*erga*). Whenever the latter are out of harmony with the former, they provoke contempts, and in addition bring destruction (*prosnariousin*) upon the truth. But when, on the contrary, words (*logoi*) are not only true, but in harmony with deeds, they persuade, and urge on towards a life in accordance with them [1172a35–b7]. Surely, the doctrine of this passage is ineluctably part of any serious effort to revive the study of political philosophy, in the spirit of Leo Strauss.

In the second book of the *Politics*, Aristotle takes to task one Hippodamus who, he says, was the first man, not engaged in political activity, to speak of the best regime. Among Hippodamus' proposals, was one which would honor anyone who discovered something useful for the city. Some of the most profound sentences Strauss ever wrote are in his interpretation of Aristotle's critique of Hippodamus, in *The City and Man*. "On the basis of some observation made nearer to home," Strauss wrote, for example, "one might suspect a connection between Hippodamus' unbridled concern with clarity and simplicity and his unbridled concern with technological progress." How near to home was Strauss's suspicion, perhaps not even he suspected. What could be more evident than the advantage of having something better, whether it be a mousetrap or a law? And how better to have something better, than to reward its inventor? Strauss is at some pains to expound Aristotle's account of Hippodamus' simplemindedness in his failure to understand the difference between improvement in the arts, and improvement in the laws. It is comical self-contradiction moreover, to make a proposal implying the possibility of unlimited change in what is supposed to be the best regime. Yet even supposing the desirability of change in the laws, Aristotle asks, is it proper to introduce change into all laws, or only into some? Into every regime, or not into every regime? And is anyone to introduce these changes, or only some people? [*Politics*, 1269a25–28] Aristotle does not answer these questions here. Yet is it not clear that by proposing a contest for honor, in the city, by the city, Hippodamus is proposing what is necessarily a *political* contest? How can any such contest differ in its essential nature from any other political contest for honor, or office? The reason why Hippodamus did not understand the difference between art and law, was that at the bottom he did not understand the difference between philosophy and politics. It was above all because of this that he could not become the first political philosopher.

The rebirth of political philosophy, no less than its birth, depends upon comprehending the difference between politics and philosophy. The promoters of the Leo Strauss Award, by proposing to recognize political philosophy by a political process, in so doing, have shown themselves heirs of Hippodamus, not of Aristotle or of Strauss. Yet they are excused by two apparent facts: They do not recognize what it is they are *not* promoting; and because of this, they cannot know what it is they *are* promoting in its place.

NOTES

Originally published in *Modern Age*, Vol. 21, No. 4, Fall 1977. Reprinted as the appendix to *How to Think about the American Revolution* (Durham: Carolina Academic Press, 1978).

1. Leo Strauss, *What is Political Philosophy? And Other Essays* (Chicago: University of Chicago Press, 1988), pp. 16–17.

FOUR

The Legacy of Leo Strauss

Review of Studies in Platonic Political Philosophy *by Leo Strauss with an Introduction by Thomas L. Pangle and a Foreword by Joseph Cropsey*

In 1974, the year following Leo Strauss's death, the American Political Science Association established an annual award, in his honor, for the best dissertation in the field of political philosophy. The petition in favor of such an award was signed by a solid phalanx of Strauss's students, although there was also a number who were not in any sense "Straussians." The petition observed that there was at present no award in political philosophy, and expressed the belief that the establishment of one by the Association "would signalize to the profession in general, and to graduate students in this field, its recognition of political philosophy as one of the important traditions within the discipline." The motion by which the petition was adopted spoke of "the universal recognition of Strauss's exemplary devotion to the philosophic study of politics." The irony in this hyperbole is today universally recognized in the highly publicized aphorism attributed to a member of Yale's political science department that neither Leninists nor Straussians belong in the profession!

I never saw either the petition or the motion until the Leo Strauss Award had become an accomplished fact. I cannot say whether my omission from the ranks of those invited to sign the petition was a matter of foresight, oversight, or insight. Certainly, my standing in the American Political Science Association hardly qualified me for inclusion in any representative enterprise of that august body. However, that would have been equally true of Leo Strauss. If there was any undertaking that might properly have been called "Straussian," it was the *History of Political Phi-*

losophy edited by Strauss and Cropsey. Moreover, Strauss had chosen me to write the chapter on "Aristotle," which immediately follows his chapter on "Plato."

Shortly after Strauss's death, Bill Buckley asked Walter Berns to organize a memorial symposium honoring Strauss in the pages of *National Review*. (It appeared in December 1973.) Berns asked Herbert Storing to write on Strauss and political science, and Werner Dannhauser to write on Strauss and conservatism. Berns asked me to write the central article on Strauss and political philosophy.[1] He also asked that in my eulogy I indicate the relationship between Strauss's work and my own. I think it worth remembering this now, because Berns has recently abused me—in the pages of *National Review* (Jan. 22, 1982)—for "presenting [myself] as the chosen spokesman for Leo Strauss." Of course, I have never done anything of the kind. But in 1973 Berns evidently thought that I was in some particular way qualified to speak of the main theme of Strauss's life and work. He even thought that in remembering Strauss it was proper that I speak of the relationship of his work and my own. Strauss's concern with the "crisis of our time, the crisis of the West" (*The City and Man*, p. 1), and mine with the "crisis of the House Divided" are certainly not unrelated. As I have pointed out elsewhere, Strauss began *Natural Right and History* not only by quoting the sentence beginning, "We hold these truths to be self-evident," but by speaking of the "nation dedicated to this proposition." That is to say, he used Lincoln's words at Gettysburg to characterize the relationship of the Declaration of Independence to the nation and government at whose birth (according to Lincoln) it had presided. Further, Strauss paraphrased Lincoln in speaking of the nation so dedicated becoming "no doubt partly as a consequence of this dedication, the most powerful and prosperous of the nations of the earth." When Strauss asked, "Does this nation in its maturity still cherish the faith in which it was conceived and raised?" he was asking the question which was the core of all of Lincoln's speeches from 1854 until his death. The crisis of the West, in its proximate form in the American regime, was represented for Strauss in the repudiation of that natural right which was embodied in the Declaration of Independence, as that natural right had been interpreted by Abraham Lincoln. Lincoln had spoken of the principles of the Declaration as "our ancient faith," and had appealed to those principles in the manner of an Old Testament prophet, calling upon his people to return to the right way. Like Lincoln (above all in his second inaugural), Strauss too would express the meaning of natural right in the language of the Bible, for the theme of *Natural Right and History* is expressed *a priori* in its epigraphs, which are taken from II Samuel and I Kings. I do not pretend for a moment to speak for Leo Strauss, but I am perfectly convinced that Strauss shared the conviction that Lincoln's appeal, in his greatest speeches, to the Declaration of Independence and to the Bible—to Reason and to Revelation—was the very model of wise statesmanship at the highest level. It was, in particular, a model of that statesmanship in its bearing upon the crisis of the West, the crisis of that civilization constituted at its core by the coming together of doctrines derived from the Bible and from the idea of autonomous human reason. The connection between prophecy and statesmanship, which Strauss himself first learned from the Islamic scholars of Plato, and which he first taught to me in 1945, was the ground upon which my study of Lincoln began. Strauss always taught the importance of "unhesitating loyalty to a decent constitution." He also taught that such a constitution, however modern, would nonetheless require "powerful support from . . . the premodern thought of our western tradition." That support had to come from both Jerusalem and Athens. I do not think that Strauss believed that without such support a decent constitution could remain decent or sustain loyalty to its decency. Again, I do not pretend to speak for Strauss when I express the conviction that Strauss's entire work pointed toward rescuing the *political practice* of the modern world from the consequences of the *political theory* of modern philosophy. The core of Strauss's interpretation of modern political philosophy, understood in the light of its Machiavellian origins, was that it attempted to guarantee the actualization of the goals of political life, first by lowering them, and second in finding institutions whose successful functioning would dispense with the need for virtue. "Scientific" political science has had as its goal the discovery of mathematical necessities in "political matter" that paralleled the necessity in the matter studied by the natural sciences. A properly designed constitution, like a properly designed automobile—or nuclear fission device—would do what it was designed to do because it could not do otherwise. All the virtue of the regime would be in its original design: thereafter it would function without virtue. Human beings would seem to be perfectly free, because they would be obeying the dictates of necessity without being in the least conscious of doing so. This is what Marx's "leap into freedom" means. But human beings would seem to themselves to be free, because they would be denied none of those things that had hitherto been denied them because of the requirements of virtue, as traditionally understood. No one would, for example, be required to be brave or temperate or just: the state would protect you; medical science would repair you; and the economy of abundance would supply you with everything you wanted. Perfect freedom would mean the absence of any conscious self-denial. The fact that no one would ever choose to be brave or temperate or just (or gentle or kind or generous) would simply go unnoticed.

Strauss's critique of modernity pointed toward both its undesirability and its impossibility. This was the meaning of his oft-quoted maxim from the Roman poet Horace: that no matter how often nature was expelled with a pitchfork, it would always return. This maxim of course implied the truth of what radical modernity denied: namely, that there was a nature that placed limits upon human freedom, a nature that was unconquerable. Modernity, however, meant the conquest of nature. Strauss was convinced that the deepest reason in modernity for wanting to conquer nature was a mistaken reason, for he was convinced that even if the technical means for dispensing with virtue were perfected (e.g., if the doctor could always cure you of the consequences of your intemperance), the result would be a combination of boredom and fanaticism, but it would not be happiness. I think, incidentally, that the history of the American Political Science Association in the last thirty years bears out this prophecy, for it is divided between behavioralists, who bore everybody (including themselves), and "caucuses" for black rights, women's rights, "gay" rights, peace, the Third World, etc. One might characterize the state of the profession—the profession that annually awards a prize in the name of Leo Strauss—as one divided between those who pursue facts uncontaminated with values and those who pursue values uncontaminated by facts.

Strauss's work pointed therefore toward the restoration of statesmanship, as exemplified in the lives of such men as Lincoln and Churchill. It pointed toward the restoration of prudence, as that combination of intellectual and moral virtue that is the necessary attribute of statesmanship. More precisely, it pointed toward the restoration of both statesmanship and citizenship. It pointed toward rhetoric, as the art by which the statesman vindicates the rule of law by securing consent to wise decisions. But Strauss never believed that men could be governed by speeches alone, or that the art of rhetoric could ever be separated from the art of war. He liked to point out that Xenophon, the pupil of Socrates, could rule both gentlemen and non-gentlemen. And he often cited Aristotle's criticism of the sophists, for thinking that men could be ruled by speeches alone. Lincoln's and Churchill's speeches could never be studied profitably apart from their deeds. Strauss had nothing but contempt for someone who, like John F. Kennedy, could profess an unbounded admiration for Churchill and could even do a commendable imitation of Churchill in his inaugural address, but who then called off the air cover for the invasion at the Bay of Pigs.

One of my many objections to the Leo Strauss Award was that it assumed that political philosophy meant the study of the works of political philosophers, and did not extend to the study of the speeches and deeds of political men. It did not consider that one principal end and aim of political philosophy, as Strauss understood it, was to provide guidance to political life.

Clearly, the establishment of the Leo Strauss Award represented a sharp change in the attitude toward his work, of many of those who had studied with him. No doubt many voted for the award, simply to express a pious regard for his memory. But no one who actually took note of the meaning of the words, either of the petition or of the resolution, and who had any understanding of Strauss as he understood himself, could have voted for it. That is to say, no one who in any way understood Strauss as he understood himself, and *sympathized* with that understanding, could have done so. It was, among other things, a white flag, by those who had grown weary of Strauss's unrelenting contentiousness, and who wanted now to be at peace with the mainstream of the profession. By accepting the designation of "one" (but only one) of the innumerable disciplines of political science, they accepted the character of a group engaged in the esoteric cultivation of its own garden, who posed no threat to the mainstream.

Lest there be any mistake about it, here is how Strauss himself had referred to that mainstream, in the peroration of his most famous diatribe: "Only a great fool," he had written,

> would call the new political science diabolic: it has no attributes peculiar to fallen angels. It is not even Machiavellian, for Machiavelli's teaching was graceful, subtle, and colorful. Nor is it Neronian. Nevertheless one may say of it that it fiddles while Rome burns. It is excused by two facts: it does not know that it fiddles, and it does not know that Rome burns.[2]

The Leo Strauss Award is a fiddler's award, by those who—like Walter Berns—think that the burning of "Rome" (viz., Jerusalem and Athens) is no concern of the "philosopher." The core of Berns's attack upon me was his allegation that "Strauss did not believe that he, or political philosophy, could save Western civilization," or that it could "reverse 'the decline of the West.'" Such "hopes," Berns declared, "distort the quest for the truth." The "theme of philosophy" according to Berns is "Eternity, not history." Berns's contrast between "eternity" and "history" corresponds, I believe, to a distinction between "theory" and "practice." As Berns here drops the adjective "political," with reference to philosophy, he seems to imply that Strauss was not a political philosopher at all. Or, perhaps, he implies that political philosophy for Strauss meant an exclusive concern with philosophy, and with the protection of "the class interests" of philosophers, but not with the moral and political interests of men and citizens.[3] However, Strauss, in his exchange with Kojève, made it clear that the decline of the West—culminating in the universal and homogeneous world state—would culminate in the complete eclipse, if not the extinction of philosophy. Moreover as Hilail Gildin has written recently:

> [I]t would be a mistake to conclude that Strauss cared about the fate of constitutional democracy only to the extent it was linked to the fate of philosophy. Like Socrates, he was just in more than one sense. His support of liberal democracy can be compared to his support of political Zionism. No one who knew Strauss ever doubted the depth and genuineness of his concern for Israel. Nor could anyone who knew him

> think that this concern was based upon his belief that the fate of philosophy in some mysterious way depended upon the fate of Israel. He thought no such thing. ("Leo Strauss and the Crisis of Liberal Democracy," State University of New York, Geneseo, New York, October 7, 1983)

Strauss cared about the fate of liberal or constitutional democracy and about Israel, as a moral and political man, as he cared about the fate of philosophy, as a philosopher. Indeed, *political* philosophy meant precisely the combination of these concerns, rightly understood. As we shall see, it is the denial of the propriety of this combination that lies at the heart of Thomas Pangle's Introduction to *Studies in Platonic Political Philosophy*, as it lies at the heart of Berns's diatribe against me.

My opinion of the Strauss Award, written immediately after the event, was expressed in an essay entitled "Political Philosophy and Honor." In that essay I pointed to the "Hippodamus Award" celebrated in the second book of Aristotle's *Politics* and to Strauss's commentary upon it in *The City and Man*. In it I pointed to the absurdity of having "the city" decide "what is political philosophy," if it is a purpose of political philosophy to guide "the city." The American Political Science Association—as Strauss hinted broadly in *The City and Man* (viz., "On the basis of some observations made nearer home, one might suspect a connection between Hippodamus's unbridled concern with clarity and his unbridled concern with technological progress," p. 22)—was itself very much a Hippodamean city. And Hippodamus, according to Strauss, failed to become the founder of political philosophy or political science because he failed to distinguish the political from the non-political; for, according to Aristotle, it is impossible to understand the moral and political things without understanding their non-mathematical character (*Nicomachean Ethics* [*NE*] 1094b23 ff).

The Rome that Strauss said was burning, we repeat, was "the West," whose "decline" was central to his concern, as a citizen of a liberal democracy, as a Jew, as a man, and as a political philosopher. "[I]n our age," he had written, in the Introduction to *The City and Man*, "it is much less urgent to show that political philosophy is the indispensable handmaid of theology than to show that political philosophy is the rightful queen of the social sciences, the sciences of man and of human affairs." Notwithstanding the presumption in favor of Revelation, vis-à-vis Reason, with which Strauss here (as elsewhere) begins, he meant to restore political philosophy to its rightful estate among the human disciplines. This meant, of necessity, its restoration as the "architectonic discipline" described in the first book of the *Nicomachean Ethics*. Just as the architect gives commands to the builders, so does the art of the *politikos* "ordain which of the sciences should be studied . . . and which each class of citizens should learn and up to what point" (*NE* 1094a28 ff). To concede, as the promoters of the Strauss Award did, that political philosophy is "one among many" disciplines, the *aggregate* of which constitutes political science, is to concede that it has no practical or political function at all. As I have pointed out elsewhere, the unity of political philosophy, among the human disciplines—the fact that it cannot be counted as "one among many"—is the indispensable condition of its authority. It is the condition of its authority in the same way that the authority of the Biblical God is grounded in the truth that He cannot be counted as "One among many." In Aristotle, political philosophy cannot be counted as "one among many" human disciplines for the same reason that happiness or the human good—of which it is the art or science—cannot be counted as "one among many." Happiness is not a sum or aggregate of good things, nor can its goodness be increased by the addition of any good thing (*NE* 1097b19). Rather it is the good in virtue of which all other goods (e.g., health or wealth or virtue or freedom) become good for man. To concede that political philosophy is "one among many" of the "sciences of man and of human affairs" would imply that there was no comprehensive human good. All individual good things become then, with respect to their goodness, discrete. One cannot then say, as Aristotle says, that one should not pray for wealth or health or freedom, but that one should pray that such things are good *for us*. Aristotle means by this that only as health or wealth or other individual goods lead toward happiness are they genuinely beneficial. To put this in the language of simple morality, good things are good for the good, but bad for the bad. Health, a good thing, was bad for Hitler. Political power, which made Churchill better, made Hitler worse. We also know that there are human beings who, being healthy, wealthy, and free, nevertheless commit suicide. Their blessings were not blessings for *them*. These simple common-sense reflections are, I believe, a key to Strauss's understanding of what is political philosophy. In a sense, the entire "Straussian" enterprise can be understood as an attempt to restore to political philosophy the authority of such common sense reflections upon experiences available to everyone. It is these reflections which lead to the idea of an overarching good, in virtue of which all contingent goods become genuine goods. Without such an idea, there can be no common measure of the goodness of good things, and in this negative sense all "goods" become equal. From this it is a short step to the doctrine that all goods are subjective, or that all goods are "values" and not "facts." The abandonment of the idea of a *summum bonum*, of happiness, or of the idea of the good, is both the necessary and the sufficient condition of radical modernity, of that moral relativism, positivism, and historicism, against which Strauss's entire life was a protest. Strauss would often say that what political life needed primarily was the art of the gentleman, of the man whose decent opinions and good character arose directly from these elementary experiences. Political philosophy, in one sense, became necessary only when "sophistry" undermined the gentleman's unsophisticated attachment to his gentlemanship. False theories, against which gentlemen as gentlemen had no defense, made necessary political philosophy. Modern philosophy had denied the gentlemen—and the citizens whom the gentlemen ruled by consent and right of nature—access to the self-understanding of their own gentlemanship. This, in part, is what Strauss meant by saying that modern man had dug a cave beneath the "natural" cave, and that what he was trying to do was to make possible a return to that original cave. His work can therefore be understood, at least in one of its fundamental aspects, as a refutation of all those false modern theories that prevent gentlemen from exercising the authority that is rightfully theirs. And the great statesmen of the modern world were precisely those who, by some divine dispensation, acted like responsible gentlemen, notwithstanding the theoretical obstacles to their so doing. For example, when, before World War II, Churchill called Hitler "that bad man," the left-wing intellectuals fell out of their chairs laughing, while the right-wing appeasers smiled their smiles of supercilious sophistication. When the bombs fell on London, shortly thereafter, Churchill's speeches were the only thing that gave them the courage that enabled them to survive. No one patronized Churchill then. Nature had indeed returned! (It has of course been subsequently expelled.)

If Strauss's career as a political scientist had any center or focus, it was in his critical destruction of the distinction between "facts" and "values." It was this achievement of Strauss which became the ground, within the profession, of the revival of classical political philosophy—which meant, of course, the revival of the idea of political philosophy as the architectonic practical discipline, as "the queen of the social sciences." Strauss, I maintain, intended not only to revive, but to restore such a discipline. For maintaining this, Walter Berns accuses me of "doctrinairism." "Strauss," he writes, "raised the possibility that ancient thought might be superior to modern thought. Jaffa, however, takes the possibility to be a certitude, thereby making what was supposed to be a fresh openness into just another dogma."[4] But Strauss wrote to Karl Löwith in 1946 (in correspondence published in 1983 in the *Independent Journal of Philosophy*), "I *really* believe, although to you it appears fantastic, that the perfect political order, as Plato and Aristotle sketched it, is the perfect political order" (emphasis by Strauss). Strauss goes on to say that he knows "very well that *today* [such an order] cannot be restored." Yet he nonetheless argues that the knowledge of the regime that is best by nature is decisive for making the right political decision concerning the most fundamental alternative that is open *today*. Strauss's argument in the letter to Löwith is substantially the same as in the famous reply to Kojève. But it is also substantially the same as in Walter Berns's own 1956 essay, "The Case Against World Government" (later versions of which were published in *National Review* in 1960 and 1983). I leave it to the reader to decide whether Strauss's overwhelmingly expressed conviction that "the completely modern solution is *contra naturam*" and therefore bad, is adequately characterized as a "fresh openness" to just another "possibility."

The book before us is entitled *Studies in Platonic Political Philosophy* (University of Chicago Press, 1984). It has fifteen chapters, each a separate essay or article by Leo Strauss. It is followed by a bibliography of Strauss's writings, and an index of the names of authors mentioned in the preceding text. The fifteen chapters are preceded by a foreword by Joseph Cropsey that occupies less than one page. The foreword is followed by an introduction by Thomas L. Pangle, of twenty-six pages. This is accompanied by a page giving the "Abbreviations [of] Works by Leo Strauss Cited in the Introduction." The references cited by Pangle are as interesting for what they omit as for what they include, but we have no time to pursue this matter here. Given fifteen chapters, the central one is the essay entitled "Note on the Plan of Nietzsche's *Beyond Good and Evil*." But Cropsey, in his foreword, tells us that it had been Strauss's intention to have added two more chapters: "a projected paper on Plato's *Gorgias* . . . was to have been placed after the paper on the *Euthydemus*." This "would have brought to three the number of essays on Platonic dialogues." Strauss did not live to write this, nor "the introduction that would . . . have explained his choice of title." If we assume that the Introduction would have been chapter I, and the paper on the Gorgias chapter 4, the chapter entitled "Jerusalem and Athens: Some Preliminary Reflections," instead of being chapter 7 (of 15) would have been chapter 9 (of 17). In short, it appears to have been Strauss's intention that the Jerusalem and Athens chapter be the center of this, his final book. That he called the reflections in this chapter "preliminary" is characteristically Straussian.

In his Introduction (p. 19) Pangle notes Strauss's declaration, in 1965, that since the time of his first work on Spinoza (i.e., since his mid-twenties) "the theological-political problem has remained *the* theme of my investigations." Pangle's quotation is from Strauss's autobiographical Preface to the English translation of Spinoza's *Critique of Religion* (1965), which had been published in German in 1930. The preface, however, is dated 1962, not 1965. Notwithstanding the foregoing, the problem Strauss declared so emphatically to be his theme par excellence is not treated as such by Pangle. Although "Jerusalem and Athens" is the intended center of this book, "The Theological-Political Problem" is discussed by Pangle in the sixth of the seven titled sections into which his Introduction is divided. Why Pangle does not regard the theme of "Jerusalem and Athens" as central is explained by him, in the section on "The Theological-Political Problem" thus: "What is most essential in the quarrel between Plato and the Bible is already present in the quarrel between Plato and the poets." In short, Pangle thinks that the quarrel between philosophy and poetry is *the* theme of Strauss's "investigations," and the opposition of Jerusalem and Athens, or of Revelation and Reason, is only a particular example of that conflict. Consistently with this, "The Quarrel between Philosophy and Poetry" is *the* central section of Pangle's Introduction.

Pangle, in short, thinks that the Bible is only one particular kind of "poetry." Pangle is not unaware of the shocking character of this assertion. He tries to soften it by saying "Strauss did not overlook, he rather brought out and stressed, the enormous differences between biblical thought and the thought of the Greek poets." Nevertheless, "he regarded those differences as, in the final analysis, secondary" (p. 20). Is Pangle right about this?

Professor Cropsey, in the foreword, declares that Pangle's Introduction was intended "so far as possible [to] replace the statement that [Strauss] was prevented from writing." And he concludes that "Professor Thomas Pangle's brilliant essay does that as well, I believe, as anything written by any living author could do." This is a very considerable claim. In "The Primacy of the Good: Leo Strauss Remembered" (*Modern Age*, Summer/Fall 1982, p. 266), I wrote "The character of [Strauss's] work, no less than its merit, has become matter of ever-increasing controversy. . . . It would then be less than candid to conceal from my readers that I myself appear to be at or near the center of the disputations about Strauss. Anything I write should then be taken with all the caution with which one approaches the views of a partisan." Pangle may be right about Strauss, and Cropsey may be right about Pangle. But no one can claim canonical status for his opinions in these matters. Each must bear the burden of such argument as the case may require.

At the center of Pangle's position is the judgment that, according to Strauss, the Bible is only "one of many" kinds of "poetry." He seems to imply that it must be subjected to "philosophy" in the same way that poetry is subjected to philosophy by Plato, whether in the *Republic* or in the *Laws*. But there is more than a suggestion that Pangle really believes, not in a Platonic conquest of poetry by philosophy, but in a Nietzschean conquest of philosophy by poetry (the "will to power"). This is as much as to assert, in explicit opposition to Strauss—or by implying that Strauss's explicit statements in this matter are all "exoteric"—that the Biblical argument for revealed truth as the ground of genuine wisdom is not serious. However, to say that there is no serious argument for the Bible may also be to say that there is no serious argument for classical political philosophy, for the skepticism—the Socratic knowledge of ignorance—that is the rational ground of classical political philosophy is also the rational ground upon which the argument for faith in the Biblical God stands. Strauss argued again and again that the modern rationalistic critique of the Bible—beginning with Spinoza—assumed that the Bible was a book like other books and that miracles were impossible. But these were assumptions and as such no more nor less in need of proof than the contrary assumptions of the pious believers. In a series of writings—of which "Jerusalem and Athens" is one—Strauss demonstrated the internal integrity of the Bible, not as a book among books, but as a perfect product of perfect piety. From the point of view of poetic art, all the matter of the art is in the service of its form, and its form in the service of its end. Not chance, but necessity, dominates "poetry," properly understood. There are no irrelevancies, and no contradictions—except such as are intended to bring to light an underlying noncontradictory intention. From this rationalist viewpoint, the Bible is not a work of poetry (i.e., of deliberate making). The Bible is not addressed to unbelievers, and "from the point of view of the Bible the unbeliever is the fool who has said in his heart 'there is no God.'" The Bible, says Strauss, "narrates everything as it is credible to the wise in the Biblical sense of wisdom." As such, it is perfectly intelligible, but not as poetry. To attribute to Strauss—as Pangle does—the view that the Bible is a species of poetry—no different from Greek poetry in the most essential respect—is profoundly mistaken.

The ultimate conflict or tension between the Biblical and the philosophic meanings of wisdom is what Strauss meant by "the theological-political problem." In his chapter on Max Weber in *Natural Right and History* he argued that the apparent insolubility by reason of this problem was the underlying cause of the fact-value distinction, as it existed in Weber's mind. He also argued—in my mind, conclusively—that this was not a sufficient reason for adopting the fact-value distinction, and that in this Weber had erred. But Weber did not therefore regard all "value judgments" as merely subjective. In this, he had not erred in the manner of his latter-day followers. They do not see, as Strauss put it, that because you cannot tell which of two mountains, whose peaks are shrouded in mist, is the higher, that you cannot tell the difference between a mountain and a mole hill!

The issue between poetry and philosophy is presented to us most lucidly in Plato's *Euthyphro*. There it is reduced to the alternative of the ideas, on the one hand, and fighting gods on the other. Unless the gods themselves are subject to intelligible necessity, there is nothing to prevent either their multiplication or their division. There is nothing about the gods that enables them to solve the question of the right way of life for man. Only as the gods become the exoteric names for the permanent and unchanging attributes of nature—above all of the sun, the moon, and the stars—can they supply such guidance. Then they become but the names for the intelligible necessities which are not gods, but ideas. But it is precisely on this issue that the Bible differs both from Plato and the Greek poets; for the Bible affirms the unity of God and denies that this unity is subject either to multiplication or division. Why this is so is a mystery. There is no intelligible necessity that accounts for God, and hence there can be no "science" of God. "I shall be that I shall be" is Strauss's translation of the name of God. God is not bound by anything other than His own will. Hence the highest "science" is not metaphysics, but Torah: the study of God's promises to man, as the ground of the knowledge of the right way of life. Strauss's account of Genesis focuses on the depreciation of the heavens and the heavenly bodies in favor of the earth and man. The story of Genesis is the story of what God has made and done for man, and why fear of the Lord and not wonder is the beginning of wisdom. God has made what He has made, and done what He has done. It is no more possible for man to fathom this than to fathom God Himself. Fear and loving obedience are what is demanded of man, and actions following from such fear and love are informed by true wisdom and constitute the right way for man. Philosophy on the other hand consists in "articulating the riddle of being." For the philosopher there are only eternal questions. The evidence for these questions is always greater than the evidence for any answers to them. Hence there is never any sufficient reason to decide that the quest for the answers is the answer to the quest for the right way of life. Philosophy, as the quest for evidence as to what is the right way of life, rests upon an unevident premise. The Bible rests upon the premise that faith and not reason is primary, because God, Who is unknowable, is the ground of all reality. As Strauss says in *Natural Right and History* (p. 75), it is "the thesis of faith, that there is no possibility of consistency, of a consistent and sincere life, without belief in revelation."

The issue between Plato and the poets is, to repeat, the issue between the ideas and gods who fight among themselves. The issue between Plato and the Bible is that between the ideas and the One God. The God of the Bible not only is One, but is unknowable precisely because He is One: What is unique is, from Plato's own point of view, unknowable. In Plato, an idea, properly so-called, is the class characteristic of a number of objects, with respect to which there are both resemblances and differences. It is the intelligible link between what is otherwise unintelligibly idiosyncratic. The idea of the Good, like the Biblical God, may be One and beyond Being. However, as an idea, it represents something common to many things that are—perhaps even to everything that is—whereas the Biblical God is at once unique and absolutely separate from the universe He has created. The uniqueness and separateness of the Biblical God excludes the possibility of philosophic knowledge of God. Knowledge of God must therefore, to repeat, consist of knowledge of God's ways, of His speeches and deeds, as they are set forth in the Bible.

Pangle, having admitted that for Strauss the theological-political problem is central, treats it as peripheral. The opposition of Revelation and Reason, or of Jerusalem and Athens, becomes merely a subsidiary aspect of "The Quarrel Between Philosophy and Poetry." The section of Pangle's Introduction that bears the foregoing title is (as noted) its central section. This central section has five paragraphs: two, three, and four are the central paragraphs, and three is *the* central paragraph. In this central section there are references to Strauss only in paragraphs one and five, but none in two, three, or four. Pangle, we know, places great weight upon whatever is "central," and tends to regard what is near the beginning or the end as "rhetorical" or "exoteric." We are confident therefore that the following account of "The Quarrel between Philosophy and Poetry" represents a nonexoteric understanding of that quarrel. The first sentence of the first paragraph says that "From a long study of the evidence available Strauss concluded that philosophy originally represents a thoroughgoing, if muted, rebellion against the spiritual authority of civil society (*NRH*, chap. 3)." This sentence, unobjectionable in itself (and in its reference to *Natural Right and History*) is, however, the *only* reference to Strauss before Pangle's account of the great "Quarrel" is complete. Here now is the very heart of the difference, as Pangle presents it. It comes from the central paragraph of the central section of the Introduction.

> When viewed in the light of this distinction between what is by nature and what is by artifice or convention, the gods appear to be merely the fictions of the poets and their sponsors or listeners. Belief in the gods is seen to veil from man the evidence whose reasonable interpretation would lead toward knowledge of the true causes of things. In particular, it seems plausible to suppose that the gods are needed as supporters of nobility and justice because nobility and justice lack intrinsic support in the hearts of men—in their natural and not simply imagined needs and inclinations. After all, that which men incontrovertibly seek and need is not the noble but, rather, personal pleasure, security, and comfort. The concern for the noble can best be explained on the basis of speculations about its origins. Then one recognizes that the noble was in all likelihood the semi-conscious invention of primitive men, who congregated and gradually devised civil societies in order to further their several individual interests: in the process, they found that it was necessary to encourage, through praise, honor, and habituation, some among themselves to sacrifice their original, natural good for the sake of others. Over long ages, and given the plastic power of custom, the concern with being held to be noble or at least not ignoble has gained such strength that it now competes with man's natural, spontaneous, and uninvented desires, and obfuscates the calculation which naturally serves and guides the latter. Yet through piercing, uncompromising thought and iron self-discipline some men can liberate themselves from the sway of opinion and learn to content themselves with the pursuit of the pleasures that are truly or intrinsically sweet. Since man does, by nature, need the assistance of society, the truly free man will continue to dwell among and profit from his deluded neighbors; but spiritually, he will live a life apart.

Here then is the reason for the quarrel of philosophy and poetry—according to Pangle, but not, as we shall see, according to Strauss. The quarrel arises, we are told, because of the philosopher's attachment to "nature" and the "knowledge of the true causes of things." To underline what this means, Pangle gives us what he regards as a philosophic account of those most interesting things—the things called noble and just. These, Pangle tells us, "lack intrinsic support." Intrinsic support, as Pangle understands it, would be support in man's "natural and not simply imagined needs." These natural needs are most emphatically *not* for the noble (or, more generally, for the moral), "but, rather, [for] personal pleasure, security, and comfort." According to Pangle then, man is by nature radically hedonistic, egocentric, and a-social. But according to the account for which, near the end of his life, Strauss declared himself still to have an unshaken preference (in the September, 1970 preface to the reprinting of *Natural Right and History*) man is by nature social. And by reason of his social nature, he is bound to distinguish between the pleasant and the good. According to the classics, it is according to the nature of man, that he sometimes chooses the opposite of what Pangle says is natural, and that he prefers what is painful but noble to what is pleasant but base.

Pangle gives us a genetic account (complete with all the logical attributes of the genetic fallacy) of the noble and the just things. They were, he says, "the semi-conscious invention of primitive men." This certainly sounds like Rousseau's *Second Discourse*. It implies that the "congregation" of men into civil societies, and their invention of morality, was prompted by the necessities of the body or by "efficient causality," but not by the needs of the soul, or by human dignity. It implies therefore that the coming into being of moral codes cannot be attributed to nature and cannot be according to nature. However, Aristotle says that what comes into being last may nonetheless be first in the order of being, or of nature. But Pangle follows Rousseau—and modern science generally—in considering only what comes into being first, what is first in the order of generation, as according to nature.

According to Pangle, the admiration for the noble and just things is not according to nature, but is the result of "the plastic power of custom," which over long time has come to be mistaken for nature. This power of custom, he says, "obfuscates the calculation which naturally serves and guides" the original, and truly "natural, spontaneous, and uninvented desires." But Strauss, expounding classic natural right in *Natural Right and History* (p. 128), says exactly the opposite. "There are things that are admirable, or noble, by nature, intrinsically," Strauss says. Of these things admirable or noble by nature, Strauss continues, it "is characteristic of all or most of them that they contain *no* reference to one's selfish interests or that they imply *a freedom from calculation*" (emphasis added). Where Pangle speaks of custom "obfuscating calculation," Strauss asserts without qualification that there is, by nature, "freedom from calculation." No opposition of views could be more direct.

"The phenomenon of admiration of human excellence," Strauss writes, is so far from being the effect of the "plastic power of custom" that it "cannot be explained on hedonistic or utilitarian grounds," viz., the grounds upon which Pangle has attempted to explain it. The attempt to do so, says Strauss, requires "*ad hoc* hypothesis."

> These hypotheses lead to the assertion that all admiration is, at best, a kind of telescoped calculation of benefits for ourselves. They are the outcome of a materialistic or crypto-materialistic view, which forces its holders to understand the higher as nothing but the effect of the lower, or which prevents them from considering the possibility that there are phenomena which are simply irreducible to their condition.

That "It is safer to try to understand the low in the light of the high than the high in the light of the low" is, perhaps more than any other, the thematic proposition of Strauss's life work. Pangle's account of the noble and just things is, however, nothing but an account of the high in the light of the low.

Pangle's supermen are those who, as he says, "through piercing, uncompromising thought and iron self-discipline . . . liberate themselves from the sway of opinion." (viz., "the concern with being held to be noble or at least not ignoble.") Having done so, they will have learned "to content themselves with the pursuit of pleasures that are truly or intrinsically sweet." Having learned to treat with contempt the opinion with which Leo Strauss associates himself, these "philosophers" will have nature's bonbons at their disposal. Exactly what these bonbons are, we are not told. But it does not take a great deal of imagination to run through one's mind a list of things widely regarded as naturally or intrinsically sweet, yet forbidden by custom or by law in decent societies. Aristotle says (*NE* 1107a16) that there is no such thing as "committing adultery with the right woman, at the right time, and in the right way," but Aristotle, like Leo Strauss, apparently lacked the iron self-discipline to liberate himself from the sway of opinion. For that, we turn to Hugh Hefner and *Playboy*.

Pangle's hero—his "truly free man" (viz., free from any inner attachment to anything noble or just)—does, by nature, need the assistance of society, and he will therefore "continue to dwell among and profit from his deluded neighbors; but spiritually he will live a life apart." Here then is Pangle's "heroic Epicurean." He has absolute contempt for "his deluded neighbors," whom he looks upon merely as subhuman instruments to his need for "personal pleasure, security, and comfort." But for those who believe, with Leo Strauss, that admiration for noble and just things is according to nature, this monster—"beast-god"—is himself simply contemptible.

In the third of the three central paragraphs of his alleged account of "The Quarrel Between Philosophy and Poetry," Pangle begins a shift from this more to his less esoteric account of this quarrel, by trying to make his anti-conventionalist Epicureanism more respectable. He writes:

> Man's material requirements are by nature few, and he who understands this can devote most of his life to the deepest genuine pleasure—that of the thinking which liberates itself from every delusion or false hope, and thus comes to bask in the austere light shed by increasing knowledge of the unfailing nature of things.

But, one must ask, on what substantive reality does this "austere light" fall? In truth, the reductionism which Pangle has practiced to explain the moral phenomena, when applied to the universe as a whole, can result in nothing but modern nihilism. Classical Epicureanism was grounded in classical materialism: Its hedonism was in theory at least an ascetic doctrine. It regarded the moral things as conventional—as does Pangle—but it regarded the universe as an intelligible reality, unchangeable by human will or reason. A classical Epicurean might then retire to "cultivate his garden," that is, contemplate this universe. This, however, assumes—at the very least—the plausibility of classical materialism, or classical atomism. But I know of no one who today adheres to classical materialism in the presence of its modern scientific counterpart. The word "atom" means "the uncut," and who, after the splitting of the atom, actually believes that the "atom" or anything else is the ultimate and intelligible material constituent of the universe? Modern science, even in its most theoretical branches, does not provide ground for the contemplative activity that was common to the idealism of Platonists and the materialism of Democriteans. Pangle's Epicureanism, to repeat, points toward modern nihilism. It does so because the reductionist mode of explanation, always seeing the high in the light of the low, always ends by seeing everything in the light of nothing. Actually, of course, one can see nothing in the light of nothing, and nihilism therefore always in the end substitutes "resolute action" for contemplation. This action must be in the service of self-willed myths: hence the ultimate triumph of poetry over philosophy, for only by resolute action in the name of self-willed myths can one overcome the emptiness, the boredom, the suicidal loneliness of an existence free "from every delusion or false hope"; i.e., free from every belief in the intrinsic dignity of noble thought or action, and from every hope that in obeying the moral law one might do what is acceptable to the living God. The resoluteness of the resolute action justified by the nihilist philosopher will differ from all previous resoluteness, by the complete absence from it of any moral inhibitions, of any sense of objective limits upon the will of the willing agent. "Then everything includes itself in power,/ Power into will, will into appetite,/ And appetite, a universal wolf,/So doubly seconded with will and power,/ Must make perforce a universal prey,/ And last eat up himself."[5] Heidegger's Hitlerism and Kojève's Stalinism are examples that come to mind.

Pangle's account of the quarrel between poetry and philosophy has nothing whatever in common with anything that might be attributed to

Leo Strauss. For Pangle it is the quarrel of one or another species of Epicureanism with *both* Jerusalem and Athens, with the morality of *both* the Bible and classical political philosophy. ("One can say. . . that the Bible and Greek philosophy agree in regard to what we may call, as we do call in fact, morality" [Strauss, in "Progress or Return," *Modern Judaism*, vol. 1, 1981, p. 34]). In his autobiographical Preface (*Spinoza's Critique of Religion*, p. 29), Strauss makes one of his memorable demonstrations of how Spinoza's critique of the Bible rests upon an unproved assumption: The unproved assumption that the orthodox belief in an omnipotent God is mistaken. Strauss argues here that the premise of orthodoxy could be refuted only by a philosophical system that would show

> man . . . himself theoretically and practically as the master of the world and the master of life; the merely given world must be replaced by the world created by man theoretically and practically. Spinoza's *Ethics* attempts to be the system but it does not succeed; the clear and distinct account of everything that it presents remains fundamentally hypothetical. As a consequence, its cognitive status is not different from that of the orthodox account.

According to Strauss, there is no cognitive—i.e., philosophic—ground for choosing between Spinoza (or any of his successors) and the Bible. "Hence the antagonism between Spinoza and Judaism, between belief and unbelief, is ultimately not theoretical but moral."

"For the understanding of that moral antagonism," Strauss continued, "the Jewish designation of the unbeliever as Epicurean seemed to be helpful . . . Epicureanism is hedonism, and traditional Judaism always suspects that all theoretical and practical revolts against the Torah are inspired by the desire to throw off the yoke of the stern and exacting duties so that one can indulge in a life of pleasure." This suspicion, we suspect, is eminently applicable here. Strauss characterizes Epicurean morality as "mercenary," and contrasts it with traditional Jewish morality in which the reward for fulfilling a commandment is the commandment itself. But this closely parallels the Aristotelian view that the reward for each act of every virtue lies in the act itself. It is true that for Aristotle each act of virtue is pleasant to the man possessed of that virtue, but its pleasantness is due to its goodness and not the other way around.

Pangle recognizes that the defense of Jewish orthodoxy is moral, but not that it may be Strauss's. Hence he does not see that the form of this defense may be a form of political philosophy. He observes:

> Strauss seems to have regarded Yehuda Halevi as perhaps the greatest directly antiphilosophic thinker in Judaism; and of Halevi he concluded, "His basic objection to philosophy was then not particularly Jewish, nor even religious, but moral." In this connection Strauss also remarked: "Moral man *as such* is the potential believer." (Pangle's italics.)

One must, I think, look more closely at the argument and action of these passages in "The Law of Reason in the Kuzari" (chapter 4 of *Persecution and the Art of Writing*). Strauss wrote "One has not to be naturally pious, he has merely to have a passionate interest in genuine morality in order to long with all his heart for revelation: moral man as such is the potential believer." I believe that both Yehuda Halevi and Leo Strauss were such men as Strauss here characterizes. Whether or not "potential" believers become actual believers is not here the question. What is crucial is the connection between Halevi's and Strauss's undeniable moral passion and their intellectual vision. Socrates, sitting in prison, rejected Anaxagoras' philosophy because Anaxagoras' explanation of why he was sitting in prison made no sense to him as a moral man. Anyone who takes with full seriousness human responsibility for human action will recognize the fundamental importance of the distinction between the just and the unjust, the noble and the base, for the exercise of that responsibility. In the sentence immediately following the one we have just quoted, Strauss wrote, "Halevi could find a sign for the necessity of the connection between morality and revelation in the fact that the same philosophers who denied the Divine lawgiver, denied the obligatory character of what we would call the moral law." The *Kuzari* is indeed, as Pangle indicates, a polemic against philosophy. But its adversary is determined by its addressee. It is addressed to a naturally pious man in a state of doubt (*Persecution and the Art of Writing*, p. 111). We may compare it, in part, to such a polemic as that which Strauss found in Rousseau's *First Discourse* ("On the Intention of Rousseau," *Social Research*, December 1947). According to Strauss, Rousseau there attacked philosophy in the name of morality. But he did so, partly in the interest of morality, but mainly in the interest of philosophy itself. Philosophers must be taught—sometimes even by chastisement—how to act in a responsible manner. In the study of Halevi, Strauss goes to some length to distinguish the different kinds of "*kalam*," that is, the different medieval Islamic systems or methods by which reason might be employed to defend faith. One of those systems, Halevi's, is essentially in defense of morality even though it embraces the defense of revelation. More generally, it is in defense of the political life which makes the moral life binding by means of Law. Of Halevi, and his *kalam*, Strauss concluded: "In defending Judaism, which, according to him, is the only true revealed religion, against the philosophers, he was conscious of defending morality itself and therewith the cause, not only of Judaism, but of mankind at large." This kind of defense of morality—and, therewith, of the cause of mankind at large—is, I believe, ultimately indistinguishable in Strauss's mind from the practice of political philosophy, as he wished to revive that practice.

Strauss speaks at the very end of Halevi's "basic objection to philosophy," which, he says, was "not particularly Jewish, nor even particularly religious, but moral." Halevi's objection becomes Strauss's, when we substitute for philosophy such contemporary representatives of "philosophy" as "scientific social science." In general, however, Strauss's project is far more difficult than Halevi's. In the eleventh century, philosophy, in some of its widespread manifestations, had irresponsibly endangered the moral order. An attack on philosophy would not adversely affect the Socratics—for they would not only support, but if possible direct the appeal to revelation. They would do so by means of what it would not be too misleading to call a "Socratic *kalam*." In our time, there is no traditional piety which can form the moral substratum for any such "*kalam*." Modernity's prejudice against traditional piety is equally a prejudice against traditional moral philosophy, and the reason which informed it. Religious fundamentalism tends to be anti-rational; but what we might call contemporary academic philosophical fundamentalism is equally so!

It has often been said that Leo Strauss regarded Heidegger as the greatest philosophic intelligence of the twentieth century. I think that this is true. Its significance however must be measured against the equally undeniable fact that Strauss considered Winston Churchill to be the greatest man of the twentieth century. Nothing I can think of brings into sharper focus the questionable status of philosophy divorced from the morality of "the Bible and Greek philosophy," for Heidegger was a Nazi and remained one after Hitler's death. By a kind of inversion of language, we might call Heidegger "a Nazi on principle," even if (perhaps) the only one. In "Philosophy as Rigorous Science," the first chapter of *Studies in Platonic Political Philosophy*, Strauss observes that "There is no room for political philosophy in Heidegger's work." Of course this absence signifies an absence of all moral concern in that work. Strauss speaks of "the facts" of Heidegger's Nazism, and says that "We cannot help holding these . . . against" him. Strauss holds the facts of Heidegger's Nazism against him all the more because "one is bound to misunderstand Heidegger's thought radically if one does not see their intimate connection with the core of his philosophic thought." This connection, we believe, is essentially that expressed above: between the "nothingness" to which unqualified reductionism leads (understanding the high in the light of the low) and "resolute action" as a substitute for contemplation.

Churchill was the supreme enemy of Hitler and everything Hitler stood for. He was the supreme enemy of Hitler because in the decisive respects he was not touched by modern philosophy. For him, the moral distinctions, as they are discovered by gentlemen in practical life—above all, political life—are the primary ground for their understanding of life and the world. In 1946 Strauss wrote to Karl Löwith (in the correspondence published in the 1983 *Independent Journal of Philosophy*), "I know from my experience how incomprehensible and foreign Aristotle's concept of *megalopsuchia* was to me originally, and that *now* I not only theoretically, but also practically, *approve* of it. A man like Churchill proves that the possibility of *megalopsuchia* exists today *exactly* as it did in the fifth century, B.C." (All emphasis is by Strauss.) Strauss's earlier alienation from Aristotle was due to his earlier "sophistication," his earlier belief (such as he attributes to Löwith in the letter) in the "culture bound" quality of moral judgments. But Strauss had become persuaded of the genuine possibility of a "culture" that was independent of time and place. Just as he had by 1946 come to believe that "the perfect political order" was the one that "Plato and Aristotle have sketched," so was he persuaded that the great-souled man simply was the one described by Aristotle in Book IV of the *Nicomachean Ethics*. There was, however, this difference: He knew that the perfect political order was not now possible; but the great-souled man was not only possible but actual. Churchill as the embodiment of *megalopsuchia* is of decisive importance, theoretically no less than practically, in Strauss's argument against historicism, against radical modernity. His example is equally decisive in favor of classical political philosophy, as the necessary condition of a decent politics in modernity. Above all, it is decisive for establishing the importance of the moral and political phenomena as the theoretical, no less than the practical, ground of philosophic wisdom. The example of Churchill was decisive for Strauss, as evidence "that there are phenomena which are simply irreducible to their conditions."

As editor of *Statesmanship: Essays in Honor of Sir Winston Spencer Churchill*, I was privileged to publish as its epigraph the eulogy that Strauss had delivered in his class on January 25, 1965, the day following Churchill's death. His remarks are, I believe, spontaneous. Yet they surpass—I believe—everything anyone else has said about Churchill. And in certain respects they are as authentic—perhaps more authentic—in what they reveal of Strauss himself, as anything more deliberately composed. I believe a review of his words on this occasion a fitting way to end this account of Strauss's "legacy."

"The death of Churchill is a healthy reminder to academic students of political science of their limitations, the limitations of their craft." Strauss begins with this ironic conjunction of death and health. But the limitations of political science—as we shall see—are precisely those, of nature and of fortune, that Machiavellianism in all its dimensions was dedicated to abolish. Strauss begins the essay on "Jerusalem and Athens" by saying the task he has set himself "goes much beyond my power." However, "we cannot define our tasks by our powers, for our powers become known to us through performing our tasks; it is better to fail nobly than to succeed basely." The ground of the moral and political life is the distinction between noble failure and base success. Churchill, in *The Second World War*, says that in war it is impossible to guarantee success, it is possible only to deserve it. But clearly this applies to peace no less than to war. This "practical" judgment of Churchill touches the profoundest level of Strauss's theoretical understanding, for it is the intervention of chance which, according to Aristotle, causes "noble and just actions" to "admit of much variety and fluctuation of opinion," and to permit virtuous men to suffer catastrophe. It was Machiavelli's project to conquer Fortune (who, as a woman, could be dominated by a sufficiently virile if sufficiently unscrupulous male). Of course, Machiavelli's successors turned the conquest of Fortune into the conquest of nature. As we have seen, Strauss's critique of modernity implied that Science's abolition of the physical limits of man's power was always understood to imply the abolition of the need for morality from human life. As we know from Swift's "Struldbruggs," the modern project looked from an early moment to the abolition of death—not, as in Biblical religion, by promising eternal life in another world, but by promising it in this one. Churchill's death, like his life, is first of all a lesson in limits, in mortal limits. But it is only within these limits that actions can be noble and just, for such actions can properly bear such names only if we do them in some sense for their own sake, and not solely for their extrinsic benefits. The phenomenon of disinterested admiration, of which Strauss makes so much in *Natural Right and History*, is a function both of man's mortality and of the role that chance plays in determining the outcome of his deeds.

"The tyrant stood at the pinnacle of his power," Strauss continued. "The contrast between the indomitable and magnanimous statesman and the insane tyrant—this spectacle in its clear simplicity was one of the greatest lessons which men can learn, at any time." Strauss calls the confrontation between Churchill and Hitler both a spectacle and a lesson; that is to say, an object both of theoretical and practical wisdom. As the latter, it teaches us how to act: that we should not submit to evil ("Never, never, never, never!"). But it also teaches us that chance, which permits good actions to fail, for reasons over which the agent has no control, can also befriend the good, by bringing successful outcomes where there is no probability—where, indeed, there may seem even to be no possibility—of success. After the fall of France, Britain stood absolutely alone, Stalin was the ally of Hitler in every respect except open belligerency, and the United States was wrapped in thousand-fold isolationism. There were ten thousand reasons of prudence why an almost completely defenseless Britain should have reached an accommodation with Hitler, who was himself anxious to make Britain his "Aryan" junior partner in the "thousand-year Reich." No one in 1940 could have foreseen that Hitler would gratuitously attack his loyal partner, Joseph Stalin, that Japan would gratuitously attack the United States at Pearl Harbor, and that Hitler would complete the cycle of folly by gratuitously declaring war against the United States. But chance works both ways. We see virtue fail, despite deserving success; but we also see virtue succeed, sometimes against every rational expectation. Strauss invites us to contemplate, with him, the spectacle of Churchill defying Hitler at the height of his power, thundering his maledictions against the tyrant, giving hope to all mankind—at the very nadir of all hope—that all would yet be well. Strauss speaks of the "simplicity" of this spectacle: It is the simplicity of good in its starkest contrast with evil. Our admiration for the good, and our detestation of the evil, Strauss implies, are grounded in our nature. Such admiration—or detestation—is, as he says in *Natural Right and History*, inherently disinterested. That both are such is exemplified in the story of Nathan and David, which Strauss used as one of the two epigraphs for *Natural Right and History* and to which he returned in the concluding passage of "Jerusalem and Athens." The "plastic power of custom" may obstruct or it may facilitate the access of our natures to the pleasure intrinsic to contemplating what is by nature noble and just, but nature and not custom is the original ground of such pleasure.

"No less enlightening," Strauss went on, "is the lesson conveyed by Churchill's failure, which is too great to be called tragedy. I mean the fact that Churchill's heroic action on behalf of human freedom against Hitler only contributed, through no fault of Churchill's, to increase the threat to freedom posed by Stalin or his successors. Churchill did the utmost that a man could do to counter that threat." Of course, Churchill's failures are all ultimately of a piece with his successes. We are reminded of the "locust years" which preceded "the war years." We are reminded of Churchill's campaign to "strangle the infant Bolshevism in its cradle," more than a decade before his warnings against Hitler, as well as his unheeded warnings against that same Bolshevism, now grown so great, at the end of the Second World War. The still, small voice of Churchill's wisdom, in peace and in war, elicits our admiration even more than that "lion's roar" of defiance that greeted the Nazi tyranny when it seemed about to devour the world. In the end, Churchill's wisdom and Churchill's courage illuminate the human condition itself, beyond the transient generations whose mortal fate he shared.

Strauss also paid tribute to Churchill's writings, "above all his *Marlborough*," for "their inexhaustible mine of political wisdom and understanding." Then he concluded:

> The death of Churchill reminds us of the limitations of our craft, and therewith of our duty. We have no higher duty, and no more pressing duty, than to remind ourselves and our students, of political greatness, human greatness, of the peaks of human excellence. We are supposed to train ourselves and others in seeing things as they are, and this means above all in seeing their greatness and their misery, their excellence and their vileness, their nobility and their triumphs, and therefore never to mistake mediocrity, however brilliant, for true greatness.

Strauss's eulogy of Churchill thus ends as it begins: with a reminder of "the limitations of our craft." This reminder, however, is not a depreciation of that craft. It is, we have seen, a rejection of Machiavellianism, and of radical modernity, of those forms of human thought that would make the noble and just things irrelevant to human life. And so it is a reminder of "our duty." In his eulogy of Churchill, Strauss reminds us, as Churchill would remind us, of duty as an inescapable feature of the right way of life. The duty to which we are here called is said to be at once the highest and the most pressing. It represents therefore what might be called a peak demand, equally of theory and of practice. It flows from our obligation "to train ourselves and others in seeing things as they are." Seeing things as they *are* implies the Socratic enterprise, of asking "what each of the beings is" (*NRH*, p. 122). Seeing the low in the light of the high here means seeing things in the light of the moral distinctions, as they become visible in such spectacles as are furnished by such lives as Winston Churchill's.

Strauss ends by a condemnation of "mediocrity," which however brilliant we must never, he says, mistake for true greatness. Nothing begets this kind of mistake more than does cynicism about morality, or the deprecation of politics. Churchill was himself deprecated during much of his career for his frequently unabashed ambition. If he had disguised that ambition, as a more sophisticated man would have done, by ideological justifications (preferably socialistic and pacifistic), no one would have objected—or perhaps even noticed. But he was a great-souled man, and claimed honor as his right, even though—as a great-souled man—he knew that the highest merit transcended any honor, for honor, like moral virtue, points beyond itself. The great-souled man can be indifferent to honor, even as he claims it. His invincibility to evil, he knows, represents a rendezvous with eternity, in which success and failure are themselves insignificant, and "Greatness is all," for greatness resonates being, the understanding of being—of seeing things as they are, which always means seeing the low in the light of the high. Such understanding is the legacy of Leo Strauss.

NOTES

Originally printed in the *Claremont Review of Books*, Vol. III, No. 3, Fall 1984.

1. See "Leo Strauss Remembered," p. 39 ff of this volume.
2. Leo Strauss, *Liberalism Ancient and Modern* (Chicago: University of Chicago Press, 1968), p. 223.
3. Walter Berns, "Reply to Harry Jaffa," *National Review*, Vol. XXXIV, Issue 1, 1982.
4. Berns, *National Review*, 1982.
5. William Shakespeare, *Trolius and Cressida*, Act III, scene ii, 119–124.

FIVE

The Platonism of Leo Strauss

A Reply to Harry Jaffa

Thomas L. Pangle

The editor has invited me to respond to Harry Jaffa's attack in his "Legacy of Leo Strauss" (*Claremont Review of Books*, Vol. III, No. 3, Fall 1984). I do so after considerable hesitation. My initial instinct was to follow the advice implicit in the sage words of Solomon (Proverbs 29:9). But the urging of friends whose judgment I respect, and my own second thoughts, have inclined me to the view that I cannot avoid replying—if only to defend my good name and to warn unsuspecting readers of the fallaciousness of Jaffa's authoritative-sounding censure. The truth is, Jaffa is guilty of gross misinterpretation: For reasons known only to him and to God, he has distorted beyond recognition my interpretation of Strauss and of the political philosophizing Strauss resuscitated.

Jaffa characterizes my interpretation in these terms: "According to Pangle, the admiration for the noble and just things is not according to nature . . . Pangle's account of the noble and just things is . . . nothing but an account of the high in the light of the low" (Jaffa, op. dr., pp. 18–19). Now, near the beginning of my essay, I spoke as follows:

> What then is Plato's conception of the problem of justice, according to Strauss? Justice in the fullest sense comes to sight, in what men say about it, as an object of aspiration; as the "common good" which binds men together in mutual dedication in a political community. Most of the time, to be sure, the concern with justice is limited to much more partial questions about mine and thine. But these questions depend on some implicit answer, however imprecise, to the question of the overriding purposes of the community. These highest goals cannot be ade-

quately defined in terms of the requirements which are ubiquitous in social life and which, for this reason as well as because of their urgency, present themselves as at first sight the most reasonable candidates for primacy—viz., the needs for physical comfort and safety. Man is such a being as cannot orient himself merely by the good, understood as what is useful for survival, health, and material ease. He is always aware of sacred restraints on the means he may employ to pursue these needs; what is more, he is aware that it is sometimes necessary, nay, praiseworthy and admirable, to relinquish or sacrifice the satisfaction of these needs. The choice of means, and the capacity for sacrifice, is dictated by the human concern for virtue or excellence. The virtues are indeed useful, for the pursuit of the mundane goals mentioned; but they are also valued as ends in themselves. They are honored as being noble. It is this dimension of what man values—the noble, the estimable or precious that cannot be reduced to the good or useful—which displays man's peculiarly moral mode of being. It is no accident that in Greek the word for noble (*kalon*) designates at the same time "beautiful." The noble and the beautiful originally belong together. We experience the noble as preeminently deserving of or calling for adornment and enshrinement; and the decorative or "aesthetically" pleasing we experience as in need of a seriousness which it finds only in association with the noble. Hence the *kalon* comes into its own in the works of the artists, and especially the poets: the *demiourgoi*, the "public workers" of the highest order. It is there that a people sees in the least fleeting and least nebulous way what kinds of human beings it reveres. Nevertheless, the peculiar luminosity of the virtues as they appear in the "imitations" of the artists does not necessarily promote a clear account of the noble. It remains much easier to point to particular instances of the noble or virtuous than to explain what the noble as such is; and the noble is never free for long from controversy. The source of the dispute is usually not doubt as to whether the virtues exist, or even what they are in general: there is remarkably broad agreement on the nobility of attributes such as courage, generosity, wisdom, law-abidingness, and so on. Battles tend to develop rather over the specifications, and, what is graver, the relative ranking of the virtues (e.g., the virtues of war vs. those of peace; humility vs. pride; generosity and love of leisure vs. thrift and industry). These quarrels mingle with, at once elevating and intensifying, the more frequent causes of discord arising from competition for scarce resources. The disputes thus become, in more concrete terms, disputes over the superiority of distinct human types or classes and their claims to highest moral and political authority: priests, soldiers, merchants, small farmers, gentry, lawyers, wage laborers, etc., vie for preponderance in the political order. Insofar as each of these factions possesses a comprehensive vision of the proper distribution of goods and the ordering of the ways of life in the whole community, each is understood, in Platonic terms, to represent a specific "regime" (*politeia*). The conflicts among the various "regimes" are the decisive conflicts at the root of all political life; and it is the aim of Platonic political philosophy in the narrow or strict sense to arbitrate these conflicts.

> It does so chiefly by setting forth a single standard, the "best regime by nature," in the light of which the competing regimes that emerge in history can be judged, categorized, and—in favorable circumstances—"mixed" in judicious compromises. (pp. 6–7)

Willfully ignoring this and other kindred passages, Jaffa adduces a long quotation from my Introductory Essay, a quotation literally ripped out of context. In its context, the passage is obviously and explicitly meant to summarize Strauss's account of pre-Socratic philosophy, the philosophy *against* which Socrates, according to Strauss, turned.

Unfortunately, this is by no means the worst of Jaffa's falsifications. The leitmotif of my essay, and I believe of Strauss's work, is made explicit in the culminating section of my essay (a section entitled "The Theological-Political Problem"). There I define this "Problem" as follows:

> it signifies, most simply put, the apparently irresolvable conflict between the claims of reason and of revelation. That conflict, Strauss learned first from Spinoza, is as much a political as it is a "theological" or "philosophical" problem. For revelation cannot be adequately understood if it is approached merely as "religious experience" in the sense of William James and other "psychologists of religion." Revelation is the authoritative disclosure to man of Divine Law—the Torah, the Chari'a, the "Old Law" and the "New Law"; this rule of law claims to give the ultimate direction to the whole of man's existence, collective as well as individual or familial. (pp. 19–20)

I proceed to raise and attempt to answer the question, "Why then does the theological-political problem dominate the project of Platonic political philosophy as Strauss understands it, and just what form does the problem assume?" (pp. 19–20). Jaffa, however, informs the unsuspecting reader that "Pangle, having admitted that for Strauss the theological-political problem is central, treats it as peripheral" (Jaffa, p. 18). He supports this claim with an argument so contrived that it strains one's faith in his sobriety: since "The Theological-Political Problem" is discussed by Pangle in the sixth of the seven titled sections into which his Introduction is divided" (p. 17), the problem is not treated as central. But Jaffa does not stop at this. He goes on to manufacture a quotation: "At the center of Pangle's position is the judgment that, according to Strauss, the Bible is only 'one of many' kinds of 'poetry.'" The phrase in quotations, in this sentence, appears nowhere in the text of my essay. And at no point, even by implication, do I commit the absurdity of "attributing to Strauss" the "view that the Bible is a species of poetry" (Jaffa, p. 17). On the contrary, I say: "Strauss did not overlook, he rather brought out and stressed, the enormous differences between biblical thought and the thought of the Greek poets" (Pangle, p. 20); four pages later I lay stress on the fact that Strauss regarded the "faith of his fathers," the "Torah," as "the most profound and intransigent version of the alternative to philosophy posed by revelation."

But I also say—and here we reach a serious issue—that according to Strauss, "what is most essential in the quarrel between Plato and the Bible is already present in the quarrel between Plato and the poets or in the muted dispute between Socrates and Ischomachus *the* perfect gentleman or *kaloskagathos* in Xenophon's *Oeconomicus*" (Pangle, p. 20). To this thought Jaffa takes strong exception, and this thought, I contend, is the very core of Strauss's rediscovery of what he intransigently held to be the *full* adequacy of the Platonic understanding of the ultimate questions for man as man. Plato never read or heard of the Bible; but despite this, Strauss was convinced of the truth of the solemn asseveration of Avicenna which Strauss chose as his epigraph for the last book published in his lifetime: "the treatment of prophecy and the Divine Law is contained in . . . the *Laws*." (I might add that in quoting Avicenna, Strauss condenses so as to make the point even more relentless than it appears in the very bold original.) Strauss's full meaning becomes clear only after a close and thorough study of *The Argument and the Action of Plato's Laws*, but a passage near the beginning (pp. 6–7) is especially helpful in teaching us about Platonic "dialectic" and its most serious theme, what Strauss in *Xenophon's Socratic Discourse* (p. 192) called "the most serious of all arts or sciences, theology." The Athenian Stranger, Strauss says,

> proceeds like Socrates, who prefers to take issue with the poets' stories about gods and heroes rather than with the stories embodied in public worship. . . . The Athenian . . . engages in a kind of dialogue with Tyrtaios who, being a poet, had praised not the fruits of war but the virtue of war. The conversation thus turns from war (or peace) to virtue as choiceworthy for its own sake as the end of legislation. . . . the Athenian quotes Theognis, a poet of a later age. . . . Since he does not take issue with Theognis, he does not engage in a dialogue with him. . . . Every legislator who is not entirely worthless, and hence in particular the Cretan legislator, who was instructed by Zeus, will give his laws with a view above all to the greatest virtue. . . . To the Cretan's remark, which is free from indignation, that this demand amounts to a condemnation of the Cretan legislator, the Athenian . . . *appeals as it were from the accepted interpretation of revelation to revelation itself, which discloses its true meaning only to those who never forget that, being divine, it is supremely reasonable*. . . . The Athenian delineates now what we may call the *natural* beginning of an inquiry into divine *legislation as distinguished from the beginning imposed on him by the opinion of his interlocutors.* The latter beginning, concerned with the origin of the Dorian laws, led to what the Cretan regarded as the most just answer. The *natural* beginning is concerned with the end with a view to which divine laws *must be supposed* to have been given; it leads to an answer that is both true and just. (My emphasis)

If Jaffa believes that the "most essential" issue regarding prophecy or the Divine Law emerged only after the time of Plato, or in texts unknown to Plato; if he supposes that the most essential issue was not and could not have been addressed by Plato's philosophic spokesman in his dialogue with the poets and the statesmen and gentlemen who are the poets' followers—then it seems to me Jaffa has either broken with Strauss's teaching or failed to comprehend it.

The disservice Jaffa has tried to do me is probably less significant, in the long run, than this misunderstanding or misrepresentation of Strauss. The serious disagreement I have with Jaffa's reading of Strauss will become more fully apparent to anyone who reads my Introductory Essay with care and with the requisite attentiveness to the texts of Strauss I cite. Here I will only add the observation that Jaffa's attempt to explain what Strauss meant by the "theological-political problem" seems to me fundamentally confused. Jaffa is aware, somehow or dimly, that the Bible and Plato are deeply at odds over "the right way of life"—that they disagree, in the final analysis, over what is right and wrong. For the Bible, as Jaffa says, "God's promises to man" are "the ground of the knowledge of the right way of life." Accordingly, "fear and loving obedience are what is demanded of man, and actions following from such fear and love . . . constitute the right way for man." But "for the philosopher there are only eternal questions" (Jaffa, pp. 17–18). Now Strauss, in *Studies in Platonic Political Philosophy*, links this profound difference to the fact that, as regards moral virtue, what is taught by the Bible represents "a very different message" from what is taught by Aristotle's *Ethics*.[1] Strauss underlines Aristotle's praise of magnanimity and depreciation of shame, in contrast to Isaiah's "implicit condemnation of magnanimity" and "implicit vindication of the sense of shame": "Who is right?" Strauss asks, "the Greeks or the Jews? Athens or Jerusalem?" (p. 210; cf. the epigraph to Jaffa's early work, *Thomism and Aristotelianism*).[2] Jaffa, however, wishes now to insist that the Bible and Plato (or Aristotle) form a common moral front—not just for many or most practical issues (as of course they do)—but on the very highest level, for the decisive issue. In particular, he argues that Platonic political philosophy joins piety in condemning unqualifiedly "Epicureanism," or ancient philosophic materialism. Jaffa goes so far as to declare that Strauss or his Platonism joins in Halevi's moral attack on "the philosophers" (Jaffa, pp. 19–20).

Jaffa is able to do this—to identify without qualification Plato's moral stance, or conception of the best life, with that of the Bible—only by in effect abandoning Plato's claim that philosophy (Socrates) gives *the* guidance to human existence; Jaffa erroneously claims that because "for the philosopher there are only eternal questions," it follows that "there is never any sufficient answer to the quest for the right way of life" (Jaffa, pp. 19–20). The Platonic Socrates arrived, on the contrary, at the following "momentous" conclusion (as Strauss calls it): "the greatest good for a human being is this—each day to make arguments about virtue and about the other matters concerning which you have heard me examining myself and others." (*Apol. Soc.* 38a; cf. *Studies in Platonic Political Philosophy*, pp. 14, 21, 50, 138–39, 210). It is ultimately—though only ultimately—on this basis that the Athenian Stranger can claim to know the criterion or goal by which "revelation"—not just this or that revelation, but "revelation itself"—can and must be judged or validated.

To obscure this is to take the heart out of Platonic political philosophy, to mask or remove the truly fundamental issue—the quarrel between the Bible and Plato over the right way of life for man as man. Having done this, Jaffa is driven to characterize the quarrel in abstract and metaphysical, rather than in concrete moral or political or human terms: "The issue between Plato and the Bible is that between the ideas and the one God" (Jaffa, p. 18).

Against this view, I believe, stands the teaching of Strauss, a teaching reaffirmed in his last book. Strauss was unswerving and unhesitating in his confession of indebtedness to Maimonides' and Farabi's interpretation of Plato and of the relation between Plato's philosophy and Biblical revelation. It was Farabi—Strauss stressed—who first dared to present Plato's philosophy as a whole without any reference whatsoever to the Ideas. What Strauss learned in this regard from Farabi he summed up in what Homer would have called winged words:

> It would be rash to maintain that the foregoing observations suffice for establishing what Farabi believed as regards any *substantiae separatae.* They do suffice however for justifying the assertion that his philosophy does not stand or fall with the acceptance of such substances. For him, philosophy is the attempt to know the essence of all beings: his concept of philosophy is not based on any preconceived opinion as to what allegedly real things are truly real things. *He has infinitely more in common with a philosophic materialist than with any un-philosophic believer however well-intentioned.* (My emphasis). . . . A man such as Farabi doubtless had definite convictions . . . but what made him a philosopher, according to his own view of philosophy, were not those convictions, but the spirit in which they were acquired, in which they were maintained and in which they were intimated rather than preached from the housetops. Only by reading Maimonides' *Guide* against the background of philosophy thus understood, can we hope eventually to fathom its unexplored depths. ("Farabi's Plato," pp. 36–37)[3]

Both the Bible on the one hand, and Farabi's or Maimonides' and Strauss's Plato, on the other hand, firmly support civic and moral virtue: but in what spirit, with what end or ends in view, and, above all, for the sake ultimately of what way of life?

With another interlocutor, one might fruitfully pursue these and related questions. But Jaffa's shrill polemics render him ineligible as a dialectical partner, for Jaffa seems to have lost his understanding of, or his capacity for, philosophic disputation. He seems to have become incapable of vigorously arguing issues in moral and political theory without labeling his opponents or their views immoral. The tone and methods that mark his argumentation are becoming all too familiar to those who take wearisome note of his ceaseless logomachy. But he seems to be descending to new levels: not only the misuse of quotations wrenched from their contexts, and the bare-faced invention of false quotations, but in addition the deployment of textually unsupported innuendo, designed to convince the reader of the opponent's knavery: "there is more than a suggestion that Pangle really believes not in a Platonic conquest of poetry by philosophy, but in a Nietzschean conquest of philosophy by poetry (the 'will to power')" (Jaffa, p. 17). And then finally, of course, after the reader has been suitably prepared by such innuendo, comes the outright character assassination: "Pangle's supermen are those who . . . having learned to treat with contempt the opinion with which Leo Strauss associates himself . . . will have nature's bonbons at their disposal. . . . Aristotle says that there is no such thing as 'committing adultery with the right woman, at the right time, and in the right way,' but Aristotle, like Leo Strauss, apparently lacked the iron self-discipline to liberate himself from the sway of opinion. For that, we turn to Hugh Hefner and *Playboy*. Pangle's hero—his 'truly free man'—is free from any inner attachment to anything noble or just . . . this monster—'beast-god'—is himself simply contemptible" (Jaffa, p. 19).

If nothing can excuse, can anything explain this performance? The mischievous cleverness that is at work in Jaffa's "review" rules out any possibility that his present speech is the sad result of declining mental powers. The problem lies not in Jaffa's mind but in his heart. I do not pretend to read hearts or hidden motives, but Jaffa's lack of restraint is so great that at the outset of his piece he cannot forbear expressing the fierce and wounded sense of self-importance that animates his reaction to his having not been chosen to write the Introduction to Strauss's last work: referring to the Strauss-Cropsey *History of Political Philosophy*, Jaffa petulantly reminds us that "Strauss had chosen me to write the chapter on 'Aristotle,' which immediately follows his chapter on 'Plato'" (Jaffa, p. 14). Why do I draw attention to this unseemly *mikropsuchia*? Because the time has come when Professor Jaffa's followers and friends (including the editors of this journal) ought to face the unseemly truth and reflect on their duty in regard to it. I conclude by addressing to those followers and friends of Professor Jaffa a serious plea and question. Years past, Professor Jaffa wrote books from which we all have learned and which deserve to be passed down, in honor, to posterity. For the sake of protecting the reputation of those works and their author, cannot more be done—is it not your obligation to do more—to dissuade your elder from appearing before the world in such demeaning postures, and in the grip of such disfiguring passions?

NOTES

Originally printed in the *Claremont Review of Books*, Vol. IV, No. 1, Spring 1985.

1. Leo Strauss, ed. Thomas Pangle, *Studies in Platonic Political Philosophy* (Chicago: University of Chicago Press, 1983), p. 210.

2. Harry Jaffa, *Thomism and Aristotelianism* (Westport: Greenwood Press, 1952).

3. "Farabi's Plato" appeared originally in 1945, in the *Louis Ginsberg Jubilee Volume* of the American Academy for Jewish Research; it has been reprinted in Arthur Hyman, ed., *Essays in Medieval Jewish and Islamic Philosophy: Studies from the Publications of the American Academy for Jewish Research* (New York: KTAV Publishing House, 1977).

SIX

"The Legacy of Leo Strauss" Defended

Harry V. Jaffa

Thomas Pangle declares that, in "The Legacy of Leo Strauss" (*Claremont Review of Books*, Fall, 1984), I am "guilty of gross misinterpretation" of his "interpretation of Strauss and of the political philosophizing Strauss resuscitated." Pangle quotes me, correctly, as writing that his (Pangle's) "account of the noble and just things . . . is nothing but an account of the high in the light of the low." But, he says, what he had written about Strauss and his legacy was almost exactly the opposite of what I had attributed to him. To prove this, he quotes a lengthy passage from "near the beginning of [his] essay." The substance of this passage supports his contention. It does represent a viewpoint opposite to the one that I had attributed to him, one which I had found, not near the beginning, nor near the end of his essay, but at its very center. The question then is, which of these conflicting and contradictory interpretations, both of which are to be found in the same essay, is the careful reader intended by the author to take as true or authoritative? Let me say at the outset that I was wholly aware of this problem—of how to read Pangle's essay—and never for a moment assumed the truth of the interpretation I adopted as the correct one. After all, one of the main themes of Leo Strauss's work was the discovery, not only that philosophic writings frequently abound in contradictions, but that these contradictions—contrary to appearances—are often, if not always, symptomatic of a noncontradictory intention. The greater writers are not the ones whose work is most free of contradictions. The greater writers are the ones whose contradictions are intentional, and who guide their more intelligent readers through the contradictions to their noncontradictory intention. I do not for a moment think that Professor Pangle is a great writer. He is, on the contrary, a lesser writer infatuated, if not intoxicated, with what he thinks he has learned about Socratic or Platonic rhetoric. In commenting on his text, I thought it best to expound his true argument, without going through the wearisome process of disentangling it from its sophistical cocoon, or from what Churchill would have called its "bodyguard of lies." I displayed what I was confident was the anatomy of Professor Pangle's argument, without *a priori* distinguishing it from its fig leaves.

In distinguishing the center of his text from its periphery, I was, Pangle says, making "an argument so contrived that it strains one's faith in [Jaffa's] sobriety." In doing so I was, however, following Professor Pangle's example. In a public lecture at Claremont, about three years ago, Pangle declared that Nietzsche was *the* philosopher, according to Strauss, and that it was in Nietzschean—that is to say, historicist—concepts that Strauss believed one must look for a solution of the dilemmas of contemporary social sciences and, indeed, of the dilemmas of modern man. This represented to me a reversal of nearly everything I believed I had learned from Strauss, and about Strauss, in an association of nearly thirty years. Strauss's distinctiveness—indeed, his uniqueness, I had thought—lay above all else in the fact that he was the first great critic of modernity whose diagnosis of the ills of modernity did not end by seeking a solution of those ills through a radicalization of the principles of modernity. Strauss was, in this decisive respect, unlike his great predecessors, Rousseau and Nietzsche. To be told by Pangle that he was in the decisive respect, not their opponent, but their follower, was astounding. In the discussion following Pangle's lecture, I raised objections to what I had heard. I cited the Introduction of *Natural Right and History* in which Strauss declared that "the contemporary rejection of natural right leads to nihilism—nay, it is identical with nihilism." I said I had always understood that to imply a rejection of Nietzsche's rejection of natural right, however more sophisticated Nietzsche's rejection may have been than any merely "contemporary rejection." Pangle began his reply by declaring that he was obliged "to pull rank" on me. (These, his exact words, were my first intimation that "Straussians" were ranked.) He then said that Strauss never returned to the theme of natural right "in his later and mature works." Apparently among the ranks of the cognoscenti *Natural Right and History* was an early and immature work.

This reply of Pangle's is, however, contradicted by Strauss himself in the Preface to the 7th impression of *Natural Right and History* published by the University of Chicago Press in 1971. In that Preface, written some eighteen years after the book it precedes was completed, Strauss observed that "It almost goes without saying that if I were to write this book again, I would write it differently."[1] From the phrase "it goes without saying" one would normally infer that Strauss means by this that almost any author would write a book differently eighteen years after its original composition. But, Strauss ended, "Nothing I have learned has shaken my inclination to prefer 'natural right' especially in its classic form, to the reigning relativism, positivist or historicist." (The word "positivist" is misprinted "politivist.") I think Strauss here disavows any such change in perspective as Pangle has imputed to him. In the Introduction to *Studies in Platonic Political Philosophy,* Pangle comments (p. 9) on the 1970 Preface to *Natural Right and History* thus:

> twenty years later Strauss had come to believe that the book could have been rewritten in an improved version. His own understanding of "natural right and history" had "deepened" in the interval; and apparently the most important aspect of the deepening had resulted from his "concentration on the study of 'classic natural right,' and in particular on 'Socrates.'"

But Strauss in this Preface does not himself apply the word "deepened" to his studies of classic natural right and Socrates. Strauss wrote that his "deepened . . . understanding applies in the first place to 'modern natural right.' My view [he wrote] was confirmed by the study of Vico's *La scienza nuova seconda.*"[2]

Strauss thus characterizes his "deepened" understanding—"in the first place"—as a confirmation of his view that "natural right . . . is not properly approached and understood by those who take 'the historical consciousness' for granted." Strauss then remarks that since he has not written anything on Vico, he refers his readers instead to his articles on Hobbes and Locke in *What Is Political Philosophy?* (1959). "I refer particularly to what I wrote on the nerve of Hobbes's argument (p. 176n)." Now the Hobbes article was first published in 1954, and the one on Locke in 1958. Both antedated that "last ten years" (preceding 1970) in which Strauss devoted himself to classic natural right and Socrates. Thus Pangle's broad hint that Strauss's understanding of "natural right and history" was transformed by his studies of Socrates and of classic natural right in the decade before 1970 is not borne out by what Strauss himself says in this Preface.

But what is that "nerve of Hobbes's argument"? It is to be found, according to Strauss, in Hobbes's assertion that "the only natural peculiarity of man's mind" is the faculty of discovering cause and effect in the nonteleological or modern scientific sense of those terms. Hobbes, Strauss says, regarded teleological thinking as "common to man and beast"! I believe that what Strauss meant by referring us to this footnote to his 1954 essay, in the 1970 Preface to *Natural Right and History,* was to point to the importance in modern thought of this Hobbesian redefinition of human nature. Hobbes himself preceded the discovery of history and the historical consciousness, but Strauss believed that the key to these concepts lay nevertheless in Hobbes. For Hobbes's redefinition meant that man was the being who could—as Marx declared in his famous thesis on Feuerbach—change the world instead of merely interpreting it. It meant that the distinctively human faculty was a faculty of increasing power, not one of abstract knowing, or of contemplating imaginary "essences." Contemplation, for Hobbes—and Marx—belonged not to reason but imagination, and the imagination was a faculty which man shared with other animals. But the ability to change the world by the conquest of nature meant that man alone was not fated to live in nature, but instead could inhabit that world of transformations arising from his own power called history. Strauss therefore saw this turning of philosophy into science in the 17th century as the theoretical root and origin of the idea of history and of the historical consciousness. If *Natural Right and History* had been rewritten in the 1970s it might then have featured a deepened understanding of the ground of history and the historical consciousness. Strauss says nothing, however, to lead us to believe that this would have contributed to a deeper sympathy with radical modernity, or a lesser sympathy with classic natural right. Or, I might add, that his studies of Socrates had led him to see an affinity he had not seen before between radical modernity and Socrates—for this is the esoteric thesis at which Pangle is continually driving. Pangle's misinterpretation—and misrepresentation—of the 1970 Preface is symptomatic of his whole misreading of Strauss.

In another discussion, in which Pangle tried to depreciate natural right in favor of history (and to depreciate *Natural Right and History*), I also cited, to the contrary, the beginning and the end of *Thoughts on Machiavelli*. In the former, Strauss had declared himself "inclined to the old-fashioned and simple opinion according to which Machiavelli was a teacher of evil." In the latter, Strauss indicated his continuing rejection of Machiavellian modernity by concluding that "It would seem that the notion of the beneficence of nature or of the primacy of the Good must be restored." But Pangle brushed aside these quotations, declaring that whatever Strauss said at the beginning or the end was merely rhetorical (or exoteric). His real opinions, Pangle said, were radically different from these, and were to be found at or near the center of the book. There, he said, Strauss showed his profound agreement with Machiavelli. Now I too have studied the center of *Thoughts on Machiavelli*, although not perhaps as someone of Professor Pangle's rank. I have found there nothing inconsistent with its beginning or its end. I was, however, persuaded by Pangle to look for just such a striking difference as he had imputed to Strauss, between the center, on the one hand, and the beginning and the end, on the other hand, of anything that *he* would write. Indeed, having spoken as openly as he did, about Strauss, as both a Nietzschean and a Machiavellian, I wondered why he had bothered, in writing the Introduction to *Studies in Platonic Political Philosophy*, to drape the body of his argument in such prudish vestments.

The central section of Pangle's Introduction to *Studies in Platonic Political Philosophy* to which we have called so much attention in "The Legacy of Leo Strauss," is, we recall, entitled "The Quarrel Between Philosophy and Poetry." In the central paragraph—the third of five—of that section, Pangle wrote:

> *The concern for the noble can best be explained on the basis of speculations about its origins. Then one recognizes that the noble was in all likelihood, the semiconscious invention of primitive men.*

In what follows, Pangle makes clear that, according to the speculations of the philosophers, the noble and just things are essentially "artificial" goods. Their goodness is essentially an illusion—Marx would call it ideology—an illusion generated by the necessities of civil society, necessities that require that some men sacrifice themselves, if others are to enjoy "personal pleasure, security, and comfort." As the analysis proceeds, it appears that only the latter goods are truly or naturally good. The "goods" that are ostensibly the fruits of self-sacrifice—the goods that are praised but not really prized—are not goods by nature, but by convention only. But this account, Pangle now says, is not what he himself really meant, or really meant to endorse, or really meant to attribute to Strauss. This passage, he says "is obviously and explicitly meant to summarize Strauss's account of *pre*-Socratic philosophy, the philosophy *against* which Socrates, according to Strauss, turned."

But if Pangle meant this account to characterize only pre-Socratic philosophy, why is it that he never once uses the term "pre-Socratic" to characterize it? Why does he not call the quarrel, "The Quarrel Between *Pre*-Socratic Philosophy and Poetry"? How can he say that he "obviously and explicitly meant to summarize Strauss's account of *pre*-Socratic philosophy" when he never once uses pre-Socratic to identify the philosophic account he summarizes? It is true that, in the parallel account in Chapter III of *Natural Right and History*, Strauss also speaks of "philosophy." But Strauss, unlike Pangle, is at pains to make clear that the philosophy under consideration is pre-Socratic. E.g., "It seems that the answer which prevailed prior to Socrates was the negative one, the view which we have called 'conventionalism'" (p. 93); "The crucial pre-Socratic text." (p. 93); "To illustrate the point by . . . the best-known pre-Socratic doctrine" (p. 94). Pangle does not do this. I am reminded in this of Lincoln's attack on Taney's opinion in *Dred Scott*. The Chief Justice had declared that "the right to property in a slave is distinctly and expressly affirmed in the Constitution." But how, Lincoln asked, could this be true, if the words "slave" or "slavery" never occur in the Constitution? How then can Pangle's account of "The Quarrel Between Philosophy and Poetry" have been meant "obviously and explicitly . . . to summarize Strauss's account of pre-Socratic philosophy" when the word "pre-Socratic" is never used to characterize that quarrel?

The word itself occurs only once in this central section, in the last paragraph. It is in the context of a discussion of the attack on Socrates in

The Clouds, where—according to Pangle—Aristophanes imputes to Socrates a more radical atheism "than that of other 'pre-Socratic philosophers' like Parmenides and Empedocles." This is the only time the word "pre-Socratic" occurs in the section called "The Quarrel of Philosophy and Poetry."

The next section of Pangle's Introduction is entitled "The Socratic Turn." One would expect to find here the account of how Socrates became the man Pangle now says turned "against" pre-Socratic philosophy. If the section on the quarrel between philosophy and poetry corresponded in some sense, to Chapter III of *Natural Right and History*, this section ought in the same sense to correspond to Chapter IV. But this is very, very far from being the case. What we have instead is a thematic treatment of classic natural right by Pangle which suggests—not very subtly—how *Natural Right and History* ought to have been rewritten. Thus rewritten, it would have obscured, if it would not have finally wiped out, any important meaning to the distinction between pre-Socratic and Socratic philosophy.

The "Socratic turn" begins by saying that "Plato and Xenophon defend a conception of the philosophic life that has been altered in the light of what was learned from Aristophanes." They portray, he says, quoting the *Second Letter*, a "Socrates become beautiful and new." But, he adds immediately, "the closer one looks, the more difficult it becomes to spell out precisely in what the newness consists." To which we would add, that as one continues looking, the difficult turns into the impossible! What has been altered in the light of what has been learned from Aristophanes is not—according to Pangle—the nature of philosophy itself, but the need for prudence in concealing itself from the citizens, whose morality it undermines. Thus Pangle: "The mature, Platonic Socrates did not abandon a dedication to a life of inquiry so consuming as to make him appear very, very strange—even inhuman—he did not rejoin the regular citizenry as an enlightened leader . . . Nor did he ever become a teacher of civic virtue." These statements are not untrue in themselves, but they become entirely misleading as they are combined with an ever greater insistence that the "new" Socrates was not genuinely concerned (and in a philosophical sense which marked him off from his predecessors) with the understanding of the moral and political things. Strauss emphasizes that the distinction between the things that are by convention and the things that are by nature, was as important for Socrates as for the pre-Socratics. But he adds immediately, that for Socrates, what is just or right by nature takes precedence over what is just or right by convention only, and not by nature. Socrates' defect in loyalty to any actual regime—including that of Athens—arose not from contempt for the city as city, but from awareness of the difference between any defective city compared to the perfect city. But Pangle does not repeat this element of

Strauss's characterization of the difference between Socrates and his predecessors.

"What is new," Pangle says, "is Socrates' emphatic admission that his idiosyncratic way of life has to be justified according to standards acceptable to the city and its moral-religious beliefs." But does "has to be justified" refer *only* to the rhetorical exigencies of philosophy, or does it also refer to a necessity lying at the heart of the philosophical understanding of reality? In *Natural Right and History* it was Socrates' refusal to accept the pre-Socratic reductionist understanding of the moral phenomena which constituted the Socratic revolution—or, if one prefers, "turn." In the *Phaedo*, Socrates rejects the Anaxagorean—or pre-Socratic—system of explanation, because it cannot account for his reasons for regarding it to be *good*, that he refuse to run away, but accept instead the judgment of the laws of Athens. Socrates demands an account of the goodness of right action, a goodness rooted in the goodness of being as such. For this, the core of philosophy itself must indeed take a new "turn." Pangle's account of the Socratic turn imputes to it little more than a new skill in inventing the myths by which one conceals the real nature of philosophy—which itself remains unchanged. It says nothing about discovering a ground in nature for human excellence, whereby the philosopher might become a lawgiver, or a teacher of lawgivers (like the Athenian Stranger), and thereby *the* teacher of civic excellence *par excellence*.

That the "Socratic turn" is, according to Pangle, no real turn at all, is virtually conceded in the next paragraph: "not for one moment does Socrates suppose that moral and political virtue can be made philosophic, or that a healthy society can become rational. . . . He knows that he cannot do more than induce in a few nonphilosophers . . . a respect for a certain poetic image of philosophy. The new Socrates has learned the lesson in political and psychological prudence that Aristophanes sought to teach." That "a healthy society [cannot] become rational" may of course mean that there cannot, as James Madison put it, be "a nation of philosophers." That, however, a healthy society cannot be founded upon principles discovered by reason and held by reason is certainly not the teaching of classical political philosophy. The Socratic enterprise in the comprehensive sense is that enterprise whereby codes of decent human conduct are recognized as exercises in reason requiring, so far as circumstances permit, that human conduct be made to conform to nonarbitrary standards. It is that enterprise in which, as our Declaration of Independence proclaims, "the laws of nature and of nature's God" become of paramount consideration in the deliberations of statesmen.

For Pangle, "the new 'political' philosophy originated by Socrates is preoccupied to an unprecedented extent with . . . rhetoric." Indeed, the very word "political" when applied to philosophy is, according to Pangle, rhetorical. That Socratic philosophy is greatly concerned with rhetoric is certainly true. But the nature of that rhetoric is itself misunderstood if one thinks of it solely, or almost solely, in terms of the defense of a philosophy unchanged in its own inner nature. Pangle, near the end of "The Socratic Turn," asks finally *the* question, "To what extent was the *core* of Socratic philosophizing affected by the Socratic turn?" After citing the end of Strauss's 1945 essay, "On Classical Political Philosophy," Pangle concludes "Strauss can thereby be understood to imply that the core of Socratic philosophy was not decisively altered by the Socratic turn." In accordance with this observation, Pangle finds Strauss "suggesting . . . that the mature Socrates, when not under the obligation to keep company with gentlemen-citizens, pursued investigations into the paradoxical nature of light and liquids, and into the question, 'Are the beings numbers?'" That is to say, the core of Socratic philosophy remained decisively pre-Socratic, and the quarrel between pre-Socratic philosophy and poetry was, in unmuted form, the quarrel between philosophy and poetry. So much for Professor Pangle's indignant accusation against me for willfully misrepresenting him.

Professor Pangle is at least as angry with me for misrepresenting him in the matter of Jerusalem and Athens, as in the matter of philosophy and poetry. He quotes me as follows: "At the center of Pangle's position is the judgment that, according to Strauss, the Bible is only 'one of many' kinds of 'poetry.'" Pangle then adds: "The phrase in quotations, in this sentence, appears nowhere in the text of my essay." There then follows a series of fulminating denials, not merely at the allegedly spurious attribution, but at the thought contained in it. Now it is true that the phrase "one of many" is not in Pangle's essay. But then I did not quote it as being in Pangle's essay. I had used the expression "one among many" at least five times in an earlier paragraph of "The Legacy of Leo Strauss," and had placed inverted commas around it there. I had commented upon the award that had been established in honor of Leo Strauss by the American Political Science Association, and which had been hailed by some of Strauss's former students for the recognition it had given political philosophy "as one of the important traditions within the discipline." In "Political Philosophy and Honor" I had commented extensively upon the absurdity of this language, and in particular upon that aspect of it which implied that political philosophy was "one of many" subdivisions or branches of political science. The very idea of political philosophy, as a practical science, was inextricably connected with the idea of an architectonic science, standing in the same relationship to other practical sciences as that of the architect to the builders, viz., the carpenters, masons, plumbers, etc. But the idea of an architectonic practical science originated in and was inseparable from the idea of a single comprehensive human good: happiness, according to Aristotle. Happiness, Aristotle says, to translate as literally as possible, "is not to be numbered together [with other good things] since it is clear that if it were to be so numbered it would become more choiceworthy with the addition of the least of [other] goods . . . [and hence could not be the final good]." (*Nicomachean Ethics* 1097b17 ff.) The common English rendering of the first part of the last sentence is that "happiness is not to be counted one among many good things." To complete the thought, happiness is that good in virtue of which other good things—e.g., health or wealth or freedom—become good "for us." When I put the phrase "one among many" (or "one of many") in quotation marks, I was recalling one of Aristotle's most memorable locutions in connection with his doctrine of the *summum bonum*. I did no more than I would have done had I written that Professor Pangle had questioned whether one ought "to be or not to be," without adding that this was Shakespeare and not Pangle. All this heavy weather over the quotation marks, however, is a diversion from the substantive issue: that classical political philosophy cannot be "one of many" practical disciplines, and that the *summum bonum* cannot be one of many good things. The idea of a *summum bonum* itself, however, implies that such a good is objective, not subjective, and that it stands in opposition to all modern relativism—including Nietzsche's "will to power." The proposers of the Strauss award thus had tacitly abandoned the ground upon which classical political philosophy stood, the ground upon which alone Strauss's career made sense.

Political philosophy—to repeat—cannot then be "one among many" political disciplines, for the identical reason that happiness—the *summum bonum*—cannot be "one among many" human goods. If we turn from Reason to Revelation, from Plato and Aristotle to the Bible, we find that all the authority of the latter is derived from the fact that the biblical God is not "One among many." I have written elsewhere of the absurdity of supposing that, when Moses said, "Hear O Israel, the Lord our God is One," he might have substituted "one and a half," or "one point zero zero one." The unity of God, and the uncompromising denial of other gods, are inseparable from the authenticity, and therewith the authority, of Revelation. When therefore Pangle wrote, in his Introduction, that "What is most essential in the quarrel between Plato and the Bible is already present in the quarrel between Plato and the poets" I felt entirely justified in saying that he had asserted that the Bible, in regard to what is "most essential," falls under the same genus as that to which the work of "the poets" belonged: viz., poetry. Being "a" form, it was "one of many."

Pangle's bluster is designed to divert attention from the fact that in his "Reply to Jaffa" he not only repeats the contention that the Bible is one of many species of poetry, but insists that this is Strauss's contention as well. He insists, furthermore, that "this thought . . . is the very core of Strauss's rediscovery of what he intransigently held to be the full adequacy of the Platonic understanding of the ultimate questions for man as man.

"To this thought," Pangle writes, and writes truly, "Jaffa takes strong exception." Pangle is unclear as to the extent to which the understanding of the "ultimate questions" implies an answer to the ultimate question, What is the right way of life? Strauss, however, was clear that this question is answered differently by Reason and by Revelation. That is to say, it is understood differently by Plato and Aristotle on the one hand, and by the Bible on the other hand. However, Pangle to the contrary notwithstanding, Strauss denied that the answer of Plato and Aristotle (or either of them) was evidently superior to the answer of the Bible. Indeed, no classical philosopher ever attempted the kind of argument that might have proved the superiority of Reason to Revelation. That attempt was left to modern philosophy. To be evidently superior, Strauss held, Reason would have to be able to refute the possibility of Revelation, and therewith the possibility that the answer of Revelation is the true answer. And this he denied had ever been done. That he was skeptical that it could be done, is an understatement. As a philosopher, Strauss may have had an "inclination to prefer" the answer of the classics: but as a philosopher, he denied that any argument for the philosophic life was sufficient to decide in favor of the claims of philosophy. The claims of the Bible had not, he thought, been refuted. In a well-known—but only recently published—lecture, "On the Interpretation of Genesis," he wrote:

> Revelation is a miracle. This means, therefore, that before we even open the Bible we must have made up our minds as to whether we believe in the possibility of miracles. . . . The question as to whether miracles are possible or not depends on the previous question as to whether God as an omnipotent being exists. Many of our contemporaries assume tacitly or even explicitly that we know that God as an omnipotent being does not exist. I believe that they are wrong; for how could we know that God as an omnipotent being does not exist? Not from experience. . . . There is then only one way in which belief in an omnipotent God can be refuted, by showing that there is no mystery whatever, that we have clear and distinct knowledge, or scientific knowledge, in principle of everything, that we can give an adequate and clear account of everything, that all fundamental questions have been answered in a perfectly satisfactory way, in other words that there exists what we may call, the absolute and final philosophic system. According to that system (there was such a system; its author was Hegel), the previously hidden God, the previously incomprehensible God, has now become perfectly revealed, perfectly comprehensible. I regard the existence of such a system as at least as improbable as the truth of the Bible. But, obviously, the improbability of the truth of the Bible is a contention of the Bible whereas the improbability of the truth of the perfect philosophic system creates a serious difficulty for that system. (*L'Homme*, janv.-mars 1981, XXI (1), pp. 5–20)

Variants of this argument appear many places in Strauss's writings. We think that Strauss is unequivocal on the proposition that "human reason cannot prove the nonexistence of God as an omnipotent being," and that it is "equally true that human reason cannot establish the existence of God as an omnipotent being." The claims of the Bible, however, do not require the establishment by reason of the existence of God as an omnipotent being. On the contrary, the Bible affirms the mysteriousness of God and His incomprehensibility by human reason as the very ground of its authority. Philosophy, however, needs to establish the nonexistence of such a God as the ground of its authority. And this, according to Strauss, it cannot do. So long as this is true, Strauss, as a philosopher, could not have held, unambiguously and unequivocally, to "the *full* adequacy of the Platonic understanding."

To support his contention, Pangle points to the epigraph of *The Argument and Action of Plato's Laws*, which is from Avicenna: "[T]he treatment of prophecy and the Divine Law is contained in . . . the *Laws*." Then he quotes from Strauss's commentary, and emphasizes it as follows: "[T]he Athenian . . . appeals as it were from the accepted interpretation of revelation to revelation itself, which discloses its true meaning only to those who never forget that, being divine, it is supremely reasonable."[3] It is clear to anyone with eyes to see, that the epigraph of Avicenna means that it is the *philosophical* treatment of prophecy and Divine Law which is treated in the *Laws*. To say that revelation itself is supremely reasonable is—according to Strauss—to assume that the cause of everything attributed to revelation is intelligible, and not mysterious. It implies that belief in revelation does not require faith. But the very unity of God, as affirmed by the Bible, implies that God is, at one and the same time, a particular and a universal, hence a unique being, and as such not accessible to reason as reason, from the point of view of reason itself. For reason can attain to universals only by abstracting from particulars, which is not possible if the living God is One. In "How Farabi Read Plato's *Laws*," Chapter V of *What is Political Philosophy?* (p. 144), Strauss explains the problem confronting medieval Muslim readers of Plato's *Laws* as follows:

> The *Laws* contains a teaching which claims to be true, i.e., valid for all times. Every serious reader of the *Laws* has to face this claim. Every Muslim reader in the Middle Ages did face it. He could do this in at least three different ways. He could reject Plato's claim by contending that Plato lacked completely the guidance supplied by Revelation. He could use the Platonic standards for judging, or criticizing, specific Islamic institutions, if not for rejecting Islam altogether. He could contend that Islam, and Islam alone, lives up to the true standards set forth by Plato, and on this basis elaborate a purely rational justification of both the content and the origin of Islam.

Every reader of Strauss's "Persecution and the Art of Writing," knows that "rejecting the claims of Islam" was not a feasible alternative, for medieval Islamic writers who wanted to avoid persecution, any more than it is a feasible alternative today in Khomeini's Iran. But it was unfeasible also because most of them believed—with Plato—that the effectiveness of law in most cases depends upon the conviction, in the minds of those subject to the law, that it is divine law. Thomas Aquinas declared that the Second Table of the Decalogue was part of the natural law, and knowable by unassisted human reason. But he said it was incorporated by God into the Divine Law, for the sake of the unphilosophic, and to make it more effective. Returning to the three alternatives, we observe that theologians who rejected Plato's claim would not write commentaries on the *Laws*. The philosophers who did write commentaries in fact did judge and criticize Islamic institutions. Mindful however of the necessity of preserving the divine authority of the *Laws*, they did so by contending "that Islam . . . alone lives up to the true standards set forth by Plato." In this way they protected the safety of the philosophers and the piety of the citizens, while making the laws more reasonable in and through their interpretations. The Islamic interpreters of the *Laws* were however only following the example of the Athenian Stranger himself, who attributed perfection to the laws of Zeus, as a way of piously discovering which laws were in fact most perfect—because most reasonable. This assumption, however, which may in fact have decided the question between Plato and the poets (and the divine law or laws as seen from the perspective of Plato) did not decide that more comprehensive question between Jerusalem and Athens, between Revelation and Reason.

In "The Legacy of Leo Strauss" I called attention to Strauss's having said, in "Progress or Return," "that the Bible and Greek philosophy agree in regard to what we may call, as we do call in fact, morality." I did not think that Strauss had forgotten the profound difference between magnanimity and humility, or any of the other differences between biblical and philosophical ethics. It is then with an ill grace that Professor Pangle accuses me of forgetting such differences. Strauss did think that, in the absence of any refutation of Reason by Revelation, or Revelation by Reason, that a civilization characterized by the dynamic tension between the two was in fact the highest civilization: This was what he meant by the West which it was our duty to defend, protect, and preserve. It is precisely by the attempt of modern philosophy to transcend the difference between Revelation and Reason that the West is above all endangered, for if the contention could be maintained that there is no mystery to justify the belief in God, it would follow that there was no ground to doubt that philosophy had been transformed into wisdom. To believe that philosophy had been transformed into wisdom leads necessarily to the unqualified claim of wisdom to rule: the claim of the universal tyrant. In the face of this challenge of radical modernity, the fate of Socratic philosophy and of the Bible are linked in both their separateness and their combination. This I think was clearly Strauss's conviction, in his great disputation with Kojève, in *On Tyranny*. In "The Legacy of Leo Strauss" I pointed out the irresponsibility from Strauss's point of view, of philosophy as represented by Heidegger. I think it fair to add also that Kojève was a partisan of Stalin—or at least of Stalinism—as much as Heidegger was of Hitler and of National Socialism. Strauss and Kojève shared a deep personal affinity and friendship, notwithstanding their differences. Nevertheless, Strauss was convinced that Kojève's Hegelianism, culminating in the acceptance, if not the advocacy, of the universal homogeneous state, pointed toward a consummation of evil in this world, quite as much as the victory of Hitler would have done. In resisting this consummation, the cause of Revelation and of Reason do indeed become One.

NOTES

Originally printed in the *Claremont Review of Books*, Vol. IV, No. 1, Spring 1985.

1. Leo Strauss, *Natural Right and History* (Chicago: University of Chicago Press, 1950), p. vii.
2. Strauss, *Natural Right and History*, p. vii.
3. Leo Strauss, *Argument and Action of Plato's Laws* (Chicago: University of Chicago Press, 1975), p. 7.

SEVEN

The Politics of Moderation

Strauss's Esotericism

John A. Wettergreen

To the Editors:

At the end of his "Reply to Harry Jaffa" (*Claremont Review of Books*, Spring 1985), Thomas Pangle threatens that Harry Jaffa is so immoderate that he is in danger of being stricken from the list of philosophers. Accordingly, he pleads with Jaffa's friends and followers to prevent him from publishing more essays like "The Legacy of Leo Strauss." As one of Jaffa's long-time followers, I am writing to say that, before I read his "Reply," I might have been sympathetic to Pangle's plea. Having read it, I am more convinced than ever of Jaffa's moderation.

It is hard not to sympathize with Pangle, the Straussians, and others who have felt the sting of Jaffa's words. However, in important matters like those under dispute, we put aside our merely personal feelings in order to ask: Did they deserve to be stung?

According to Professor Pangle, in a philosophic dispute on moral and political questions no one deserves to be stung: "labeling [one's] opponents or their views immoral" is forbidden by him. Anyone who dares to label, he believes to be "ineligible as a dialectical partner." But this means that if one is in a dispute with someone whose position is truly immoral, one must conceal that truth. Now I have heard that Professor Pangle is a believer in Leo Strauss's doctrine of philosophic esotericism, according to which philosophers are supposed to conceal their true views from the uninitiated; e.g., by putting them at the very center of their writings. So let me say, without, in any way wishing to pull rank on Pangle, that Mr.

Strauss told me—in perfect confidence—the whole truth about esotericism: It is the means of defending morality. (*I put the previous sentence at the very center of this letter, in order that it not be concealed from any Straussian.*) Pangle seems to suppose that Straussian esotericism could obfuscate immorality. Strauss would never have taught such a thing, because that would have contradicted his teaching that philosophic wisdom and political moderation are harmonious. Acting accordingly in his dispute with Machiavelli, Strauss scarcely hesitated to declare his inclination to the view that he was an evil teacher of evil. Of course, Machiavelli was not alive to be stung by Strauss's hard words. However, Jaffa is far more gentle with Pangle than Strauss was with Machiavelli.

After all, Jaffa does not claim that Pangle "is free from any inner attachment to anything noble or just," but only that "Pangle's hero" is. In fact, Pangle's understanding of the nature of philosophic disputation confirms the truth, and so the justice, of Jaffa's "labeling" of his position. For to claim, as Pangle does, that a worthy "dialectical partner" is indifferent to moral distinctions is to claim, theoretically, that morality—the noble and the just—is not a matter worthy of serious philosophic concern and to claim, practically, that we should not help our friends, even by means of disputations, to be as good as they can be. Harry Jaffa has devoted a good part of his life to trying to help his friends by means of philosophic disputes on the nobility and justice of their actions. This is a sign of his amazing moderation; i.e., of his adamantine devotion to the achievement of the best good that can be had in the present circumstances, and by the mildest of means.

That Pangle believes Jaffa's unusually kind and helpful words to be the products of "disfiguring passions," that he supposes Jaffa's almost profligate use of his time to correct Pangle's essay to be "*mikropsuchia*," is symptomatic of the very blindness to the moral phenomena which "The Legacy of Leo Strauss" is intended to correct.

NOTE

Originally published in the *Claremont Review of Books*, Vol. IV, No. 2, Spring 1985.

EIGHT

Leo Strauss's Churchillian Speech and the Question of the Decline of the West

> The probability that we may fall in the struggle ought not deter us from the support of a cause we believe to be just; it shall not deter me. If ever I feel the soul within me elevate and expand to those dimensions not wholly unworthy of its Almighty Architect, it is when I contemplate the cause of my country, deserted by all the world beside, and I standing up boldly alone, and hurling defiance at her victorious oppressors. Here, without contemplating consequences, before High Heaven, and in the face of the world, I swear eternal fidelity to the just cause. . . . Let none falter, who thinks he is right, and we may succeed. But, if after all, we shall fail, be it so. We still shall have the proud consolation of saying to our consciences, and to the departed shade of our country's freedom, that the cause approved of our judgment, and adored of our hearts, in disaster, in chains, in torture, in death, we never faltered in defending.
>
> —Abraham Lincoln, Springfield, Illinois, December 26, 1839

In a "Reply to Harry Jaffa" (1982), Walter Berns declared that Leo Strauss "did not believe that he, or political philosophy could save Western civilization (or reverse 'the decline of the West')."[1] "It is precisely hopes of this kind," Berns continued, "that distort the quest for truth. Eternity, not history, is the theme of philosophy, which, Strauss believed, must beware of wishing to be edifying." I was denounced as being "like" Marx, since, said Berns, I wanted to "change the world" rather than "interpret it." Here Berns echoed the most famous of Marx's "theses on Feuerbach," and in doing so appeared to accept Marx's dichotomy between change and interpretation.

In the "Primacy of the Good: Leo Strauss Remembered" (1982, 26:3–4), I have, I think, sufficiently refuted these charges made against me. If I had wished in some sense to reverse the decline of the West, it was only because I believe it the function of political philosophy to distinguish good action from bad and promote the one and avert the other. In short, I believed that political philosophy, as distinct from philosophy simply, was possible. If I was "like" Marx, then Strauss, and indeed Aristotle, were also guilty of this reproach. Marx's distinction between interpreting the world and changing it, however, has little to do with the concern with right action, as I (or Strauss, or Aristotle) understand it. Political philosophy, in its classic form, attempts to inform human action with human wisdom, first of all by clarifying the meaning of such terms as noble and base, just or unjust, good and bad. All such distinctions Marx dismissed as ideology, mere epiphenomena of the relations of production. Political philosophy stands or falls by the belief that human actions are in the decisive sense free, that they are not under the control of a power outside the human soul, over which the soul itself has no power. Marx believed that the human will was a mere plaything of a historical dialectical process constituting providential order within which and by which human life was ordered. Nothing is more instructive in this regard than to compare and contrast the idea of a right to revolution, as that idea is implied in the American Declaration of Independence, and the idea of revolution in the *Communist Manifesto*. As Harvey C. Mansfield Jr., has argued—in chapter 5 of *The Spirit of Liberalism* (1978)—there can be no right of revolution properly so called in Marx's doctrine. There is a necessity of revolution, arising from history. But what is necessary is not a matter of moral choice. One does not speak of a right to be mortal, although one does speak of a right to life.

In the Declaration, the people have a right to alter or to abolish governments, insofar as those governments fail to secure certain inalienable rights. But such action ought to take place only in accordance with the dictates of prudence. A right can be exercised wisely or unwisely. Abraham Lincoln, in his first inaugural address, argued that there was no constitutional right in any state to withdraw from the Union. Nevertheless, he conceded that the people in each state did have a natural, or revolutionary right, to withdraw their allegiance from the Union. This they might do if there was a greater threat to their lives and liberties from remaining in the Union than by withdrawing from it. But Lincoln, in a point by point examination of the case, argued that there was in fact no threat to their legitimate interests in or by the Union. Lincoln invited deliberations upon a matter of moral and political choice. For Marx—and, according to Mansfield, for Burke as well—no such dialectical examination of alternative courses of action can determine whether a revolution ought to be made. In Mansfield's words, "When revolution is a right it must be a choice." Burke's view of the Revolution of 1688 is thus closer to Marx than to Jefferson, according to Mansfield, because Burke said of the Whig leaders' acceptance of William to replace James, that it "was not properly a *choice*; . . . it was an act of *necessity*, in the strictest moral sense in which necessity can be taken." And that sense, to recall Aristotle, is one in which neither praise nor blame is appropriate. For praise and blame belong only to those actions for which we are responsible, where the moving cause of our actions lies in ourselves, and where our will may be held accountable to our reason.

Aristotle says that we deliberate only about things capable of being otherwise. We do not deliberate about whether we shall be mortal beings, but we do deliberate about how to avoid death by violence or disease. If the West's decline is judged a symptom of morality, if it is held to exhibit metaphysical necessity, then to think of reversing it would indeed be foolish. I think it fair to point out that it is in the interest of Marxists to persuade us that such is the case, but I am at a loss to understand why Walter Berns would wish to do so. If, to repeat, the course of history expresses a dialectical necessity, then it does indeed become a field of thought, but not of action, a subject of contemplation, but not of moral or political choice. It becomes a subject of philosophy, but not of political philosophy. But to put Leo Strauss among those who thought that history was primarily a subject of thought, and not at all one of action, would be to put him among those who held a view of history like that of Marx.

To say that Strauss did not accept the West's decline fatalistically, does not, however, mean that he was an optimist in regard to its prospects. But the essence of the West, the essence of that civilization constituted at its core by Reason and Revelation, is found in nothing more than in the distinction between noble failure and vulgar success.[2] Acting in time, however, does not mean that they are indifferent to eternity or that they are indifferent to eternal truth. Nor does it mean that in their hopes for well-being or happiness in this world, hopes contingent upon right action, they distort their quest for the truth that transcends time. The revolution in human understanding represented by the name of Socrates, that revolution to the understanding of which Strauss's life may be said above all to have been devoted, was a revolution in the way of understanding eternal things, no less than the human things. Strauss began his chapter on "Classical Natural Right," which Richard Kennington has rightly pointed to as the central section of *Natural Right and History*[3] by referring to a passage in Cicero's *Tusculan Disputations*. "Socrates," Strauss wrote, "is said to have been the first who called philosophy down from heaven and forced it to make inquiries about life and manners and good and bad things. In other words, he is said to be the founder of political philosophy."[4]

Here is the passage which Strauss abridged:

> from the ancient days down to the time of Socrates . . . philosophy dealt with numbers and movements, with the problem whence all things came, or whither they returned, and zealously inquired into the size of the stars and all celestial phenomena; Socrates on the other hand was the first to call philosophy down from the heaven and set her in the cities of men and bring her also into their homes and compel her to ask questions about life and morals (mores) and good things and bad things. (Cicero, Bk. 5, chap. 4)

Strauss, in this reference, omits Cicero's characterization of pre-Socratic philosophy. Cicero mentions three things about pre-Socratic philosophy: first, its preoccupation with mathematics; last, its preoccupation with astronomy; central, its problem of "whence things came, or whither they returned" (1971, 20). We are reminded of the biblical, "from dust thou art, and to dust thou shalt return."

The Old Testament, however, knowing not nature, attributes the breath of life in man to God. Man's being—to use the language of philosophy—is not originally in man but in a Being upon whom man is dependent. Man is made in the image of God: man is that part of God's creation that reflects God's own being. Man's humanity is above all to be found in his divine image, which sets him apart from and above the rest of creation. For man to "know himself" then, he must know the divine image in himself. To learn what this image is, he must turn to the Original of the image: he must turn to God. But he cannot see God directly. To attempt to look directly at God would be like trying to look directly into the sun: the result would be blindness, not light. He must learn the ways of God in the ways that God has appointed him to know these ways. For a Jew, certainly this means to study Torah. The philosophic injunction, for the pious Jew or Gentile, can be obeyed only by studying God's word. I believe it proper to mention this because Strauss was a Jew, who began his scholarly career as what we might call a pre-Socratic (or Spinozistic) Jew, who later became a Socratic Jew.

Through Strauss's study of Spinoza, he learned how to read the Bible "scientifically," by the same method one would attempt to understand any phenomenon of nature. The Bible, approached in this way, was merely a human book. But Strauss became convinced that Spinoza's reading of the Bible would not reveal how the Bible was intended to be understood. Later, Strauss would insist, as the supreme hermeneutic principle, that we understand the great books exactly as their authors understood them, before attempting to understand them differently or better. In the case of the Bible, this meant that no understanding of it was possible that was not grounded in a pious reading of the Bible. Spinoza's break with tradition eventually led to Strauss's break with Spinoza. It led him to Maimonides, as a profound interpreter of the Bible, for the very reason that Maimonides, unlike Spinoza, continued—and did not break with—the tradition he interpreted. A pious Jew is above all concerned with right action. A pious Jew naturally—one is tempted to say—identifies obedience to the Law with a concern for eternal things, because he grounds that obedience upon his understanding of the Eternal One. A pious Jew would regard with horror the idea that because of his concern with the fate of the Holy City—and every right action is a manifestation of this concern—he was somehow distorting the quest for truth. Strauss's discovery of the superiority of Orthodox Judaism to Spinozistic or liberal Judaism prepared the way for his discovery of Socrates and of classical political philosophy altogether. (His way was from Maimonides to Al-Farabi to Plato.)

Strauss's discovery of the Socratic ground of classical political philosophy was simultaneous with, and not ultimately distinguishable from, his discovery of the ground of biblical revelation. His interpretation and critique of modern philosophy—which took many years to complete and was completed, in a sense, in his study of Machiavelli—proved that Reason and Revelation, the core of the West, were untouched in their intrinsic claims by modern philosophy and modern science. For Strauss, the question of the right way of life remained what it had always been. The decline of the West meant the turning away from the question of the right way of life. But the decline of the West would be irreversible, or final, only if this question had lost its meaning. If, however, I read him rightly, Strauss never conceded the authority of any argument that attempted to prove that this was possible or that the question of the right way of life had been altered or transformed in any way by modern philosophy or modern science.

In *Natural Right and History*, the Socratic revolution is characterized as follows:

> Socrates deviated from his predecessors by identifying the science of the whole, or of everything that is, with the understanding of "what each of the things is." "To be" means "to be something" and hence to be different from things which are "something else"; "to be" means therefore to be a part. Hence the whole cannot "be" in the same sense in which everything that is "something" "is"; the whole must be "beyond being." . . . If "to be" is "to be something," the being of a thing, or of the nature of a thing, is primarily its What, its "shape" or "form" or "character," as distinguished in particular from that out of which it has come into being. The thing itself, the completed thing, cannot be understood as a product of a process leading up to it, on the contrary, the process cannot be understood except in the light of the completed things or of the end of the process. . . . This view makes possible, and it favors in particular, the study of the human things as such. (Strauss, 1971: 122–123)

Later Strauss added the following comment, that he applied equally to pre-Socratic and post-Socratic science or philosophy. Such science or philosophy, he said, "forces its holders to understand the higher as nothing but the effect of the lower or prevents them from considering the possibility that there are phenomena which are simply irreducible to their conditions, that there are phenomena that form a class by themselves" (1971: 129).

Socrates can be called the founder of political philosophy, according to Strauss, because he attempted to understand the whole, and the ground or basis of the whole, differently from the philosophers who preceded him. Socrates became identified with that view of the whole that called the ground of becoming—itself beyond being—"the idea of the Good." Assertions about "the beings" depended upon their dependence upon insight into the goodness of such beings. Any assertion about a chair, for example, beginning with the assertion that this particular object is indeed a chair, not a table, or a floor, or a house, depends upon the "idea of the chair." Recognizing that a chair is a chair, means recognizing that there are an infinite number of possible chairs, different from this chair, that yet are chairs. "Chairness" is then something different from any possible particular chair, and yet it is this "chairness," seen by the eye of the mind, that is the necessary condition for speech and reason about crucial chairs. But the identity of the chair is also indistinguishable, in the final analysis, from its goodness. What makes all chairs chairs, even as they differ with respect to what makes each individual chair individual, is the function or work implied in the idea of the chair: the ability to support the human body in a semirecumbent posture. A defective chair can do this ill, a good chair can do it well. Calling a chair a real chair, like calling a man a real man, is the most emphatic form of the superlative.

Reality is goodness from the Socratic perspective. The *logoi* are constituted by an immaterial reality, which is the ground of all material reality, and in these *logoi* the goodness and the being of things coincide. Because the being of the beings is ultimately grasped by reference to their goodness, concern with the human things, moral philosophy and political philosophy, becomes the center of philosophy. In it the questions of goodness and the question of being coincide nominally as well as really. Philosophy, and moral and political philosophy, may not be one and the same. But it is from the consideration of the question of right human action that one is led to that realm of being that transcends human action. The prototypical example is supplied by Socrates sitting in the prison to which the Athenians had condemned him to death. The friends of Socrates had made it possible for him to walk out of the prison and live safely in exile. But Socrates chose to remain in prison and suffer the fate appointed him by Athens's laws. No explanation of his behavior was possible on the basis of any pre-Socratic or post-Socratic doctrine. No doubt someone would today hypothesize a subrational, or non-rational explanation of Socrates' decision to suffer death, as a death wish, or an inverted Oedipus complex, etc. But Socrates had denied *a priori* the validity of such explanations. For Socrates, the cause of his behavior was an ordering of his will by his reason. This ordering is to be found in the *logos* embodied in the *Crito*, a *logos* that may be understood more comprehensively in the context supplied by the *Euthyphro*, *Apology*, and *Phaedo*. By uncovering the ground whereby he was satisfied that his was a right action was in some sense a reflection of rightness as such. But the being of a right action was not different from the goodness of that action. And the goodness of any good thing (like the chairness of any chair) could only be what it was, because of the good simply. Just as the idea of a chair "is" in a different sense, so the idea of the good "is" in a different sense than any good thing "is." The idea of the good is beyond being. Any good thing, like any chair, belongs to the material world and is subject to change and to corruption. But the idea of the good, beyond being, is incorruptible and eternal.

Socrates discovered in the idea of the good the unchanging ground of all actual and all changing things. But it was Socrates' seriousness about the moral and political things that disclosed to him something at least of the eternal ground of reality. Before Socrates, the human things, the moral and political things, were considered conventional and not natural by the philosophers. Because of this, they were not considered a serious concern of philosophers. Pre-Socratic philosophy did indeed draw the distinction that Walter Berns draws, between concern for the fate of the Just City and "the quest for truth" whose theme is "eternity, not history." Socrates' decision to remain in prison and suffer execution is the human action, which is recognized as that central event in history, disclosing the possibility of a human life lived well because guided by human reason. It is recognized as such because in it we see a concern with what is right and good, everywhere and always. For this reason, Socrates' temporal fate has been stamped with eternity. Socrates, we may well conclude, was a bad citizen of Athens, even as he obeyed its laws: but if he was, it was because he was a good citizen of the just or beautiful city, the city in speech, which is ungenerated, incorruptible, and forever.

Although Walter Berns thinks that I "distort the quest for truth" with "hope" that "political philosophy could save Western civilization" or "reverse 'the decline of the West,'" he has acted on a principle that he would deny to me. In "The New Pacifism and World Government" (1983), Berns returns to a theme that he first set forth, according to my recollection, in an essay entitled "The Case Against World Government." It was included in a book of readings on international relations edited by Robert A. Goldwin and published by Oxford University Press some time in the mid-1950s.[5] A version of the same essay was, I believe, also published in *National Review* in 1960. It was directed against the position of a movement for World Federalism, that was identified with no one more than the late Robert M. Hutchins. Hutchins was for many years president, and then chancellor, of the University of Chicago. Later he became famous, or infamous, as the head of the Center for the Study of Democratic Institutions at Santa Barbara, California. One of the main preoccupations of the Center, for many years, was the drafting of a constitution for world government. In his earlier years, Hutchins was identified with reviving the study of the Great Books at the core of liberal education. He was the leading opponent—with Mortimer Adler—of the influence of John Dewey and pragmatism on American education. His *The Higher Learning in America,* originally the Storrs Lectures at Yale University, delivered during the academic year 1935–1936 (my freshman year at Yale), was and remains the most thoughtful book on higher education by an American college president during the twentieth century. Hutchins was something of a neo-Thomist who had the hardihood to assert, in the most anti-metaphysical of times, that metaphysics was the discipline most deserving of thoughtful men's attention. Unfortunately, he was influenced more than he should have been by Dante's *De Monarchia.* Dante there argues, not only for monarchy, but for universal monarchy as the crown of world government. Dante built the most extraordinary case for world government from arguments taken from Aristotle's *Metaphysics,* ignoring all the while Aristotle's *Politics.* A similar transportation of a discipline, from its proper to its improper subject matter, seems to have taken place in Hutchins's mind. The results were even more grotesque, since in other respects Hutchins was a democrat after the fashion of Tom Paine, rather than a medieval monarchist. Hutchins's most lasting achievement by far was bringing Leo Strauss to the University of Chicago in 1949. Strauss ended his career at Chicago as the Robert M. Hutchins Distinguished Service Professor. No two men could have differed more profoundly than Strauss and Hutchins on the desirability, or even possibility, of world government. Yet in arguing the case against such a world government, the high honor of carrying his master's banner fell to Walter Berns.

It may appear at first that arguing the case against world government is not identical with exercising the discipline of classical political philosophy to the end of preventing or reversing the decline of the West. Yet anyone who has read Strauss's "Restatement" in the 1963 edition of *On Tyranny,* will know that in his reply to Alexander Kojève, the great Hegelian scholar, Strauss rejected, utterly and completely, the doctrine that historical necessity, in any form or in any sense, required or justified the universal homogeneous state. Yet Strauss's rejection of history in a sense culminating in Hegel and Marx, but anticipated in Hobbes (and ultimately in Machiavelli), was long prepared in the whole body of his writing. The most eloquent rejection of historical necessity, of anything that might be called "the wave of the future," even if this wave was attributed to divine providence, is what I have called "Strauss's Churchillian speech." It is to be found in his critique of Edmund Burke, in *Natural Right and History.*

If the fundamental human choices are not made for man by history, and if choices need not be the result of blind fate or of will unguided by reason, then classical political philosophy necessarily becomes the guiding human discipline concerned with the right or best regime. And it is precisely in the spirit of Strauss's rejection of history that Walter Berns discusses the question of the eligibility of world government, as advanced by the World Federalists or by nuclear disarmers. In this he is a practicing classical political philosopher.

Berns's argument against the desirability of world government rests upon the demonstration, ably presented, that a world government would be a tyranny. No conception of historical necessity, nor of the Hobbesian analysis of the passions, leads him to call tyranny "monarchy misliked." A world government would not only be a tyranny, it would far exceed any tyranny hitherto known, because it would be a tyranny in a world in which there were no tyrannies. The world behind the Iron Curtain would be infinitely more terrible if there were no Free World beyond it offering some hope and some possible refuge. As Berns argues, the World Federalists have never been able to agree among themselves upon a world constitution that might conceivably rest upon the consent of the governed, the only basis of a free constitution. How could the United States—or, for that matter, the USSR—join a legislature in which one man, one vote would serve as the basis of representation? China would have double the voting power of these two powers combined. And how could there be a federal senate in which Chad, or Libya, or Israel had the same number of votes as the USSR, the United States, and China? But today's nuclear disarmers see world federalism arising out of the nuclear disarmament, self-imposed, by the nuclear powers. This would mean transferring the manufacture, possession, and deployment of nuclear weapons (and presumably, other cataclysmic weapons, such as chemical and biological) to some international agency. Berns ably argues that this agency, however originally constituted, would have to take extraordinary measures to safeguard its monopoly. For today, he remarks, a Princeton undergraduate can design a hydrogen bomb using information available in most public libraries. An agency designed to keep nuclear weapons out of the hands of the rest of the world would have to have powers of inspection that extended into every area of the world. There could not be any room that its agents could not enter at any time, without a warrant, and without knocking. The authority of such agents, however, could not be maintained by a monopoly of nuclear weapons alone. If resistance to its authority would not need to be enforced with nuclear weapons, there would have to be a hegemony, if not a monopoly, of other weapons. If the end of this world agency is the removal of nuclear war, then it must have all the powers necessary and proper to carry out this mission. Such powers would have to be unlimited in theory as in practice.

A subsidiary argument—which Berns does not make—is that the danger of nuclear war would not, in all likelihood, actually be lessened by such a regime. The danger of nuclear war would only become a danger of civil war, within the universal regime, rather than one of international war, as at present. There is no reason to think that the agents of this tyranny would not fall out among themselves. If they did, there would be none of those restraints upon them, that act upon the governments of nuclear powers, which are the free governments. But it is worth pointing out that the government of the USSR is today restrained indirectly by the restraints imposed upon free governments, by the opinions of the governed. Knowing, as Konstantin Chernenko knows, that the United States will not act preemptively with nuclear weapons, he is under no incentive to anticipate such action with preemptive action of his own. But if the only governments or persons in charge of nuclear weapons were as irresponsible as his own government, Chernenko would become a much more unstable and trigger-happy tyrant. By their own standards, the nuclear disarmers, and the world government advocates would make the world far more dangerous than it now is. This substantially, is Berns's conclusion. But Berns's conclusion goes beyond this: he agrees with Thomas Jefferson that "resistance to tyrants is obedience to God." We have a transcendent duty to resist tyrants. We have this duty, because death is not the greatest evil. Acting well in this life means acting, not out of fear, but out of concern with what is noble and good.

The culmination of Berns's argument against the nuclear disarmers and the world government advocates is not prudential. Or, to be more precise, it is not prudential in the modern sense of prudence, which means especially cowardice. The principles of constitutional democracy, the principles of political and moral decency, are he says worth fighting for, no matter what the dangers and no matter what the price. That, says Berns, was

> the view of "our fathers" who founded this country, and of the "sons" who, at places like Gettysburg, fought and died. Do we now regard them as fools? They, like the others, who avoided the battle, are long since dead, as dead as if they had been killed in a nuclear war, but it was they, and not the others, whom Lincoln asked us to remember—and whom we do remember, and whom we can honor only by dedicating ourselves to the cause for which they gave their lives. The new pacifism can only teach us about risks, but life without risk is inconceivable, and the risks we take to preserve an honorable way of life are both necessary and noble.[6]

In what he has written here, Berns and I are in complete agreement. Our way of life is honorable, because, in the cause of right, it does not place preservation of the body in this world above the steadfastness of the soul. It ranks honor above life, whether that honor is received in this world, in the memory of posterity, or in the next world, in the Kingdom of God. Our way of life is the way embodied in our Constitution, in the principles of our regime, as we received them from the Founding Fathers, and as they were transmitted by Lincoln. But this is not always Berns's view. In the *Wall Street Journal*, August 2, 1982, in an article entitled "Congress is Saying, Give Peace a Grant," Berns attributed the principles of the American Constitution to the teachings of Thomas Hobbes. According to the Hobbesian dispensation, wrote Berns, the political order "would confine itself to satisfying the desires of the body, or providing conditions under which they might be satisfied." And it is precisely this Hobbesian view, that men are rational only when they pursue bodily self-preservation in preference to any other goal, that Berns characterizes as the underlying (and overarching) principle of constitutional democracy. Yet, as he now says, and well says, this is *not* the principle of the nuclear disarmers.

The history of political philosophy is characterized above all by the comparing and contrasting of ancients and moderns. The principle of the ancients, of the spiritual descendants of Socrates, can be summed up by the principle of Socrates represented by his speech and deed in his trial and death. In the prison, Socrates taught us that the decision concerning life and death should be made in light of the difference between what is intrinsically noble and just, and what is intrinsically base and wrong. Fear of death is the enemy of the noble and just, and it is what makes men act basely and do wrong. The principle of the moderns is above all that of Thomas Hobbes who taught that men act rationally and well only when they act out of fear of violent death. No two positions are more opposed. Nor is there anything difficult or esoteric in grasping the distinction between the two. But the regime whose principle is fear is tyranny—so that the attempt to produce security above all else results in absolute rule. The nuclear disarmers, seeking absolute security in world tyranny, are only the latest of the disciples of radical modernity.

Where Leo Strauss stood on this question may be seen in the passage of *Natural Right and History* to which we have referred. Strauss there criticized Edmund Burke, in the same sense as we have seen Mansfield criticize Burke. Burke, said Strauss, "comes close to suggesting that to oppose a thoroughly evil current in human affairs is perverse if that current is sufficiently powerful: he is oblivious of the nobility of last-ditch resistance." Since Strauss here says only that Burke "comes close" to making what is called a suggestion, we think it proper to observe that Strauss has not here ascribed this view to Burke without equivocation. And we know there are those—whose opinions we hold in high regard—who would dispute this interpretation of Burke. But whether the opinion in question is or is not Burke's, there is nothing equivocal as to how that opinion ought to be regarded.

> [Burke] does not consider [Strauss went on] that, in a way that no man can foresee, resistance in a forlorn position to the enemies of mankind, "going down with guns blazing and flag flying," may contribute greatly toward keeping awake the recollection of the immense loss sustained by mankind, may inspire and strengthen the desire and the hope for its recovery, and may become a beacon for those who humbly carry on the works of humanity in a seemingly endless valley of darkness and destruction.

This is not the whole of Leo Strauss's Churchillian speech. But it is enough to serve our purpose. It illuminates his thesis of "esoteric writing." For this writing is, in part at least, the writing of those who see the beacon in the midst of tyranny and learn how to find those around them who also yearn for the end of tyranny, how to communicate with them, and how to teach them, and how to strengthen their souls. But those who carry on the works of humanity humbly need to look backward towards those beacons, that their fellow men may also some day once again see the light. And those who hold up those beacons, even if they fall in the battle, shall not be forgotten. Their memory shall not perish from the earth. For the ground of noble action itself lives not in time, but in eternity. That was the faith of Churchill, of Lincoln, and of Leo Strauss.

NOTES

Originally published in *Teaching Political Science*, Vol. 12, No. 2, Winter 1984–1985.

1. Berns, *National Review*, Vol. 34, Issue 1, 22 January 1982.
2. See Jaffa on Strauss on Churchill, pp. 75-79 of this volume.
3. Richard Kennington, "Strauss's Natural Right and History," *The Review of Metaphysics*, Vol. 35, no. 1 (1981), pp. 51–86.
4. Strauss, *Natural Right and History*, p. 120.
5. Walter Berns, "The Case Against World Government," *Readings in World Politics*, 3rd edition. Robert Allen Goldwin, ed. 3 vols. (Chicago: American Foundation for Political Education, 1955), Vol. 3, pp. 62–75.
6. Walter Berns, "The New Pacifics and World Government," *National Review*, Vol. 35, Issue 10, 27 May 1983.

NINE

Response to M. F. Burnyeat's "Sphinx Without a Secret"

A Review of Studies in Platonic Political Philosophy *in the* New York Review of Books *(May 30, 1985)*

I would like, if I may, to comment on M. F. Burnyeat's review of *Studies in Platonic Political Philosophy*, by Leo Strauss. Burnyeat's opinion of Strauss was sufficiently indicated by the cartoonist, who gave Strauss two right hands—neither of which, one presumes, knew what the other was doing.

Burnyeat declares that "There is no doubt that Strauss was an inspiring teacher." But Burnyeat can find nothing in Strauss's writings—which he calls "remote and rebarbative"—to explain Strauss's extraordinary influence on nearly everyone who came into contact with him. What went on in Strauss's classes was remarkable and powerful, but as far as Burnyeat is concerned, it remains utterly mysterious.

This is neither the time nor the place for me to offer my own critique of Strauss's work. It is a subject on which I have written with increasing frequency since Strauss's death. I would like, however, to offer a few words of personal testimony as to how Strauss differed in my experience from other teachers, and why so many sat so spellbound in his classes.

I might mention that I took my first course with Strauss in the fall of 1944. For the next seven years, in both New York and Chicago, I attended virtually every class he taught, including those in summer sessions. During this period I believe I spent nearly as much time alone with him as in class. But whether in class or alone, every minute was a vital learning experience. Today, I return again and again to his writings. Contrary to Burnyeat, Strauss was a great writer, and his works abound with passages of eloquence and beauty. But he always warned us, when writing, not to sacrifice precision of meaning for mere effect.

My own books, particularly my writings on Lincoln, are often outgrowths of conversations I originally had with Strauss. In the Preface to the 1982 reprinting (by the University of Chicago Press) of *Crisis of the House Divided,* my book on the Lincoln-Douglas debates (first published in 1959), I wrote that the work had been born in my mind when I discovered—at a time when I was studying the *Republic* with Leo Strauss—that the issue between Lincoln and Douglas was in substance, and very nearly in form, identical with the issue between Socrates and Thrasymachus. Douglas's doctrine of "popular sovereignty" meant no more than that: in a democracy justice is the interest of the majority, which is "the stronger." Lincoln, however, insisted that the case for popular government depended upon a standard of right and wrong independent of mere opinion and one which was not justified merely by the counting of heads.

Lincoln once described the central proposition of the Declaration of Independence—to which, at Gettysburg, he said the nation at its birth had been dedicated—as "an abstract truth, applicable to all men and all times." This is a perfect example of what Leo Strauss meant by natural right. And Strauss believed—as did Lincoln—that it was possible to have sufficient knowledge of natural right to guide our lives, in the decisive respects, both individually and politically.

Lincoln once declared that he had "never had a feeling politically that did not spring from the sentiments embodied in the Declaration of Independence." For Lincoln, the Declaration was a timeless source of political wisdom. It was a source of such wisdom for the American people as much as were the tablets of the Law brought down by Moses from Sinai for the children of Israel. If we however turn to Carl Becker's *The Declaration of Independence,* a book perfectly characteristic of non-Straussian scholarship in political philosophy, we find the following: "To ask whether the natural rights philosophy of the Declaration of Independence is true or false is essentially a meaningless question."[1] What Becker meant—and he spoke for nearly every historian and social scientist of our time—was that to ask what is just or unjust, right or wrong, is a "value judgment," and as such "subjective" and not susceptible to rational analysis, which can deal only with "facts."

Before I met Strauss this is what I had been taught, and had never been given any reason to question. I had spent five years at Yale in the 1930s, as undergraduate and graduate student, where no one, so far as I knew, had ever doubted this orthodoxy. To study the Declaration of Independence—or Plato's *Republic*—meant to study the "climate of opinion," "the spirit of the times," the "weltanschauung" out of which the work came. Strauss however declared that we must understand the great works of the human mind as their authors understood them, before we try to understand them differently or better (although—contrary to Burnyeat—Strauss never hesitated to make such judgments when he believed he had sufficient grounds for doing so). None of the great writers of the past had believed, either in the fact-value distinction, or in the historicist fallacy that the genesis of an idea was the key to the truth about it.

Lincoln's reading of the Declaration—as embodying an eternal, and eternally applicable truth—was precisely the kind of reading that I had learned from Strauss. Thus Strauss taught me to read with ever growing wonder and gratitude, both Lincoln and the tradition of political philosophy within which Lincoln had his life and being.

It is difficult to convey to anyone who has not shared such an experience the excitement I felt—now nearly forty years ago—when I realized that I had been emancipated from the dungeon of historicism, from that dark place of the soul in which the great questions, the only questions that make life ultimately worth living, are treated as "essentially meaningless." That excitement has however never left me, and I can have only pity for those—like Professor Burnyeat—who seem likely never to know it.

NOTES

Originally published in "The Studies of Leo Strauss: An Exchange," *New York Review of Books* (October 10, 1985).

1. Carl Becker, *The Declaration of Independence* (New York: Alfred Knopf, 1942; originally published in 1922), p. 277.

TEN

"Dear Professor Drury"

Many thanks for yours of recent date. This letter is not, however, a response to it. (I will get around to that a little later on.) It is rather a response to your paper, "Leo Strauss's Natural Right Teaching," delivered to the Western Political Science Association meeting last month, a copy of which was forwarded to me by one of my former students.

I can indicate my astonishment in reading it by saying that my reaction might have been the same had I read an interpretation of the New Testament that maintained that Jesus was not the Christ, but the Anti-Christ! Certainly you could not have imputed a doctrine to Strauss more opposite to what I have always believed him to maintain. I never for a moment, in the thirty years I knew Strauss, or in any of the years since his death, during which I have been constantly rereading his work, discovered a line to support anything except a doctrine of limited constitutional government, embodying the rule of law—ruling and being ruled in turn—a rule of law guided by and embodying traditional moral principles—moral principles supported, in the main, by both Reason and Revelation.

The thesis of your paper, expressed in the Abstract, is "that Strauss's classic natural right consists *only* of the absolute right of the wise to rule without restraint of law or of any inviolable moral principles" (emphasis added). Your leading text to support this thesis is the following, from *Natural Right and History*:

> It would be absurd to hamper the free flow of wisdom by any regulations; hence the rule of the wise must be absolute rule. It would be equally absurd to hamper the free flow of wisdom by consideration of the unwise wishes of the unwise; hence the wise rulers ought not to be responsible to their unwise subjects. (p. 140)

Now these sentences are taken from near the beginning of a paragraph setting forth what Strauss calls the classics' doctrine of the best regime. He does not characterize it as an expression of his own opinion, although I myself believe that, taken as a whole, this paragraph does go to the heart of the argument for the rule of law—not tyranny—that was the ground of Strauss's political convictions. If you read on in the same paragraph you find that

> this solution, which at first glance seems to be the only just solution for a society in which there are wise men, is, as a rule, impracticable. The few wise cannot rule the many unwise by force. The unwise multitude must recognize the wise as wise and obey them freely because of their wisdom. But the ability of the wise to persuade the unwise is extremely limited. . . . Therefore it is extremely unlikely that the conditions required for the rule of the wise will ever be met.[1]

The absolute rule of the wise is then a theoretical premise, necessary for our understanding of the problem of wise or just rule, but in no sense a practical conclusion. This is shown by the immediate sequel:

> What is more likely to happen is that an unwise man, appealing to the natural right of wisdom and catering to the lowest desires of the many, will persuade the multitude of his right: the prospects of tyranny are brighter than those of the rule of the wise. This being the case, *the natural right of the wise must be questioned,* and the indispensable requirement for wisdom must be qualified by the requirement for consent. The political problem consists in reconciling the requirement for wisdom with the requirement for consent [emphasis added].[2]

Now it really was unconscionable of you to quote "the rule of the wise must be absolute rule," without noting "the natural right of the wise must be questioned." Among Straussian apothegms none was more common than that the appeal to the right of wisdom, in the political arena, leads not to the best regime, but to its negation, namely, tyranny. Equally common is the saying that the heart of the political problem is the problem of reconciling the requirement of wisdom with the requirement of consent. Indeed this is the very heart of statesmanship. But the solution to this problem—so far as there can be an enduring solution—is the very opposite of that Machiavellian force and fraud you ascribe to Strauss, namely:

> According to the classics, the best way of meeting these two entirely different requirements—that for wisdom and that for consent or for freedom—would be that a wise legislator frame a code which the citizen body, duly persuaded, freely adopts. That code, which is, as it were, the embodiment of wisdom, must be as little subject to alteration as possible; the rule of law is to take the place of the rule of men, however wise.[3]

This is the practical conclusion drawn from the theoretical premise of the unqualified right of the wise to rule. In a passage to which we will come in a moment, Strauss also says that the wise—meaning the philosophers—do not wish to rule. That is, not only can the wise not persuade the unwise to be ruled by them, but they cannot persuade themselves to rule the unwise! Thus from every point of view, the unlimited right of the wise to rule is theoretical. Hence it follows that "the rule of law [must] take the place of the rule of men, however wise." And it follows as well that anyone who advances the claims of wisdom as a ground for ruling must be an unwise adventurer, discredited in advance by the fact that he has advanced such claims.

Strauss's life work culminated in his commentary on Plato's *Laws*. But he certainly inspired me to see in the American Founding an example, perhaps the greatest of all actual examples, of that work of a "wise legislator" that he characterizes here. It is certainly true that the Constitutional Convention, working in secret, produced a completed work of great wisdom—for the acceptance of the American people. It is also true that they usurped authority—acted, if you will, in a tyrannical manner, as Plato says founders must—not only in going beyond their legal authority, from the Congress of the Confederation, but in going over the head of the existing government to secure ratification. And Madison justified this usurpation of authority in the 43rd *Federalist* (which happens to be the central number of that book) by an appeal "to the transcendent law of nature and of nature's God, which declares that the safety and happiness of society are the objects at which all political institutions aim, and to which all such institutions must be sacrificed." Some of Lincoln's actions during the Civil War can be characterized in the same way. Thus we contemplate extreme actions in defense of the rule of law by wise men whose unfettered wisdom may sometimes be the necessary condition for the establishment or survival of a decent constitutional order. But these are not justifications of tyranny, or of any immorality. And Madison's appeal to the law of nature here anticipates everything that either Aristotle or Strauss ever meant by saying that natural right—or natural law—is altogether changeable. Your attempt to discover a sinister Machiavellianism in the changeability of the precepts of the natural law is simply without any foundation. That there are no moral rules to which exceptions might not be found, where "the safety and happiness of society" are at stake, has been recognized by sound moralists at all times. (Certainly the rules of war—or the rules followed by rulers protecting their regimes—in the Old Testament bear witness to this.) These exceptions do not apply to private life. And they are exceptions that one is well advised not to advertise. Madison, for example, uses language that is characteristic of "Straussian esotericism" when answering the question of what would be the relationship between the nine States that ratify, and the remaining States that might not ratify, the new Constitution. "The second question is not less delicate; and the flattering prospect of its being merely hypothetical forbids an over-curious discussion of it. It is one of those cases which must be left to provide for itself." Unfortunately, the question that remained hypothetical in the 1790s became very nonhypothetical in 1861, when 11 States "deratified" the Constitution!

It was not only in the drafting and ratification of the Constitution that the American Founders followed the prescription Strauss describes, but in the conception of the human type required to make it succeed. Namely,

> The administration of the law must be entrusted to a type of man who is most likely to administer it equitably, i.e., in the spirit of the wise legislator. . . . The classics held this type of man is the gentleman. The gentleman is not identical with the wise man. He is the political reflection, or imitation, of the wise man . . . . The best regime will then be a republic in which the landed gentry, which is at the same time the urban patriciate, well-bred and public spirited, obeying the laws and completing them, ruling and being ruled in turn, predominates and gives society its character.[4]

I cannot think of anyone who more nearly fulfills the character of a gentleman (as aforesaid) than Washington. And there was no weightier reason for the ratification of the Constitution than the moral force of Washington's character behind it—and the belief that Washington would administer the new government in its infancy, remedying whatever was doubtful in it by his overwhelming trustworthiness.

The unfettered rule of the wise is then primarily a theoretical teaching, necessary for understanding the practical teaching, in which wisdom is modified by the requirement of consent. It is not purely or merely theoretical, however, because wise action unfettered by consent may in certain great crises become necessary in the very service of the rule of law. And the wise men who may sometimes be obliged to suspend the requirement of consent, at least momentarily—for example, such as Washington and Madison and Lincoln did—do not do so to advance the claims of wisdom as such, or in their own behalf. Their wisdom is justified only by its service to the rule of law. The practical political teaching of the classics—classic natural right—culminates in "the rule, under law, of gentlemen, or the mixed regime." And that rule succeeds only to the extent that the law breeds men of character—that is, of the highest moral rectitude—whose wisdom may remedy from time to time the defects inherent in the law as such.

One of your more extraordinary assertions about Strauss is the following. You say that, "Strauss's contempt for the morally virtuous man takes on extreme proportions when he describes the just or moral man who is not also a philosopher as a "mutilated human being." The passage to which you refer (*Natural Right and History*, p. 151) is preceded by the following:

> In the first place the wise do not desire to rule; they must therefore be compelled to rule. [Such compulsion, we learn elsewhere, is itself possible only in Plato's *Republic*, a regime that, in turn, is possible only "in speech."] They must be compelled because their whole life is devoted to the pursuit of something which is absolutely higher in dignity than any human things—the unchangeable truth. . . . If striving for knowledge of the eternal truth is the ultimate end of man justice and moral virtue in general can be fully legitimated only by the fact that they are required for the sake of that ultimate end. . . . From this point of view the man who is merely just or moral without being a philosopher appears as a mutilated human being.

Now seen in this context, this is I think a simply true statement. With the exception of Kant, there has never, so far as I know, been anyone who has maintained that morality can stand entirely or simply on its own foundation. The dignity of the moral life—with that exception—can be seen to derive, at least in part, from its service to an end that transcends morality. And Kant's attempt to make morality an end in itself is disastrous. Consider that a "rational being" of "good will" must tell a would-be murderer the truth about where he might find his intended victim! Now *that* is a mutilated human being! In "The Mutual Influence of Theology and Philosophy," Strauss writes:

> We observe first a broad agreement between the Bible and Greek philosophy regarding both morality and the insufficiency of morality; the disagreement concerns the "X" which completes morality. According to Greek philosophy, that "X" is *theoria* or contemplation, and the biblical completion we may call, I think, without creating any misleading understanding, piety, the need for divine redemption, obedient love.[5]

Is it not clear that from the point of view of the man who "loves his God, with all his heart, and with all his mind, and with all his might," the merely moral man must appear a defective human being? The pious man thinks that in obeying the moral law he is obeying and honoring God. To him, a man who in obeying the moral law merely dignifies himself must appear as less than fully human. Whether from the perspective of Reason or of Revelation, it is the capacity of the human soul to transcend time and participate in eternity that is the ultimate cause of that soul's dignity. Morality is thus elevated, not depreciated, by its link with transcendence. Morality cut off from transcendence sinks into Kantian absurdity.

In the context of your discussion of natural law, you write the following: "Deferring to Aristotle in a typically scholastic manner, Strauss remarks . . . that a natural law that would suffer deformed children to live is certainly not natural, being contrary to Aristotle's judgment on the matter." This is supported by reference to Strauss's chapter on "Marsilius of Padua" in the *History of Political Philosophy* (which is reprinted in *Liberalism Ancient and Modern*). The page reference in your paper is inaccurate. (It is on page 267 of the *History*). Here is what Strauss actually wrote: "Among the rules which can metaphorically be called "natural rights" Marsilius mentions the rule that human offspring must be reared up to a certain time; he may have regarded this rule as not unqualifiedly rational since Aristotle had held that no deformed child should be reared. Strauss does not, deferring to Aristotle, say that by the natural law deformed children should not live. He does not even say that Marsilius says this. What he says is that Marsilius *may* have thought the rule that commands parents to raise their children to a certain age was not unqualifiedly rational, because Aristotle had said that deformed children should not live. There is no justification for saying or implying that either Marsilius or Strauss advocated infanticide for deformed children, or that in this either of them deferred to Aristotle. But Marsilius may indeed have doubted—because of Aristotle—the unqualified rationality of this precept. Whether Strauss agreed with Marsilius cannot in any way be decided from this passage.

In the sentence following the one quoted above, you go on to write: "It seems that Strauss cannot help agreeing with Machiavelli and Nietzsche that Christianity is inferior to pagan religion because it has the effect of rendering the world weak." You refer to page 206 of *Thoughts on Machiavelli* for justification. The only passage on this page that seems relevant is the following: "To repeat Machiavelli's primary contention, whereas pagan religion was conducive to the triumph of the world, Christianity has rendered the world weak." If you think this constitutes evidence of Strauss's agreement with Machiavelli, then I would have to say that every time you repeat any contention of Strauss, that proves that you cannot help agreeing with him! And Nietzsche is not mentioned here.

You speak of "Strauss's Aristotelian view," which you say "implies a radical depreciation of morality." At that point, you cite *Thomism and Aristotelianism*, page 31, with the observation, "Jaffa recognizes this, but makes little of it." Now I have already denied that the subordination, of morality to trans-moral transcendental ends constitutes a depreciation of morality. I believe the opposite is true. Harry Neumann agrees with you that Aristotle's subordination of the moral life to the contemplative life implies a depreciation of morality, and we have hammered each other hour after hour, and year after year, on this topic, in our joint seminars. Neither has persuaded the other, but the students certainly get a good lesson on the meaning of fundamental differences! I am convinced, however, that my view is shared with Strauss, and you have no right to conclude otherwise merely on the basis of how you (and Neumann) read Aristotle.

As to the contention, recorded in *Thomism and Aristotelianism*, "that [according to Thomas and Aristotle] prudence, or practical wisdom cannot be, but the other intellectual virtues can be, without moral virtue," let us consider the facts of the case. The intellectual virtues, according to Aristotle, are *nous*, *episteme*, *sophia*, *techne*, and *phronesis*. The first refers roughly to inductive reasoning, the second to deductive. The third represents a combination of the first two. The fourth refers to the "know-how" of the artisan (and Aristotle recognizes no distinction between the useful and the fine arts). Clearly, none of these requires or implies moral virtue of any kind. Drunken carpenters or mathematicians are not exactly unknown to us. But what of philosophers? Consider the remarks about the gods, in Book X of the *Nichomachean Ethics*:

> We assume the gods to be above all other beings blessed and happy; but what sort of actions must we assign to them? Acts of justice? Will not the gods seem absurd if they make contracts and return deposits and so on? Acts of brave men then confronting dangers and running risks because it is noble to do so? Or liberal acts? To whom will they give? It will be strange if they really have money or anything of the kind. And what would their temperate acts be? Is not such praise tasteless, since they have no bad appetites? (1178b9–17)

Thomas Aquinas somewhere in the *Summa Theologica* says something very similar about the biblical God. He says that when the Bible says that God is *angry*, *jealous*, or *just*, these terms are used metaphorically, to express God's intentions in terms humanly intelligible. But they do not mean that these qualities exist in God as they exist in man. They could not do so, for the reason that they would imply that God is imperfect.

However, the decisive point, as far as your indictment of either Aristotle or Strauss is concerned, is that *sophia* as such is concerned with thought only, and not with action. "*Sophia*" issues no commands, and cannot be characterized by moral virtue for the simple reason that it directs no actions that can be either virtuous or vicious. Hence it follows that any claims made or asserted in behalf of the right or need of wisdom, in regard to moral or political action, by either Aristotle or Strauss, must refer to *phronesis* and not to *sophia*. And *phronesis* is ex hypothesi characterized by moral virtue in the highest degree. So your polemic against Strauss's alleged immoralism misses the point at every point!

There is nonetheless a difficult question concerning the relationship of *sophia* and *phronesis*. I myself have long believed that their separation is dialectical rather than substantial, and I think that that was Strauss's view as well. The sharp separation between theory and practice, as it exists formally in Aristotle's text, fits his own apparent understanding of the qualitative physical differences between heaven and earth, as well as the eternity of the visible universe, differences and distinctions no longer tenable in the form in which we find them in his works. I think Strauss's preoccupation with the problem of Socrates in his later years reflects the conviction that the reconstruction of classical political philosophy requires a reliance upon the moral distinctions as the key to the metaphysical distinctions. Political philosophy—meaning thereby first of all moral philosophy—must become the key to philosophy itself. We have access to theoretical wisdom only by taking the moral distinctions with full seriousness. This is very clear in that marvelous eulogy of Churchill, with which I ended "The Legacy of Leo Strauss."

> We have no higher duty, and no more pressing duty, than to remind ourselves and our students, of political greatness, human greatness, of the peaks of human excellence. For we are supposed to train ourselves and others in seeing things as they are, and this means above all in seeing their greatness and their misery, their excellence and their vileness.

"Seeing things as they are" refers to the being of things, their metaphysical reality. Yet that being is seen as goodness ("The Primacy of the Good"). The spectacle of "political greatness, human greatness" becomes then a ground of philosophy itself, because the philosopher himself looks to this spectacle to contemplate the being of things, which becomes manifest in the spectacle. The great statesman thus brings to light the distinctions that are the ground to theoretical as well as practical philosophy. In Strauss, the moral distinctions become the heart of philosophy. And statesmanship thus itself becomes part of philosophic activity, seen in its wholeness. This is Strauss's answer to Heidegger as well (as Churchill was the answer to Hitler)—in whom political philosophy finally disappears. If then we see in Heidegger the death of political philosophy (and the death of God, for they are one and the same), in Strauss, we may see their resurrection!

Strauss's eulogy of Churchill begins and ends by reminding "academic students of political science of . . . the limits of their craft." What this means is illuminated by a remark of Churchill himself in *The Second World War*. It is, Churchill said, not possible to guarantee success in war; it is possible only to deserve it. As I have often insisted, this applies not only to success in war, but to the whole of life. No one can guarantee happiness. But one can deserve it. If success could be guaranteed—if Fortuna, and Natura—could be subjected to human will—no one would deserve it. To guarantee success means to abolish human freedom.[6] To abolish the possibility of failure is to abolish the possibility of success. The abolition of the possibility of failure may be said to be the heart of the Machiavellian project. Strauss rejected this project with all his heart, and all his soul, and all his mind. To the best of my knowledge and belief, he is the only one in the last four hundred years to have done so, thoroughly, thoughtfully, systematically. Therein above all lies his greatness. It seems to me that it would be a pity, and a stultification of your own career, to persist in thinking that the greatest of all anti-Machiavellians was himself Machiavellian. And in so doing you would be giving another victory to Machiavelli!

NOTES

Originally printed in *Political Theory*, Vol. 15, No. 3, August 1987, 316–325.

1. Strauss, *Natural Right and History*, p. 141.
2. Ibid.
3. Ibid.
4. Ibid., p. 142.
5. Leo Strauss, "The Mutual Influence of Theology and Philosophy," *Independent Journal of Philosophy*, Vol. III (1979), pp. 111–118. Reprinted in *Faith and Political Philosophy: The Correspondence Between Leo Strauss and Eric Voeglin: 1934–1964*, tr. and ed. Peter Emberley and Barry Cooper (Columbia: University of Missouri Press, 1993).
6. Have you seen my essay, "On the Necessity of Scholarship of the Politics of Freedom"? It is the introduction to my 1982 book, *Statesmanship: Essays in Honor of Sir Winston Churchill* (Durham, NC: Carolina Academic Press).

ELEVEN

Crisis of the Strauss Divided

The Legacy Reconsidered

The Spring 1987 issue of *Policy Review* carries an article by Dinesh D'Souza, the redoubtable managing editor of that journal, entitled "The Legacy of Leo Strauss." I published an essay with precisely the same title in the Fall 1984 issue of the *Claremont Review of Books.* Although D'Souza certainly had a copy, I find no sign of his having read it, or that he is familiar with any of my other—now numerous—writings on Strauss. Certainly he is not familiar with how my understanding of Strauss differs from that of the "Straussians." The evidence suggests that D'Souza has spoken to those who differ with me rather than having formed an independent judgment by reading Strauss with anything like the care his books demand.

D'Souza writes:

> Unfortunately, of late, deep fissures have developed among Strauss's best students which have permanently fractured a once cohesive community. For the outsider it is poignant to watch the Straussian parting of the ways, this intellectual and even personal diaspora. Somehow it seems unworthy of these men.

To this he adds: "Central to the internecine Straussian conflict is Harry Jaffa, the *enfant terrible* of the clan." This characterization of me is further explained in this way:

> He has perhaps inflated the importance of his mission by comparing himself to Socrates as a self-avowed pest who indefatigably pursues the truth—provoking the retort from Walter Berns that . . . It is an error of logic to conclude that because Socrates was a pest, all pests are Socrates.

There is something exhilarating, to say the least, in being described as *enfant* by someone forty years or more one's junior. How does someone so young become so wise? Paraphrasing Malvolio in *Twelfth Night,* we might say that some are born wise, some achieve wisdom, and some have wisdom thrust upon them. Clearly, D'Souza was not born wise, or he would not have gone to Dartmouth. (I write this, not as a Yale man, but as one who read admiringly what Mr. D'Souza himself wrote when editor of the *Dartmouth Review.*) Nor could he have achieved wisdom: there simply has not yet been enough time. It seems then that he must have had wisdom thrust upon him—by Walter Berns, for example, as in the foregoing "retort." Unfortunately, however, I never said or wrote anything to which Berns's remark might have been a retort. For one thing, I never characterized either Socrates (or myself) as a "pest." When Mr. D'Souza has become even wiser than he is now, he will learn that it is never wise to repeat accusations (however clever they may sound) against someone without asking whether those accusations have any foundation in fact. And he should never in any case report the charges without reporting the replies (or defenses) to them. Chapter 10 of *American Conservatism and the American Founding*—a rejoinder to Walter Berns—points out that it is Berns, not I, who calls Socrates a pest. And it points out that Berns, in leveling accusations against me, cast himself in the role of the city of Athens and me in the role of Socrates. Socrates compared himself to a gadfly disturbing the repose of a great and somnolent horse (the city of Athens). The gadfly helps to awaken the horse, compelling it to shake off its lethargy and become alive. Such activity is health-giving, not pestilent.

D'Souza writes (certainly with me in mind) of the fracturing "of a once cohesive community." This fracturing he deems "unworthy." At another time and place this would be called heresy against the gods of that community. Here he is also echoing Walter Berns, who had written that I had engaged in "petty polemics" with persons I had "owed it to myself to ignore." (See *American Conservatism,* pp. 128 ff.) But these "petty polemics" concerned the question of the constitutional status of the Declaration of Independence. They concerned whether or not "the republican form of government" guaranteed by the United States to every state in Article IV of the Constitution was—or was not—defined for the Constitution by the Declaration of Independence. Berns—and other Straussians—insisted that the Declaration of Independence was not republican (or democratic) and that it was neutral toward forms of government. They said this in opposition to the explicit and unambiguous words of Jefferson, Madison, and Lincoln. (See especially *How to Think About the American Revolution,* ch. 3.) In adopting the view that the Declaration of Independence supplied "no guidance" to the framers of the Constitution, they were adopting the thesis made famous by John C. Calhoun, and adhered to until the present day by his followers and descendants (e.g.,

Willmoore Kendall and Melvin Bradford). Berns's blustering was due to the fact that he and his friends did not want it advertised that they had abandoned the position of Lincoln for the position of Calhoun. They did not want it known that, in denying that the Declaration of Independence was the source of the democratic principles of the Constitution, they were denying as well the central thesis of the Gettysburg Address, a thesis repeated, incidentally, in the first paragraph of *Natural Right and History*. Berns's personal attack upon me—which D'Souza has echoed—had no other purpose than to throw up a smokescreen to conceal the fact that he was tied "by interests he could not admit to an argument he could not defend," and that he was thereby excusing himself from his honorable obligation to debate openly the questions that divided us. D'Souza should at least have found out what the questions were that were "fracturing" the community before deciding whether it was worthy or unworthy of someone to have pursued them.

ATHENS AND JERUSALEM

Strauss's work is subtle, complex, and profound. Yet in certain fundamental respects it is also extraordinarily simple and lucid. It is built upon the distinction, within philosophy, between ancients and moderns. It is also built upon the parallel distinction, among the only ultimate principles he recognized, between revelation and reason, the Bible and Greek philosophy, Jerusalem and Athens. Strauss saw Western civilization as constituted, at its core, by the confluence of what was represented by the two cities, Jerusalem and Athens.

"No two cities have counted more with mankind than Athens and Jerusalem. Their messages in religion, philosophy, and art have been the main guiding lights of modern faith and culture." So wrote Winston Churchill in *The Second World War* (vol. 5, p. 486), expressing the theme of Strauss's life work no less than of his own. Implicit in Churchill's words, explicit in much of what Strauss wrote, was that what is valuable in modernity is an inheritance from Jerusalem and Athens. There are no guiding lights for "modern life and culture" in modern life and culture to replace the lights that have come from these two cities. By philosophy, Strauss meant not a subject matter but a way of life, above all the way of life of Socrates, the way of life of autonomous human reason. By revelation, he meant not Homer or Hesiod or any other poet (not even Shakespeare), but the Bible, the way of life of obedient love of the living God. He saw revelation and reason—the Bible and Greek philosophy—as in fundamental agreement both as to what morality was and as to the insufficiency of morality. He saw them as in fundamental disagreement as to what that X was which completed and justified morality. Socratic philosophy, however, both began and ended in knowledge of ignorance. "I know that I know nothing" remains, after 2000 years, the characteristic expression of Socratic wisdom. Socratic wisdom, therefore, although standing opposed to biblical faith as a mode of knowing, remains open to that faith, for the reason that it cannot and does not deny that revelation is possible, or that revelation might be the source of that wisdom—that truth—that philosophy loves and seeks but can never achieve. Strauss, as we shall see, was uncompromising in defending, on Socratic ground, the integrity of the way of life represented by the Bible and biblical faith.

Modern philosophy attempted to transcend the opposition of reason and revelation. Modern philosophy attempted—notably as in Descartes—to radicalize skepticism so as to transform it into a ground of dogmatism. Modern philosophy, proceeding by clear and distinct ideas from premises which it would assert to be beyond doubt, would leave no room for that doubt that accompanied the conclusion of every Socratic conversation. Socratic philosophy proceeded from premises which could be doubted to conclusions which necessarily could also be doubted. Skepticism was the very shadow of the image of Socratic philosophy. The attempt to eliminate skeptical doubt from the Socratic enterprise was like trying to jump over one's own shadow. Socrates, however, found in his very doubt of his own reason the reason to inquire, the incentive to eternal questioning. But this doubt of one's own reason could also lead, and in the Bible did lead, to faith in the living God as the source of the resolution of the very doubts that sustained the philosophic way of life.

SOCRATES AND THE PRE-SOCRATICS

D'Souza speaks of *Natural Right and History* as Strauss's best-known work but immediately shows that, in the most important respects, he himself does not know it. Consider the following:

> In [*Natural Right and History*] Strauss identifies pre-philosophic life with mindless attachment to tradition and authority. Strauss sees Socrates inaugurating philosophy by challenging the "primeval identification of the good with the ancestral." Strauss argues that the pre-philosophic approach—embodied, for example, in Homer and Hesiod—is vulnerable because it has no basis for distinguishing good traditions and bad traditions. Furthermore, its frequent appeal to revelation poses the problem of different people having different epiphanies or different oracles giving contradictory advice; how are people to arbitrate the disputes which inevitably arise over whose theology is to prevail?

One would have thought that even at Dartmouth they would have taught D'Souza that Socrates did not inaugurate philosophy! "The discovery of nature necessarily precedes the discovery of natural right. Philosophy is older than political philosophy" (*Natural Right and History,* pp. 81, 82).

The philosophic challenge to the ancestral was first made by the pre-Socratics, and Socrates comes into sight challenging not the ancestral but the pre-Socratics. Strauss, citing Cicero as his authority, apparently believed Socrates was the founder of *political* philosophy. And Socrates himself is represented in Aristophanes' *Clouds* as a pre-Socratic philosopher. The transformation in philosophy by which political philosophy (as distinct from philosophy) came into existence seems then originally to have been a change in Socrates himself. Thomas Pangle, in his introduction to Strauss's posthumous book, *Studies in Platonic Political Philosophy*, strongly implies, if he does not directly assert, that the only real change accomplished by Socrates was to place an exoteric fig leaf over the amoral atheism of pre-Socratic philosophizing. According to Pangle, this was the lesson Socrates learned from Aristophanes. According to Pangle—along with Berns, a spokesman for unfractured Straussianism—the real or esoteric Socratic philosophizing remained as indifferent to and as contemptuous of morality—and of the life of the city—as pre-Socratic philosophy. If Pangle (and his friends) are right, then Socrates—and Leo Strauss—were both frauds. (This controversy is documented in the *Claremont Review of Books*, Fall 1984 and Spring 1985 issues.)

D'Souza commits an error of cosmic significance when he says that Strauss identifies prephilosophic life with "mindless attachment to tradition and authority." Some of the most famous Platonic dialogues—e.g., the *Republic*, the *Gorgias*, and the *Protagoras*—show Socrates locked in dialectical combat with men who were known as Sophists. They were epigones of pre-Socratic philosophy and taught that there were natural causes of the phenomena traditionally attributed to the gods. The gods do not exist, and nature, as understood by the pre-Socratic philosophers, is utterly indifferent to the distinction between the just and the unjust, the right and the wrong, or to any specifically human things. According to pre-Socratic philosophy, the noble and the just are entirely conventional and have no rational or nonarbitrary foundation whatever—no foundation outside of human will. Pre-Socratic philosophy stood in exactly the same relationship to traditional morality that present-day science—especially present-day social science—stands in relationship to traditional morality. Leo Strauss's Socrates (as distinct from the Socrates of the Straussians) comes to sight then as the *defender* of traditional morality against the corrupting influence of pre-Socratic philosophy. That defense is symbolized in his thesis that "it is better to suffer than to do injustice." The death of Socrates, in voluntary obedience to the judgment of the city of Athens—however mistaken that judgment may have been—is his testimony that the morality of that city was a necessary element of the human good. In refusing to leave the prison, Socrates refused to do injustice. It is true that Socrates did not defend traditional morality on what were then traditional grounds.

Natural right is not identical with divine right. The gods of the ancient city were no longer a believable ground for morality, for Socrates no less than for the pre-Socratics. They remained believable, however, for ordinary citizens, for whom the identification of morality with belief in their ancestral gods also remained, and would so remain very largely until the advent of Christianity. For Socrates and for his followers, however, the ideas—the intelligible necessities underlying the being or goodness of things—replaced the gods as the ultimate authority. However, the doctrine of ideas was by no means atheistic, since God might be conceived, as he is in the *Timaeus*, as *demiourgos*—literally, "people worker"—acting as an intermediary between the ideas (or the Idea of the Good) and the world inhabited by man. Clearly, the Platonic paradigm of the teaching of Socrates anticipates parallel paradigms in traditional Judaism and Christianity. Meanwhile Socrates, by his discovery of natural right, poured new wine into the old bottles of ancient pantheism, and acted to preserve traditional morality from the corrosion of the scientism of pre-Socratic philosophy. It cannot, however, be emphasized too strongly that Socrates' critique of the Sophists, and his attack upon the moral relativism of pre-Socratic natural science, and Strauss's attack upon the moral relativism of modern social science, both come to sight as defenses of traditional morality. And while traditional morality might be said to be deficient in its ability to defend itself from sophistry, ancient or modern, it is certainly not properly called mindless. The essence of the Socratic revolution (its perfection to be found perhaps in the *Nicomachean Ethics* of Aristotle) lies in the discovery that there is an inherent intelligibility in the moral distinctions. There is moreover a prephilosophic attachment to morality independent of the Socratic ground in nature that is to be found in that tradition and authority called the Bible.

REASON AND REVELATION

We have cited D'Souza saying that Strauss saw Socrates "challenging the 'primeval identification of the good with the ancestral.'" This identification, according to D'Souza, with "its frequent appeal to revelation poses the problem of . . . whose theology is to prevail?" Certainly, within the context of the Platonic dialogues, the gods of the ancient cities, who quarrel among themselves, provide no sure guidance to man. In the *Euthyphro*, the dialogue on piety, we see as *the* alternative the ideas, or fighting gods. But the alternatives as presented in the dialogues were not *the* fundamental alternatives for Leo Strauss. D'Souza speaks of "revelation," "different epiphanies," "different oracles" as all on the same level. In doing so, he follows Thomas Pangle (in his introduction, cited above) in treating biblical revelation as being not essentially different from the theologies or theogonies of Greek poetry. But the epiphanies or oracles of

Greek poetry represent paganism. The arguments Socrates uses in relationship to the many gods of Euthyphro do not have the same standing in relationship to the one God of the Bible. When Strauss speaks of revelation, he is not speaking of the poetic imagination; he is speaking of faith founded in the Bible. And Strauss held that philosophy, whether ancient or modern, cannot refute biblical revelation. Within Strauss's work there are a number of presentations of the dialectical confrontation of the claims of revelation and reason. In every instance, those of revelation emerge intact as the only basis for a perfectly consistent life—even though freedom from contradiction would appear to rank among the highest claims that reason itself raises on its own behalf. Here is an example from *Natural Right and History* (p. 75):

> All arguments in favor of revelation seem to be valid only if belief in revelation is presupposed; and all arguments against revelation seem to be valid only if unbelief is presupposed. This state of things would appear to be but natural. Revelation is always so uncertain to unassisted reason that it can never compel the assent of unassisted reason, and man is so built that he can find his satisfaction, his bliss, in free investigation, in articulating the riddle of being. But, on the other hand, he yearns so much for a solution of that riddle and human knowledge is so limited that the need for divine illumination cannot be denied and the possibility of revelation cannot be refuted. Now it is this state of things that seems to decide irrevocably against philosophy and in favor of revelation. . . . To grant that revelation is possible means to grant that the philosophic life is not necessarily, not evidently, *the* right life. Philosophy, the life devoted to the quest for evident knowledge available to man as man, would itself rest on an unevident, arbitrary, blind decision. This would merely confirm the thesis of faith, that there is no possibility of consistency, of a consistent and thoroughly sincere life, without belief in revelation. The mere fact that philosophy and revelation cannot refute each other would constitute the refutation of philosophy by revelation.

And again (from "On the Interpretation of Genesis," *L'Homme,* 1981, pp. 5–20):

> before we even open the Bible we must have made up our minds as to whether we believe in the possibility of miracles. . . . The question as to whether miracles are possible or not depends on the previous question as to whether God as an omnipotent being exists. Many of our contemporaries assume tacitly or even explicitly that we know that God as an omnipotent being does not exist. I believe that they are wrong.

Strauss goes on to say that the only way the belief in an omnipotent God could be refuted would be by a perfect philosophical system in which all fundamental questions have been answered. He mentions Hegel as one who had attempted such a system, although elsewhere he has given Spinoza as an example. But he concludes, "I regard the existence of such a system as *at least* as improbable as the truth of the Bible." [Emphasis added.]

And Strauss makes clear that, while the improbability of the truth of the Bible is a contention of the Bible—otherwise there would be little merit in faith—the improbability of the truth of the perfect philosophical system is a fatal flaw of such a system. (Clearly, the belief that Marxism-Leninism "solves" all the fundamental questions of human existence is the animating principle, not merely of the USSR as a regime, but of the belief that communism will transform the human race into a higher species: men become angels when they finally learn that there are no angels!) As the aforesaid analysis is meant to show, Strauss is therefore equally a defender of both the Bible and philosophy. As we can learn from Strauss's great debate with Kojève, the belief in the perfect philosophical system leads to universal tyranny, the death of Western civilization. But it is also true that the belief in the possibility of the perfect philosophical system can be transformed by historicism into nihilism. The conviction that skeptical philosophy and biblical faith must both be replaced by a system of belief consistent with modern science requires in the end not that perfection of understanding originally envisioned (however mistakenly) by modern philosophy but its abandonment in nihilism. It is only in the light of the foregoing analysis that, I believe, one can understand Strauss's attitude toward the American Founding and of liberal democracy thus conceived.

THE THEOLOGICAL-POLITICAL PROBLEM

D'Souza writes that

> Strauss was greatly attracted to the American regime because of its closeness to the moderation and lawfulness of Aristotle's favored "mixed regime," a combination of elements of aristocracy and democracy. . . . The fundamental appeal of America for Strauss and Straussians is not that it secures the most material progress for the most people; rather it is that it resembles the ancient city, combining the exhilaration of liberty with a call to higher standards, to wisdom and virtue.

This statement, although there are elements of truth in it, is misleading. In the first place, there is no such agreement among "Straussians" as D'Souza seems to imply. Paul Eidelberg has been a vigorous exponent of the "mixed regime" thesis concerning America, notably in his *The Philosophy of the American Constitution* (1965), but he has been contradicted by other Straussians, in particular the late Herbert Storing and the late Martin Diamond. The latter cited Madison in *Federalist* #14 referring to the new Constitution as "a government wholly popular," and representation as "the basis of *unmixed* and extensive republics." On this issue, I have generally sided with Diamond and Storing, although I have insisted that the democracy of the American regime differs fundamentally from ancient democracy, in that it is based upon the natural equality of all mankind. Democracy, as characterized in Aristotle's *Politics,* represents the claims of the many who are poor, in opposition to those of the few who are rich, within the closed society of an ancient city. It does not imply recognition of rights common to rich and poor alike within the city, and it does not imply rights common to mankind, as distinct from the rights shared by those who are fellow citizens. The United States was the first regime in the world—ancient or modern—to declare its independence not by virtue of what was distinctively its own, but on the basis of rights which it shared with all men everywhere. Indeed, Athenian democracy flourished when Athens converted the alliance against Persia into a despotic empire, in which the tribute exacted from Athens's former allies enabled the poor to be paid from the public treasury so that they could afford to attend the assembly. There was no principle in Athenian democracy averse either to slavery or to imperial despotism.

The proposition that "all men are created equal" represents a secular and wholly rational correlate of the biblical tenet that all men are creatures of the one God. The ancient city, as contemplated in the works of Plato and Aristotle, ceased to be a self-sufficient form of political association for Western man with the Roman conquest of the ancient world (if not by the Alexandrian conquest which preceded it). It may be said to have ended in principle when Roman citizenship was extended to the provinces and the city of Rome became, according to its own self-understanding, the world-city. In the ancient world, each city had its own gods (or, as in the case of Israel, God). If there was only one city, however, there could be only one God. The establishment of Christianity in the Roman Empire under Constantine was a development in strict accordance with the logic of the ancient city, though it marked the extinction of the ancient city. It was, that is to say, in strict accordance with the logic of every ancient city but one—Israel. Before the establishment of Christianity, every ancient city could see the triumph of Rome as a triumph of the Roman gods, because every victory in war was regarded as a victory of the gods of the victors. No sacrifice of faith or of conscience was seen in submission to the victorious gods of the conquerors. Except in the case of the Jews. The Jews, by reason of their monotheism, could not accept any victory or defeat in this world as final. For this reason, they could not accept even a monotheism other than their own—although it should be borne in mind that to the Jews alone, Christianity, with its doctrine of the Trinity, did not appear monotheistic. Christianity, and the idea of the City of God, brought into being a cosmopolitan world—the original of that "candid [secular] world" to which our own Declaration of Independence is addressed. Henceforth, the idea of one living God for all mankind would dominate the political consciousness within which Western man would seek political salvation. For the Declaration of Independence, while presupposing the end of that connection between faith and citizenship that was the hallmark of the Holy Roman Empire—and of the national church-states that succeeded it—nonetheless presupposes a universe governed by the one God. The Declaration of Independence, no less than the Bible, presupposes a "Creator," although it leaves open whether it is the Creator of a natural or of a revealed religion.

Ancient Israel—however much its God was held to be the God of the universe—was still the source of law for a particular ancient people and a particular ancient city, whose identity was derived not only from its God but from its consciousness of its difference from the alien gentile world around it and their alien gods. The Christianity of the Holy Roman Empire claimed universality because all mankind are children of the one God. With the Holy Roman Empire, the distinction between fellow citizens and aliens (or barbarians) is replaced with the distinction between the faithful and infidels or heretics. All mankind could in principle become fellow citizens of the City of God and its secular correlate, the Holy Roman Empire. But while the City of God was spiritual, the government of this world was also material, and the common origin in the one God was not able to produce the kind of friendship—and hence the kind of political loyalties—that men shared in the closed societies of the ancient city. From the moment of the establishment of Christianity, the political problem became the theological-political problem. This was already foreshadowed when Jesus spoke of rendering unto Caesar only the things that are Caesar's, and to God the things that are God's. The separation of—and tension between—the divine law and the human law constituted an absolutely novel problem. It was a problem that became more, and not less, acute by the establishment of Christianity. Judaism was (and remains) essentially Law, whereas Christianity is essentially Faith. With this we point to the theological-political problem which Leo Strauss said was at the center of his life and work. It is in the face of this problem that the meaning of the wisdom and the moderation of the American Founding must be inferred. That is why neither Strauss's devotion to the American regime—nor mine—can be understood simply as a reflection of our devotion to classical political philosophy. Our understanding of the relevance of classical political philosophy is affected at every point by our understanding of the tension between the City of God and the earthly city. Or to restate it, it is affected by the tension between the transcendence of the City of God, based upon faith, and the immanence of the earthly city, based upon the consent of the governed. By the principles of the Declaration of Independence, there is no opposition between what is owed to Caesar and what is owed to God. Caesar's government represented taxation without representation. Once the will of the government becomes the will of the people, the relationship between one's obligation to God and to government is no longer what it was, either in the ancient city or in the pre-Christian or Christian West, before July 4, 1776.

THE PRIORITY OF RIGHTS

In 1965 Strauss published *Spinoza's Critique of Religion,* an English translation of a book that had originally made its appearance in German in 1930. For this edition he wrote what has become widely known as his "autobiographical preface." In this preface he declares that the book was written during the years 1925–1928 by "a young Jew . . . who found himself in the grips of the theologico-political predicament." Later he remarks that the theological-political problem had remained *the* theme of his investigations. What, according to Strauss, was that predicament and problem? Strauss had been a Zionist in his youth, and in one sense remained one. "The establishment of the state of Israel . . . procured a blessing for all Jews everywhere regardless of whether they admit it or not." But this establishment "did not . . . solve the Jewish problem. It could not solve the Jewish problem." Why? "Finite, relative problems can be solved; infinite, absolute problems cannot be solved. In other words, human beings will never create a society which is free from contradictions. From every point of view it looks as if the Jewish people were the chosen people, at least in the sense that the Jewish problem is the most manifest symbol of the human problem insofar as it is a social or political problem."

Of the man for whom "the Jewish problem is the most manifest symbol of the human problem," it could hardly be said that the ancient city—if by this is meant the pagan city—is the unequivocal standard of political or moral judgment. Strauss argued repeatedly that the goal of modern political philosophy was from the outset to lower the goals of political life so as to make them more attainable. Comfortable self-preservation was an end more easily agreed upon—and, with the aid of science, a goal more easily reached—than either virtue or salvation. It was a goal readily embraced by modern Jews, who saw it as a vehicle for their emancipation from sectarian prejudices (or at least their legal effects)—those of the ghetto no less than those of the Christian or Moslem worlds outside the ghetto. But lowering the goals of political life did not change the goals of human life. The ultimate goals of human life are those Strauss identified with Jerusalem and Athens, of autonomous human reason and of divine revelation. The conflict or tension between revelation and reason was, he held, the fundamental conflict within the human condition, and it was not one that could be resolved without tyrannical compulsion. Strauss had no illusion about the loftiness of political life guided by what claimed to be divine revelation. Those who played God to man usually ended by revealing the bestiality, not the divinity, of human nature. This teaching of the American Revolution was certainly accepted wholeheartedly by

Strauss. It was accepted by Strauss not, as D'Souza alleges, because he "was fiercely pro-American in the style of millions of émigrés and refugees." Whatever his personal motives, which may indeed have resembled others', it was accepted because of a life-long reflection upon the theological-political problem, and upon the human problem "whose most manifest symbol" was the Jewish problem. Moderation (informed by prudence) affirmed that "human beings will never create a society which is free from contradictions." Modern utopianism believed that the tension between reason and revelation could be transcended: Marxism is only the most visible form of this aspiration. From the point of view of Marx, Socratic philosophy—contemplation of the riddle of being—was as much an opiate of the human condition as revealed religion. "The philosophers have hitherto interpreted the world. The point is however to change it." In Marxism, revolution replaces both prayer and skeptical inquiry. The consummation of revolution purports to end the need either for prayer or speculation, because it declares that it will end all the mysteries addressed by both. But there is not an iota of support for this claim. The only support for the alleged truth of Marxism, like that of all modern doctrines ending—as does Marxism—in nihilism, is simply that it has been willed. This is Strauss's conclusion in his great debate with Kojève, the most sophisticated representative of radical modernity.

In the American Founding, comfortable self-preservation may be said to become the end of limited government. But it does not replace prayer or thought as ends or principles of human life. Nor does it replace prayer or thought as the transpolitical ends of the regime, served by government but not directed or controlled by government. Rather, by removing prayer and thought from political control, limited government emancipates political life, and therefore human life, from the oppression of those conflicts which arise as to which are the true thoughts and which are the true prayers. It is able to do so because—but only because—revelation and reason are able to substantially agree upon what morality is—as Strauss has himself declared to be the case. That morality that is the common ground of revelation and reason—of Athens and Jerusalem—becomes known as "the laws of nature and of Nature's God." It is the morality of natural rights—the rights with which all men have been equally "endowed by their Creator." It is a morality that starts from rights not because rights are prior to duties—or that "rights" is just a polite name for passions (which is the official "Straussian" or Walter Berns interpretation, based upon the unproved assumption that Hobbes is the philosophic progenitor of the American Founding). The priority of rights reflects the authority of that Creator whose endowment they represent and who demands respect for them. Our respect for the rights of others constitutes an essential element of our duty to God, our primary duty, and the duty antecedent to our rights. Only by seeing that our respect for others is required by our duty to God can there be government which combines majority rule with minority rights. "And can the liberties of a nation be thought secure," wrote Jefferson, in a famous passage of the *Notes on Virginia*, "when we have removed their only firm basis, a conviction in the minds of the people that these liberties are the gift of God? That they are not to be violated but with his wrath?"

TO BIGOTRY NO SANCTION

One reason the young Jew described in Strauss's preface was in the grip of the theologico-political predicament was because of the predicament of the Weimar Republic. It "was a liberal democracy," but

> in the light of the most authoritative political document of recent Germany, Bismarck's *Thoughts and Reflections*, the option for Weimar reveals itself as an option against Bismarck. . . . By linking itself to Weimar the German liberal democracy proclaimed its moderate, nonradical character: its resolve to keep a balance between the dedication to the principles of 1789 and the dedication to the highest German tradition. The Weimar Republic was weak.[1]

The Weimar Republic was weak because of the tension between Germany's Christian and monarchical past—above all the tradition of the German emperors who were the emperors of the Holy Roman Empire—and liberal democratic constitutionalism. In nothing did that constitutionalism express itself more characteristically than in giving Jews full citizenship, for the first time in German history. But it thereby identified Jews with democracy—and the two together with a radical break with the highest German tradition. Exactly the opposite was the case with the American Founding, in which Jews were considered full citizens for the first time, not merely in American history, but since the end of their own polity in the ancient world, more than 2000 years before. In the Virginia Statute of Religious Liberty of 1786, the principle was laid down by Jefferson "that our civil rights have no dependence on our religious opinions, any more than our opinions in physics or geometry." But it was some years before the doctrine of Virginia became the doctrine of the United States, partly by reason of the First Amendment and partly by being incorporated one by one into the state constitutions. Nor was it always as clear as it ought to have been to everyone, that Jews were in fact entitled to the benefits due to them in abstract theory. But whatever had been ambiguous or equivocal ceased to be such after President Washington penned his letter to the Hebrew Synagogue in Newport, Rhode Island, in the spring of 1790. We reproduce it in full, because it represents what may be the most remarkable testament of all time to human wisdom and virtue, seen from the perspective of "the Jewish problem as the most manifest symbol of the human problem":

Gentlemen,

While I receive with much satisfaction your address replete with expressions of esteem, I rejoice in the opportunity of assuring you that I shall always retain grateful remembrance of the cordial welcome I experienced on my visit to Newport from all classes of citizens. The reflection on the days of danger which are passed is rendered the more sweet from a consciousness that they are succeeded by days of uncommon prosperity and security. If we have wisdom to make the best use of the advantages with which we are now favored, we cannot fail, under the just administration of a good government to become a great and happy people. The citizens of the United States of America have a right to applaud themselves for having given to mankind examples of an enlarged and liberal policy worthy of imitation. All possess alike liberty of conscience and immunities of citizenship.

It is now no more that toleration is spoken of as if it were by the indulgence of one class of people that another enjoyed the exercise of their inherent natural rights, for, happily, the Government of the United States, which gives to bigotry no sanction, to persecution no assistance, requires only that they who live under its protection shall demean themselves as good citizens in giving it on all occasions their effectual support.

It would be inconsistent with the frankness of my character not to avow that I am pleased with your favorable opinion of my administration and fervent wishes for my felicity.

May the children of the stock of Abraham who dwell in this land continue to merit and enjoy the good will of the other inhabitants, while everyone shall sit in safety under his own vine and fig tree, and there shall be none to make him afraid.

May the Father of Mercies scatter light, and not darkness upon our paths, and make us all in our several vocations useful here, and in his own good time and way, everlastingly happy.

A commentary that would attempt to do any justice to this remarkable document would take many thousands of words. None shall be attempted here. Jews are told that they are full citizens by right of nature—and that the positive law of the Constitution is in this governed by the law of nature. But they are addressed as equal citizens, even before their right is proclaimed. It is not only the intrinsic meaning of what has been said here that counts above all else—or the great beauty of the language with which it is said. No one else—not Jefferson, Madison, Hamilton, Adams, or John Marshall, not even Abraham Lincoln in the days that would come—could make these sentiments matter, as they did matter, when they were said by George Washington. For Washington is the father of his country, the leader of the revolution, the president of the Constitutional Convention, and the first president of these United States. He is the man known to every school child as "first in war, first in peace, and first in the hearts of his countrymen." From no one else could such a statement about Jews have carried the authority it did carry when it came from Washington. No one could repudiate these words, once they had come from Washington, without making himself contemptible. No one but Washington could have made the natural-right doctrine of the founding so compelling. By this he assured that in time the benefit of this doctrine would also be enjoyed by black people. For if Jews could not be excluded, no one could be.

In Weimar Germany, what Bismarck represented, what was the highest German tradition, stood in opposition to the principles of liberal democracy. In the American Founding, everything represented by Bismarck, by the tradition of monarchy and Christianity, was represented by Washington. And Washington knew this. He knew that as first president, every step he took, every pronouncement he made, would make an indelible impression for the indefinite future. In founding the Society of the Cincinnati, he made the break with monarchy final and the commitment to republicanism permanent. In addressing the Jews as he did, he made the commitment to civil and religious liberty unequivocal and irrevocable. These were steps designed to assure that the teachings of the Declaration of Independence would be followed. He had given his support for the struggle for religious liberty carried forward in Virginia by Madison and Jefferson. But it was the conviction that he himself in his own person represented greatness of soul, that he combined pride in himself with respect for the equal rights of others, that gave to his patriotism a dignity that was irresistible. Aristotle has written that the great-souled man "must speak and act openly," for "to care less for truth than for what people think is a coward's part" (*Nicomachean Ethics,* 1124b26). Washington was no coward. He did not wear his piety on his sleeve, but there is no reason to believe that his life-long attendance at the services of his parish church, of which he was for many years a vestryman, was merely for the sake of appearances. Nor is there reason to think that he, any more than the signers of the Declaration of Independence, meant anything less than what he said in placing his firm reliance upon divine Providence.

Walter Berns has written that, "Madison, Washington, and Jefferson . . . were not Christians, except perhaps in the most nominal of senses." He has also written that

> The American Founders insisted on a separation of church and state not primarily because they wanted to accommodate the varieties of religious belief, but because they held it to be a self-evident truth that all men were endowed with the natural rights of life, liberty, and the idiosyncratic pursuit of happiness.
>
> . . . I would go further: the very idea of natural rights is incompatible with Christian doctrine, and by its formulators, was understood to be incompatible. In fact, Thomas Hobbes and John Locke were enemies of all revealed religions. (*This World,* Fall 1983, pp. 97, 98)

The only evidence Berns has ever offered that the Founding Fathers—and especially Washington—were not Christians is that Hobbes was not a Christian. D'Souza notes that Leo Strauss believed that we must attempt to understand Plato and Aristotle as they understood themselves. But Strauss's hermeneutic principle requires that we attempt to understand George Washington (or anyone else) as he understood himself, no less than Plato or Aristotle. Berns makes no such attempt, but simply imposes upon Washington (and the other Fathers) an interpretation derived from his reading of Hobbes. He is convinced, without evidence or argument, that Locke is merely Hobbes with a fig leaf, and removing the fig leaf we find (besides what is usually under fig leaves) virulent atheism. Since Locke followed Hobbes, and the Founding Fathers followed Locke, the Founding Fathers were virulent atheists! Berns's emendation of the Declaration to read "the idiosyncratic pursuit of happiness" is typical. By it, he implies a divorce of morality from human happiness, from "the laws of nature and of nature's God." However, in the nature of things there cannot be an idiosyncratic morality, since morality cannot mean merely "doing one's own thing."

According to Berns, it was Hobbes, the man who called tyranny "kingship misliked," who stands revealed as the philosophic progenitor of the Declaration of Independence, the greatest denunciation of tyranny ever written! But Hobbes also declared that courage was not a virtue, and that honor was not a good. And he boasted, when the civil wars in England began, that he "was the first to flee." But what is not merely absurd, but deeply offensive, is the implication that Washington's greatness of soul, so transcendently displayed in the Newport letter, was a fraud. For according to Berns's assertions, Washington's motive—the motive of all the Founding Fathers—was not the free exercise of religion, as a natural human right, but the ultimate extinction of all revealed religion, that of the Jews included. From this perspective, the motives of the Founding Fathers are hardly distinguishable from those of Karl Marx in his infamous essay "On the Jewish Question."

D'Souza has grossly misrepresented my argument with Pangle and Berns on the nature of the American political tradition. One would think, from what he has written, that I somehow opposed as unpatriotic "free argument and debate" concerning the ideas of the American Founding. He contrasts my views with those of Thomas Pangle, who, he says, writes that "The questioning of America . . . is at the very core of what it means to be patriotic." D'Souza writes: "This meets with a roar of disapproval from Jaffa and his students, who consider patriotism of this stripe to be a bloodless and weak kneed patriotism not worthy of the name."

I have never written or spoken a word to justify such a characterization. I have, however, been unsparing in my documented refutation of Berns's and Pangle's Hobbesian account of the founding. Pangle and Berns, while alleging their belief that America should be questioned, do not however take kindly to being questioned themselves. It is they who resort to personalities when the argument goes against them. D'Souza quotes Pangle saying that he will not debate with me because I am alleged to be incapable of arguing issues in moral and political theory without labeling [my] opponents and their views immoral.

I never labeled Pangle's or Berns's views at all. However, if their description of the founders' views is correct—that they were merely a compound of Hobbes's materialism, atheism, and hedonism—who can doubt that they were immoral? Do these disciples of Leo Strauss declare that I have no right to make such "value judgments"? What in the world is the point "of arguing issues in moral and political theory" at all?

Walter Berns, when I dared to contradict him for asserting that the Founding Fathers were not Christian *(This World,* Spring/Summer 1984, pp. 1-8) and that they were enemies of revealed religion, responded, "Who will rid us of this pest of a priest?" Berns's barely printable fulminations—I am confident they were unprintable before they were edited—were altogether personal. He simply refused to explain why reading Hobbes was a sufficient ground for confidently asserting that he knew what Washington's inner convictions were. It is good to know, however, that if I am to be thought a pest, I am equally one in the order of revelation as of reason!

I hope Mr. D'Souza will arrange a debate at the Heritage Foundation between me and Walter Berns (or Thomas Pangle), addressed to either or both of these questions: Is the Declaration of Independence neutral toward all forms of government? And were the Founding Fathers Christian? I am prepared to accept an invitation to such a debate at any time. D'Souza should know, however, that I have been issuing such invitations to Berns for many years with no success. But a renewed experiment should reveal at least who is sincere, in finding "questioning . . . at the core" of what is American. I believe it will not be difficult by this for him to discover more than he now knows concerning "the Legacy of Leo Strauss."

NOTES

Originally printed in *Social Research,* Vol. 54, No. 3 (Autumn 1987): 579–603. "Crisis of the Strauss Divided" is the witty invention of Professor Colleen Sheehan of Villanova University. I have appropriated it gratefully without permission.

1. Leo Strauss, *Spinoza's Critique of Religion* (Chicago: University of Chicago Press, 1997), p. 1.

TWELVE

Leo Strauss, the Bible, and Political Philosophy

What follows is my response to a remarkable letter that I received in January 1988 from two younger scholars, Larry Arnhart of Northern Illinois University and Leonard Sorenson of Assumption College in Massachusetts.[1] The questions they addressed to me about God and man, the Bible and philosophy, were more direct and comprehensive than any that had been asked me in a teaching career of some forty-five years. Their questions were prompted by an article of mine entitled "Crisis of the Strauss Divided," which had been published in late 1987. That article was the revised text of a lecture I had given at the New School for Social Research earlier in the year, as part of a symposium on the contributions of foreign-born scholars to the understanding of the American Constitution, whose bicentennial was being celebrated. I was asked to speak on the contributions of Leo Strauss.[2]

In my lecture I had taken my bearings in part from Strauss's assertions concerning the insolubility of the opposition between revelation and reason—Jerusalem and Athens—as to the highest principle of human life. I had also taken my bearings from Strauss's assertion that, according to Aristotle, the ends of the city—that is, of political life as such—are the ends of the moral virtues. And I had noted Strauss's pronouncement that, notwithstanding their theoretical disagreement as to the end or ends served by the moral virtues, revelation and reason had agreed substantially on what in practice morality was. And I had taken my bearings further from Strauss's assertion that the very life of Western civilization depended on the continuing dialogue—the eternal dialogue—between revelation and reason. But both the continuity and the beneficence of this dialogue depended on its remaining theoretical, with neither side demanding, or being entrusted with, political power with respect to the conduct of the dialogue between them. In the postclassical world, government by sectarian religious authority—or by sectarian philosophic authority (as in the case of Marxist-Leninist regimes)—were equally tyrannical and equally abhorrent. From this perspective, the intention of the American Founding, with its unprecedented separation of church and state—its guarantee of the free exercise of religion, and of freedom of speech and of the press—could be seen, as not a lowering of the goals of political life, but an emancipation of man's highest aspirations for truth from the tyranny of the political passions. In this sense it could be seen as the best regime of Western civilization. However, this regime was endangered from the outset (notably in the slavery controversy), and continues to be ever more endangered, by the moral relativism—culminating in nihilism—of modern philosophy. Strauss's critique of modern philosophy, as it seemed to me, was directed above all toward overcoming what he often called the "self-destruction of reason," so that the authority equally of classical philosophy and the Bible, with respect to virtue and morality, might be restored. This restoration, I am convinced, is also nothing less than the restoration of the perspective of the American Founding.

I should mention finally that, although I cite Leo Strauss repeatedly as the ground of my assertions, I do not claim Strauss's authority for the conclusions I draw from them. Other students of Leo Strauss draw very different conclusions—indeed, in some cases, opposite conclusions—from his writings than I have done. I only say here (as elsewhere) what I believe to be true, and what in Strauss's writings has led me to think as I do. Others must judge whether, in thinking as I do, I think truly.

Gentlemen:

In yours of January 27, 1988, you propounded a number of interrogatories (as Lincoln would call them), to which I will now respond. You flattered me greatly by addressing me as you did, but I am not so lost to all decency, not to say modesty, as to think that my responses will constitute answers. I can only hope that I may contribute something to your continuing discussion.

You ask "two general questions to which all our other questions are subordinated."

> *1. What is the specific, substantive teaching that is novel or unique to biblical revelation?*

I reply first that it is the idea of the One God who is separate from the universe, of which He is the Creator. As both separate and unique, God is unknowable. We can properly be said to know only those things that have class characteristics that identify them as members of species or genera. That is, if I say, "This is a chair," I imply that there is an infinite number of possible chairs, each different from this, but each equally a chair. Reason means recognizing the idea of a chair in the chair, and understanding thereby why the particular is different from the universal. Once I understand what a chair is, I understand why there can be many chairs besides this one. Moreover, any particular which we experience by sense perception—however unique it may be understood to be—immediately implies the possibility of the existence of other particular objects of its class. This would be true, for example, of the first electric light bulb, the first airplane, the first of anything. It would be true also of any object that can be conceived by the imagination: for example, a centaur, which is half man, half horse. I may never have experienced a centaur; but by imagining one, I know I can also imagine others that resemble this one and yet are different. But the God of the Bible is not only one, but the only possible One. As such, He cannot become an object of knowledge. And He cannot be imagined. A god that can be imagined would be a pagan deity (of which there always can be many), but not the One of the Bible. This is why the second of the Ten Commandments forbids the making of images; that is to say, it forbids any suggestion that God can become an object of knowledge by being an object of sense perception. It is *because* He cannot become an object of knowledge that He can, and indeed must, be an object of faith. There is therefore a clear and distinct epistemological reason why faith—and not reason—has primacy. To summarize: I cannot know anything of which there is and can be only one. If God is One, and if there can be no other God, there can be no idea of God. God is unique in that in Him no distinction can be drawn between the universal and the particular, which is the ground of all intelligibility within the dispensation of unassisted human reason. God is therefore unknowable. This is the fundamental premise of the Bible.

Since internal reflection, or reasoning, about human experience can never lead men to the idea of the God of the Bible—since the God of the Bible is not an idea, and He is not a cause within the order of nature—revelation as the form of communication between God and man becomes "reasonable." Revelation is marked by miracles, although Creation itself is the primary miracle. This is shown by the first sentence of Genesis, which reports something that only God could have known or witnessed. All other miracles are lesser miracles, but their reason for being is already implied in the story of Creation. God's reasons for communicating with man must be subsumed under His reason for communicating to man His account of His creation of the world—and man. If the highest things (God and the story of Creation) are unknowable, then the highest capacity or virtue of man cannot be theoretical wisdom. In Aristotle, for example, practical wisdom is in the service of theoretical wisdom. In the Bible, theoretical wisdom is replaced by—or perhaps is constituted by—the study of God's speeches and deeds, of which the Bible (or Torah, or Law) is a record.

> Blessed is the man who walks not in the counsel of the wicked,
> Nor stands in the way of sinners,
> Nor sits in the seat of scoffers;
> But his delight is in the law of the Lord,
> And on his law he meditates day and night. (Psalms 1:1-2)

Your second general question was as follows:

> 2. *If biblical revelation poses an unanswerable challenge to philosophy and therefore is—in Strauss's words—"The refutation of philosophy by revelation,"*[3] *then why should we not reject philosophy?*

The "refutation of philosophy by revelation" has some of the same ambiguity as "I know that I know nothing." Strauss has placed this "refutation" in the mouth (so to speak) of revelation in much the same way that Socrates put the argument of the laws (the Torah of Athens!) into the mouth of the laws of Athens in the *Crito*.

There is an Aristotelian maxim that goes: "When we have refuted all the errors, what remains is the truth." Refutation is the method of philosophy, rather than of revelation. (The "method" of the Bible is found in such expressions as "Thou shalt . . . " or "I am . . . ") Strauss's refutation of philosophy by revelation is a Socratic elenchus. This, however, does not mean that it is not serious, or that it is meant to subvert the argument for revelation by making it depend on philosophy. God did not create man without reason, or without making it obligatory upon him to obey reason, in all these matters with respect to which reason can be a sufficient guide. Philosophy—insofar as it is the perfection of human reason—is the perfection of a God-given gift. Only the function of philosophy is differently conceived, depending on whether that function is understood as ultimately ministerial to the teachings of divine revelation, or as identical with an intrinsic rationality that is itself the most divine thing in human life.

The context of your quote from *Natural Right and History* is important. Strauss shows how in Max Weber revelation has been transformed into "value judgments"—the sublime into the ridiculous! In restoring the dignity of revelation, Strauss shows why the conflict between reason and revelation is *not* a ground for declaring reason impotent. Because we may not be able to say which of two mountains whose peaks are covered by clouds is higher does not mean we cannot tell a mountain from a mole hill![4]

The argument for revelation becomes in Strauss a defense of the common ground on which Socratic political philosophy and the Bible both stand. "I know that I know nothing"—awareness of ignorance, of the need to know—itself leaves open the question of whether satisfying this need depends primarily on reason or on faith. Socratic progress in wisdom—such progress as may be said to result from every Socratic conversation—always is accompanied by an increased awareness of what we do not know. The mystery of the universe, the mystery of being, grows—rather than diminishes—as a result of Socratic progress in wisdom. How can a Socratic know that his "progress" is in "wisdom" if the goal of philosophy recedes with every supposed advance? Does not philosophy—confidence in the ultimate significance of reason—depend on an act of faith as much as belief in the God of the Bible? Hence, reason itself points to, and cannot reasonably deny, the possibility that the mystery of being is impenetrable, because the Author of the universe is a mysterious God who, being separated from the universe He created, is beyond being.

Modern rationalism comes to sight as the attempt to dispel the mystery of being by so radicalizing skepticism as to abolish skepticism from philosophy. It attempted (notably in Descartes, but also in Spinoza) to discover premises that could not be doubted, and to proceed therefrom both inductively and deductively to conclusions that could not be doubted and that did not require any "faith in reason." In so doing, it believes in the possibility of the ultimate transformation of philosophy into wisdom. The consummation and transformation of philosophy—love of wisdom—into wisdom itself, were it to succeed, would put an end to both Socratic skepticism and biblical faith. For in such a case, there would be nothing left either for inquiry or for faith. Strauss's critique of modern philosophy showed the impossibility of this enterprise more than any intellectual event of our times. His demonstration that the self-destruction of reason ends in nihilism proved the superiority both of Socratic skepticism and of biblical faith to the modern attempts to supersede them. Whatever opposition may be intrinsic to the difference between biblical faith and Socratic skepticism, they stand as one in their dissimilarity to modern rationalism. Both employ reason, whether as autonomous reason or as the handmaiden of revelation, to make authoritative moral judgments. And while differing as to the ultimate purpose of morality, they yet agree substantially as to what morality is. In his autobiographical preface, Strauss cites Deuteronomy 4:6. "Keep them and do them; for that will be your wisdom and your understanding in the sight of the peoples, who, when they hear all these statutes, will say "Surely this great nation is a wise and understanding people."[5] Why were the "peoples"—namely, the Gentiles—expected to say of the Israelites, that they were a "wise and understanding people"? What in them enabled them to recognize wisdom and understanding (remember Meno's dilemma!), if no direct revelation had been vouchsafed to them? And why did God expect that a comparison of the laws of different nations would disclose—presumably to a wise and understanding judge—the superior righteousness of the laws of Moses? Does not the Bible then presuppose that the recognition of wisdom is a human potentiality, and that righteousness is an object of all law, and not only of the Torah? Does it not thereby presuppose that the teachings of reason and of revelation will not contradict each other, since both reason and revelation are God's gifts to mankind? Nothing in the proposition of the One Unknowable God forbids our believing that among His deeds was creating us as reasonable beings, with access by our reason to everything implied in the idea of "the laws of nature and of nature's God." While Strauss is careful to say that the Old Testament does not have in it any word for nature, he does emphasize (in part by the epigraphs chosen from the Old Testament for *Natural Right and History*)[6] that the experience of justice and of injustice underlies all human experience. St. Paul declares, "When Gentiles who have not the law do by nature what the law requires, they are a law to themselves. . . . They show that what the law requires is written on their hearts" (Romans 2:14-15). This passage parallels Deuteronomy 4, which implies something like natural law, although that concept is not yet explicitly formulated.

From the point of view of the Bible, God's revealed Word and not autonomous human reason is the source of the highest wisdom. But the role of reason—hence of political philosophy or natural right, as distinct from metaphysics—is not thereby negated or even diminished. Consider the following from Strauss's introduction to *The City and Man*:

> It is not sufficient for everyone to obey and to listen to the Divine message of the City of Righteousness, the Faithful City. In order to propagate that message among the heathen, nay, in order to understand it as clearly and as fully as is humanly possible, one must also consider to what extent man could discern the outlines of that City if left to himself, to the proper exercise of his own powers. But in our age it is much less urgent to show that political philosophy is the indispensable handmaid of theology than to show that political philosophy is the rightful queen of the social sciences . . . : even the highest law-court in the land is more likely to defer to the contentions of social science than to the Ten Commandments as the words of the living God.[7]

Strauss here speaks of political philosophy as "the indispensable handmaid of theology." But it is much more urgent, he says, to show that it is "the rightful queen of the social sciences." I would argue that establishing political philosophy as the ruler of the social sciences has become a necessary condition for the very survival in our times of biblical religion and morality. Within the framework of historical modernity, the authority of revelation cannot and ought not to be the ground of political authority. Since the moral teachings of revelation are in great measure (as the Bible itself attests) also the teachings of reason, political philosophy provides authority, within a nonsectarian political constitution, for a moral teaching in agreement with revelation. In our time, revelation has become—as Strauss's chapter on Max Weber makes clear—confounded and confused with "value judgments." In the wake of the transformation of modern philosophy, not into wisdom but into nihilism, the Bible itself has been interpreted to mean whatever is in accordance with anyone's strongest passions. The homosexual rights movement, for example, has made great strides in persuading the mainstream churches that the injunction to "love your neighbor" is a divine justification of sodomy and lesbianism. Passionate commitment has become identified—or confused—with revelation. The irrefutability of revelation has been confounded with the alleged undemonstrability of all "value judgments" and hence is held to be another justification for rejecting all authoritative moral teaching. But deference to the authority of revelation, from the Bible's point of view, is not arbitrary. It is because God is, to repeat, both One and separate that revelation is the necessary means for communicating to man his true place in the universe and his relationship to God. Revelation, although miraculous in its origin and essence, is not subjective; God is an objective reality, and He does not authorize subjective moralities inconsistent with the teachings of unassisted human reason. The idea of authoritative traditions as the ground of human well-being is an idea flexible enough to take into account the defects of fallible human minds as the light of revelation is filtered through them. But the differences among genuine traditions—and traditions based on the Bible often do differ—must not be regarded as a justification for regarding all traditions as merely arbitrary. The idea of natural right and natural law can be seen as the means by which genuine traditions can be distinguished from the many false pretenders to that claim. We cannot suppose that revelation would authorize moralities incompatible with what we know to be naturally right.

It is clear from the foregoing, I believe, that Socratic skepticism and biblical faith stand on the same epistemological foundation. It is impossible to restore the claims of the one without restoring the claims of the other. The transformation of modern philosophy into modern rationalism, and modern rationalism into nihilism, leads to the rejection of all rational standards for human thought or human action. This it does in part because of a spurious resemblance of nihilism to the doctrine of *creatio ex nihilo*, which the Bible itself genuinely and necessarily teaches. Modern nihilism culminates in each person's being invited to create his own moral universe. Nothing inhibits man, seen in the light of the nihilistic dispensation, from himself laying claim to the attributes of God. Faith becomes then the justification equally of anything—or nothing. In this situation, only the refutation of modern rationalism and its mutation into nihilism can restore the possibility of biblical faith in its genuine bearing on human life.

Let me conclude this part of the discussion by observing that the attack on reason and rationalism (and the natural law tradition) that is the hallmark of a certain modern political conservatism is—no less than modern political liberalism—in the service of nihilism. On the surface, this conservatism appears only as a rejection of modern rationalism. It is in fact a vehicle of modern romanticism, of a preference of the heart over the head. Its preference for the heart, however, is vindicated by no systematic thought such as has informed all the great religious traditions of the West, whether it be the Talmud or the Canon Law, whether it be the *Summa Theologiae* or the *Guide of the Perplexed*. However decent these conservative Christians or Jews may be, they have no inner defense against, for example, the demand for recognition of the rightfulness of homosexuality and other forms of sexual freedom (so called). Having rejected the authority of reason, they have literally no reasons by which to object to whatever the passions may demand in the name of freedom.

I turn to what in the House of Commons would be called your "supplementary questions." They are in six paragraphs—the first being as follows, in your words:

> *You link biblical revelation to faith, law, monotheism, and divine omnipotence. Is it the combination (or some combination) of these that is unique to biblical revelation? Or is one of them more crucial than others? You emphasize faith, but it is not yet clear to us what you mean by the content of faith. To speak of the content of faith as the Bible as a whole, as obedient love of God, or as in God as the source of the resolution of the very doubts that sustain the philosophic way of life, leaves us in the dark about the unique content of biblical faith as opposed to pagan religion.*

I believe I have already answered the foregoing. I think it is clear not only that—but why—faith (accompanied by the "obedient love of God") can be "the source of the resolution of the very doubts that sustain the philosophic way of life." Of course, as Strauss says, it is also true that "man is so built that he can find his satisfaction, his bliss, in free investigation, in articulating the riddle of being."[8] Whether one *should* live one's life "articulating the riddle of being"—rather than "resolving" it by faith—remains a question. While biblical faith may be said to offer an alternative to "free investigation," human freedom requires only that one recognize either alternative as consistent with that freedom. Modern rationalism, or the nihilism into which it self-destructs, represents an abandonment or denial of human freedom.

You speak of "biblical faith as opposed to pagan religion." I think that in Plato's *Euthyphro* we find a definitive confrontation between pagan religion and philosophy. The issue is reduced to either fighting gods or the ideas. (The modern equivalent would be fighting, more commonly, "contending values.") The gods can be made to stop fighting—that is, to provide noncontradictory guidance to human life—only if they are reduced to a role ministerial to the ideas. In Plato (and still more in Aristotle), one can see the philosophers replacing the poets (and/or the Sophists) and the gods of the poets (and/or the Sophists) as the source of a noncontradictory moral instruction. Of course, the philosophers will not rule directly, but through the new breed of Sophists and poets that results from the philosophers' influence on education—or, as in the case of Aristotle, through the gentlemen whose education they will supervise. But the God of the Bible is immune to Plato's critique of paganism, for reasons I have already, I think, made sufficiently clear.

Your second set of "supplementaries" begins as follows:

> *You define and distinguish revelation as Jewish law and revelation as Christian faith. Is the uniqueness of biblical revelation found in Christian faith as opposed to Judaic law? If so, does this mean that Judaic law is fundamentally closer to pagan revelation and the ancient city?*

What you call "Judaic law" was certainly originally the law of an ancient city. Since all ancient cities (as represented by the beginning of Plato's *Laws*) claimed their laws to be of divine origin, ancient Judaism may be said in that respect to resemble other ancient cities. However, faith in God was the principle underlying and informing every aspect of the laws of Moses; hence, faith as such was never less fundamental to Judaism than to Christianity. In Judaism, however, obedience to the law was always regarded as the basic test of fidelity. Absent this legalistic orientation, Christianity placed more reliance or emphasis on tenets of faith, apart from their consequences for conduct. In its monotheism, ancient Israel was unlike any other ancient city. One effect of this unlikeness was that the Jews did not cease to have God as their God when Israel ceased to be an ancient city, when the Torah was no longer their civil as well as their divine law.

You continue:

> *You claim that the theme of Strauss's lifework was the reason/revelation issue, which you seem to distinguish from the theological-political problem, the latter of which you proceed to call the "absolutely novel" problem which was caused by Christianity. You then identify this problem as at the center of Strauss's life and work, as "the theme of his investigations." Could you clarify what you take to be the difference of these two issues and how both, if different, could be at the core of one's work?*

I have long thought that two sentences from Strauss's autobiographical preface characterize better than anything else the thrust and purpose of his lifework. "It is safer to try to understand the low in light of the high than the high in light of the low. In doing the latter one necessarily distorts the high, whereas in doing the former one does not deprive the low of the freedom to reveal itself fully as what it is."[9]

This is writing of classic beauty and simplicity. It embodies Strauss's quiet rejection of Machiavelli, while admitting—or rather insisting—that the full revelation of the low is something that political philosophy and especially statesmanship cannot afford to neglect. As we cannot too often repeat, Strauss never forgot the claims of revelation, no less than of reason, to be the "high." But a judgment with respect to these claims was ultimately dependent on speculative reason, which he did not think could in fact render any final decision. While human freedom requires recognition of the philosophical and biblical alternatives, there is nothing to compel acquiescence in one more than the other. Strauss wrote as much at the end of "Progress or Return?":

> The very life of Western civilization is the life between two codes, a fundamental tension. There is therefore no reason inherent in Western civilization itself, in its fundamental constitution, why it should give up life.[10]

I believe that Strauss devoted his life, above all else, to keep Western civilization from "giving up life." The self-destruction of reason in the ultimate "wave" of modernity meant abandoning both philosophy and revelation, and affirming the human will as the sole authority for what had been attributed either to autonomous reason or to God.

Strauss's articulation of the differences between ancients and moderns I called "practical," rather than "theoretical." The heart of the modern experiment, which had its origins in Machiavelli, was to transcend the differences between the two competing views of the high. "Transcend" may be the wrong word, however, since the human problem was now to be addressed by lowering—not elevating further—the ends of human life. The human problem was to be solved by the conquest of fortune. This conquest, as it turned out, was to be accomplished by science. Science would supply the goods that men wanted most—health, wealth, freedom—without any requirement of virtue, either in their acquisition or in their enjoyment. Science would give men here on earth what most men had hitherto expected only in heaven: the effortless enjoyment of boundless pleasure. Science would replace God. This new God would in the truest sense be a *Demiourgos*, a slave of the people, and not their master. The high would be in the service of the low.

Strauss's rejection of modern principles rested not primarily on the folly of the optimistic assumption that the boundless power promised by science would be man's servant and not his master. Machiavelli's quarrel was seen to be equally with classical political philosophy and with Christianity. He accused them both of "utopianism." What he meant by this, however, was not the difficulty inherent in the achievement of the best regime. This was essentially a straw man in Machiavelli's argument. What Machiavelli really objected to was the tyranny of moral virtue. The subordination of the passions to reason in the economy of human well-being was a doctrine common to both Athens and Jerusalem. Certainly in Aristotle, moral virtue is always subject to prudential reason. As such, it is anything but utopian. Strauss thought that Machiavelli's turning away from moral virtue, as a necessary ingredient of human well-being, was mistaken. The emancipation of the passions of the body from the restraints of reason by the conquest of nature (and fortune) was not a project that could succeed. Taking one's bearings not by what men ought to be but by what they are—or lowering the goals of political life in order to guarantee their actualization—was doomed to fail. It was doomed to failure because of its insufficient attention to, or its ignorance or forgetting of, the ineluctable character of the human soul. The project of subordinating the higher elements of the soul to the lower could only lead to a tyranny greater than anything that had existed hitherto. Machiavellian modernity meant reversing the classics by establishing the primacy of practical over theoretical reason. Science would be in the service of man's estate—but not of man himself. The idea that the passions could furnish more rational goals for human life than reason itself was essentially absurd. What Strauss meant by devoting his "investigations" to the "theological-political problem" was restoring the authority of the moral order common to philosophy and the Bible, and restoring with it the conviction that human life could be well lived only by devotion to the "high." Recognition of what was truly the "high," moreover, would engender modesty and humility, and therewith moderation.

As has been said, the authority of revelation rests on the proposition that the universe is the creation of the One God who is separate from the universe He created. Because God is separate, reasoning about the universe (going from effects to causes) will not lead to the first cause. The authority of philosophy, or of reason, arises from the perception (as, *e.g.*, affirmed in the first and tenth books of the *Nicomachean Ethics*) that reason is the best or most divine thing in us, and that the way of life devoted to its cultivation is the best way of life for man.

The establishment of Christianity as state religion in the fifth century is understandable in light of the fact that every ancient city had attributed its law to its God. When Rome became the universal city, it was consistent with previous human experience that men should now transfer their loyalty to a universal God. But experience revealed that the universal city was not a city in the sense in which previous cities had been cities. A city qua city has to be particular, not universal. Different peoples require different laws adapted to their different characters and circumstances. The homogenization of the different regimes into a single regime can take place only by means of despotism, against which human nature—a God-given human nature—must of necessity rebel. The universal city may, however, be understood in a way that does not contradict nature; it may be understood as the City of God—the city that is the eternal home of man, but not his mortal or terrestrial one. All the citizens of the different mortal or terrestrial cities may become fellow citizens of the City of God without ceasing to be good—and thus different—citizens of their particular regimes in this world. Moreover, the City of God may be understood, within the dispensation of philosophy, as the best regime—the regime that, in speech, is always and everywhere best, although it may not exist in actuality or in deed, anywhere or ever.

Although the establishment of Christianity in the fifth century was understandable, it was nevertheless inconsistent with both reason and revelation. The vitality of Western civilization, of which Strauss spoke, was the vitality arising from "arguments advanced by theologians on behalf of the biblical point of view and by philosophers on behalf of the philosophic point of view."[11] The very idea of religious establishment meant an attempt by political means—that is to say, by practical reason—to resolve theoretical questions on the nature of faith and its relationship to reason. The result was theological despotism.

The essence of modernity, on the other hand, is the parallel attempt to resolve theory on the basis of practice, by asserting that philosophy has been transformed into wisdom—as in the persons of Hitler or Stalin. The earlier attempt led to theological despotism, and the modern effort has led to ideological despotism. Political moderation is rooted in the refusal to resolve the mystery of human life by political means. It is rooted in the recognition of human freedom as grounded in the openness of the human soul to that mystery. It is rooted, as well, in the recognition of a moral order—which understands human freedom not as the mere absence of restraint, but as directed to living a human life in the light of its transcendent ends, whether these are defined by reason or by revelation.

You asked later whether the possibility of revelation is something that can be proved. I believe—with, I think, both Leo Strauss and Thomas Aquinas—that it cannot. Suppose someone had argued once upon a time that airplanes, for example, were impossible. Now, if someone had genuinely proved this to be true, then flying would be a miracle. On the other hand, since we now know that flying is indeed possible, we know that no such proof was ever possible. But at least since Leonardo, men have known that flying is possible. This is to say that, long before they knew how to fly, human beings understood what causes could bring it about that men would actually fly. By this fact, they knew that flying, when it happened, would not be miraculous. The essence of revealed truth—*qua* revealed—is that it comes from a God who, faith tells us, is outside the order of nature, within which unassisted reason alone can overcome ignorance. If we could prove that revelation is possible, then revelation would be like anything else that we might believe we can someday understand even if we have not yet understood it.

NOTES

Originally printed in *Leo Strauss: Political Philosopher and Jewish Thinker*, ed. Kenneth L. Deutsch and Walter Nicgorski (Lanham, MD: Rowman and Littlefield, 1994).

1. My response was dated 13 February 1989. In the following version I have made a few revisions, and added formal scholarly references and a few notes for the sake of readers who may not share the background of the correspondents.

2. George Kateb of Amherst spoke on Hannah Arendt, and Dante Germino of the University of Virginia spoke on Eric Voegelin.

3. The words quoted from Strauss are taken from *Natural Right and History* (Chicago: University of Chicago Press, 1953), p. 75. They emerge at the end of a long passage, and are the latter part of a sentence, not its beginning, as may be seen in the following:

> Philosophy has to grant that revelation is possible. But to grant that revelation is possible means to grant that philosophy is perhaps something infinitely unimportant. To grant that revelation is possible means to grant that the philosophic life is not necessarily, not evidently, *the* right life. Philosophy, the life devoted to the quest for evident knowledge available to man as man, would itself rest on an unevident, arbitrary, or blind decision. This would merely confirm the thesis of faith, that there is no possibility of consistency, of a consistent and thoroughly sincere life, without belief in revelation. The mere fact that philosophy and revelation cannot refute each other would constitute the refutation of philosophy by revelation.

4. I have used this familiar saying of Strauss without quotation marks.

5. "Preface to the English Translation," in *Spinoza's Critique of Religion* (New York: Schocken Books, 1965), p. 30.

6. The story of Nathan and David (2 Samuel 12) is an example of the human ability to recognize (contra Meno) even our own acts of injustice, if our own persons are disguised, and we are able to look upon those acts as a neutral observer. Strauss is telling us that the recognition of natural right does not even depend on the prior discovery of nature.

7. Leo Strauss, *The City and Man* (Chicago: Rand McNally, 1964), p. 1.

8. Strauss, *Natural Right and History*, p. 75.

9. Strauss, "Preface to the English Translation," *Liberalism Ancient and Modern*, p. 2.

10. "Progress or Return?" in *The Rebirth of Classical Political Rationalism: An Introduction to the Thought of Leo Strauss*, ed. Thomas L. Pangle (Chicago: University of Chicago Press, 1989), p. 270.

11. Ibid.

THIRTEEN

Dear Sirs:

Sir Isaiah Berlin's comments on Leo Strauss (*New York Review of Books*, May 18, 1992) are a welcome addition to the growing literature—and growing controversy—about this unique figure in twentieth century political philosophy.

Shadia Drury's *The Political Ideas of Leo Strauss* (Macmillan, 1988) has gained a great currency in publicizing the view that Strauss's esoteric teaching—his real teaching—was that of a disciple of Machiavelli and of Nietzsche. According to Drury, he was an atheist, nihilist, and immoralist, a Pied Piper who cleverly misled the young by baiting his teaching with the discovery that, whatever conventional morality might preach, neither God nor nature objected to forbidden pleasures.

Sir Isaiah, on the contrary, calls Strauss "A genuine classical and Talmudic scholar, who thought that political philosophy went gravely wrong with Machiavelli—'the teacher of evil'—and had never recovered." According to Sir Isaiah, Strauss tried "To convert me in many conversations when I was a visitor in Chicago, but he could not get me to believe in eternal, immutable, absolute values, true for all men everywhere at all times, God given natural law and the like." It is difficult to believe that the same man could have led Drury and Berlin to such opposite conclusions. I attended nearly every one of Strauss's classes for seven years, and spent perhaps as much time with him alone as in class. I must say that the Strauss I knew was much closer to the one Sir Isaiah knew.

Sir Isaiah is however mistaken in saying that according to Strauss, "no political thinker since the Middle Ages had found the true path." The American Founders, Lincoln, and Churchill—whether or not they are to be called political philosophers, were certainly political thinkers of a very high order. According to Strauss, Aristotle's political philosophy is itself based upon what it is that non-philosophic and pre-philosophic wise and good men do. Strauss himself once wrote that he was unable to understand what Aristotle meant by magnanimity until he concluded that Churchill was a perfect example of it. No one can understand Strauss who does not understand why, in that sense, Churchill—not Maimonides or Thomas Aquinas—enabled him to understand Aristotle!

In saying why Strauss failed to convert him, Sir Isaiah writes, "Perhaps there is a world of eternal truths, values, which the magic eye of the true thinker can perceive—surely this can only belong to an elite to which I fear I have never been admitted." But Leo Strauss began *Natural Right and History* by quoting the magisterial words of the Declaration of Independence, beginning "We hold these truths to be self-evident." Strauss then echoed the Gettysburg Address, in speaking of the "nation dedicated to [this] proposition," and he asked, "Does this nation in its maturity still cherish the faith in which it was conceived and raised? Does it still hold those "truths to be self-evident?" In 1774 Jefferson, in addressing the King of England, had affirmed that "the great principles of right and wrong are legible to every reader." Jefferson's great disciple, Abraham Lincoln, had saluted Jefferson on his birthday in 1859:

> All honor to Jefferson—to the man who, in the concrete pressure of a struggle for independence by a single people, had the coolness, forecast, and capacity to introduce into a merely revolutionary document, an abstract truth, applicable to all men and all times.

The idea of a truth "applicable to all men and all times" was not something Strauss found only in classical and medieval philosophy. Carl Becker, however, in his 1952 book, says that "To ask whether the Natural Rights philosophy of the Declaration of Independence is true or false is essentially a meaningless question." It had indeed become meaningless to our academic elites, but it has never been such to the common man, to whom and for whom Jefferson and Lincoln and Churchill spoke.

Leo Strauss's great achievement was to restore—to those with eyes that could see—the authority of those moral perceptions which are inherent in classical political philosophy because they are inherent in political life. They are the ground of wise statesmanship, and good citizenship, everywhere and always. That an invincible ignorance—bred of historicism and relativism—has descended upon the elites of our time is the cause of the crisis of our time. Strauss's teachings would break the power of those elites, which is why his detractors see him as a traitor to his class.

My Dear Sir Isaiah:

I thought you might be interested in the enclosed copy of my recent letter to the *New York Review*, commenting on your comments on Leo Strauss.

In the course of your interview in the *NYR* you mentioned a hitherto unpublished critique of you by Strauss. I have not heard of such a critique, although I will ask professor Cropsey—who is Strauss's literary executor, and custodian of the Strauss archive at the University of Chicago Library—about it. My conjecture is that the work you heard about is one entitled "Relativism," published originally in 1961 in *Relativism and the Study of Man,* edited by Helmut Schoeck and J. W. Wiggins (Princeton: Van Nostrand). It has recently been reprinted in a new collection of his work, entitled the *Rebirth of Political Rationalism, An Introduction to the Thought of Leo Strauss,* selected and introduced by Thomas L. Pangle (The University of Chicago Press, 1989). A major part of this essay is an examination of your argument in *Two Concepts of Liberty.* I enclose a copy.

In the interview you said you would not reply, since Strauss was dead and his followers did not interest you. May I respectfully suggest that this is not a good reason. Strauss is emerging as a much greater subject of interest than he ever was in his lifetime. In addition to countless uncollected essays and articles, I believe I can count three recent volumes of essays about him, in addition to Drury's book length study. A recent doctoral dissertation at Claremont Graduate School (by Susan Orr) is a 250 page commentary on his "Jerusalem and Athens" lectures. She followed a procedure that closely followed Strauss's own method in his studies of, for example, Farabi.

Since much of the writing on Strauss is hostile (notably Burnyeat in the *NYR* and Holmes in *TLS*),[1] he obviously engages those who disagree as well as those who are inclined to agree with him. I was struck by how much of what you said in your own right resembled formulation by Strauss. You seemed to me to attack him in part where you were actually in agreement, perhaps for carrying the argument beyond the point that you were willing to follow. In any event, I think it is a mistake to refrain from replying to Strauss because he is not here to defend himself. He believed, as I think you do, that the dialogue among truly serious thinkers was not personal, and that it transcended time—and morality. I am sure that if your reply to him is worthy of him—as I would surely hope it would be—then someone equal to the argument will in due time emerge to carry it forward (whether in your lifetime or mine does not matter!).

NOTES

A Letter to the Editor of the *New York Review of Books*, 1992.

1. M.F. Burnyeat, "Sphinx Without a Secret," *New York Review of Books* (May 30, 1985); Stephen Holmes, "Truths for Philosophers Alone?" *Times Literary Supplement* (December 1–7, 1989), pp. 1319–23.

FOURTEEN

"Relativism"

Leo Strauss

"Relativism" has many meanings. In order not to become confused by the "blind scholastic pedantry" that exhausts itself and its audience in the "clarification of meanings" so that it never meets the nonverbal issues, I shall work my way into our subject by examining the recent statement of a famous contemporary about "the cardinal issue," the fundamental political problem of our time. As a fundamental problem it is theoretical; it is not the problem of particular policies, but the problem of the spirit that should inform particular policies. That problem is identified by Isaiah Berlin as the problem of freedom.[1]

Berlin distinguishes two senses of freedom, a negative and a positive sense. Used in the negative sense, in which it was used by "the classical English political philosophers" or "the fathers of liberalism," "freedom" means "freedom *from*": "Some portion of human existence must remain independent of social control"; "there ought to exist a certain minimum area of personal freedom which must on no account be violated."[2] Positive freedom, on the other hand, is "freedom *for*": the freedom of the individual "to be his own master" or to participate in the social control to which he is subject.[3] This alternative regarding freedom overlaps another alternative: freedom for the empirical self or freedom for the true self. Still, negative freedom, freedom from, is more likely to mean freedom for the empirical self; whereas positive freedom, freedom for, has to a higher degree the tendency to be understood as freedom only for the true self and therefore as compatible with the most extreme coercion of the empirical selves to become something that their true selves allegedly desire.[4]

The freedom that Berlin cherishes is the negative freedom for "our poor, desire-ridden, passionate, empirical selves":[5] "a maximum degree of noninterference compatible with the minimum demands of social life"[6] or the "freedom to live as one prefers."[7] He seems to cherish that freedom as "an end in itself" or "an ultimate value."[8] He certainly does not believe that the older reasoning in favor of negative freedom is valid. For, contrary to the older view, negative freedom is not the "necessary condition for the growth of human genius": "Integrity, love of truth and fiery individualism grow at least as often in severely disciplined communities or under military discipline, as in more tolerant or indifferent societies"; negative freedom is a peculiarly Western ideal and even a peculiarly modern Western ideal, and even in the modern Western world it is cherished by some individuals rather than by large masses; there is no necessary connection between negative freedom and democracy.[9]

Berlin finds the true justification of negative freedom in the absurdity of the alternative. The alternative is the notion that men can be free only by participating in *the* just, *the* rational or *the* perfect society in which all just or rational ends of all members of society are harmoniously satisfied or in which everyone obeys only himself, i.e., his true self. This notion presupposes that there is a hierarchy, and therefore a fundamental harmony, of human ends. But this presupposition is "demonstrably false"; it is based on a "dogmatic and *a priori* certainty"; it is "not compatible with empiricism," i.e., with "any doctrine founded on knowledge derived from experience of what men are and seek"; it is the root of "the metaphysical view of politics" as opposed to the "empirical" view.[10] Experience shows us that "the ends of men are many, and not all of them in principle are compatible with each other. . . . The necessity of choosing between absolute claims is then an inescapable characteristic of the human condition. This gives its value to freedom . . . as an end in itself and not as a temporary need."[11]

Experience, knowledge of the observable Is, seems to lead in a perfectly unobjectionable manner to knowledge of the Ought. The allegedly empirical premise would seem to be the equality of all human ends. "Mill, and liberals in general, at their most consistent . . . wish the frontiers between individuals and groups of men to be drawn solely with a view to preventing collisions between human purposes, all of which must be considered to be equally ultimate, uncriticizable ends in themselves. Kant and the rationalists of his type do not regard all ends as of equal value." From the context it appears that the ends that are to be regarded as equal include "the various personal aims which their individual imagination and idiosyncrasies lead men to pursue."[12] Interference with the pursuit of ends is legitimate only to the extent to which one man's pursuit of an end collides with another man's pursuit. Yet it appears that such collisions cannot possibly be prevented: "The possibility of conflict—and of tragedy—can never be wholly eliminated from human life, either personal or social."[13] Not all collisions, but only certain kinds of collisions can and ought to be prevented by social control: "there must be *some* frontiers of freedom which nobody should ever be permitted to cross."[14] The frontiers must be of such a character as to protect a reasonably large area; it would not be sufficient to demand that every man must have the freedom to dream of the pursuit of any end he likes.

Yet the primary question concerns, not the location of the frontiers, but their status. Those frontiers must be "sacred."[15] They must be "absolute": "Genuine belief in the inviolability of a minimum extent of individual liberty entails some . . . absolute stand."[16] "Relativism," or the assertion that all ends are relative to the chooser and hence equal, seems to require some kind of "absolutism." Yet Berlin hesitates to go quite so far.

"Different *names* or *natures* may be given to the rules" that determine those frontiers: they may be called natural rights or the word of God, or Natural Law, or the demands of utility or of "the deepest interests of man"; I may believe them to be valid *a priori*, or assert them to be *my own subjective ends, or the ends of my society or culture.* What these rules or commandments will have in common is that they are accepted so widely, and are grounded so deeply in the actual nature of men as they have developed through history, as to be, by now, an essential part of what we mean by being a normal human being. Genuine belief in the inviolability of a minimum extent of individual liberty entails *some such absolute stand.*[17]

That is to say, the demand for the sacredness of a private sphere needs a basis, an "absolute" basis, but it has no basis; any old basis, any "such absolute stand" as reference to my own subjective will or the will of my society will do. It would be short-sighted to deny that Berlin's comprehensive formula is very helpful for a political purpose—for the purpose of an anti-Communist manifesto designed to rally all anti-Communists. But we are here concerned with a theoretical problem, and in this respect we are forced to say that Berlin contradicts himself. "Freedom from" and "freedom for" are "two profoundly divergent and irreconcilable attitudes to the ends of life . . . each of them makes absolute claims. These claims cannot both be fully satisfied. But . . . the satisfaction that each of them seeks is an ultimate value which . . . has an equal right to be classed among the deepest interests of mankind."[18] The absolute claim for a minimum private sphere cannot be fully satisfied; it must be diluted, for the opposite claim has an equal right. Liberalism, as Berlin understands it, cannot live without an absolute basis and cannot live with an absolute basis.

Let us consider more precisely the basis of liberalism as Berlin sees it. "What these rules and commandments [*sc.* that determine the frontiers of freedom that nobody should ever be permitted to cross] will have in common is that they are accepted so widely, are grounded so deeply in the actual nature of men as they have developed through history, as to be, by now, an essential part of what we mean by being a normal human being."[19] But Berlin had told us earlier that "the domination of this ideal has been the exception rather than the rule, even in the recent history of the West,"[20] i.e., that the ideal of negative freedom is not natural to man as man. Let, then, the rules in question be natural to Western man as he is now. But what about the future?

It may be that the ideal of freedom to live as one wishes . . . is only the late fruit of our declining capitalist civilization: an ideal which . . . posterity will regard with . . . little comprehension. This may be so; but no sceptical [sic] conclusions seem to me to follow. Principles are no less sacred because their duration cannot be guaranteed.[21]

But it is also true that principles are not sacred merely in virtue of the fact that their duration cannot be guaranteed. We are still waiting to hear why Berlin's principles are regarded by him as sacred. If these principles are intrinsically valid, eternally valid, one could indeed say that it is a secondary question whether they will or will not be recognized as valid in the future and that if future generations despise the eternal verities of civilization, they will merely condemn themselves to barbarism. But can there be eternal principles on the basis of "empiricism," of the experience of men up to now? Does not the experience of the future have the same right to respect as the experience of the past and the present?

The situation would be entirely different if one could assume the possibility of a peak of experience, of an absolute moment in history, in which the fundamental condition of man is realized for the first time and in principle fully. But this would also mean that in the most important respect history, or progress, would have come to its end. Yet Berlin seems to take it for granted that in the most important respect history is unfinished or unfinishable. Hence, the ideal of negative freedom can only be "relatively valid" for him: it can be valid only for the time being. In entire accord with the spirit of our time, he quotes "an admirable writer of our time" who says: "To realize the relative validity of one's convictions and yet stand for them unflinchingly, is what distinguishes a civilized man from a barbarian."[22]

That is to say, not only are all our primary ends of relative validity; even the end that suggests itself as necessary by virtue of the absolute insight into the relative validity of all our primary ends is likewise only relatively valid. On the other hand, the latter end, or the right position toward any primary end, is so absolutely valid that Berlin or his authority can build on it the absolute distinction between civilized men and barbarians. For this distinction, as set forth in the quoted passage, is obviously meant to be final and not to be subject to revision in the light of future experience.

Berlin cannot escape the necessity to which every thinking being is subject: to take a final stand, an absolute stand in accordance with what he regards as the nature of man or as the nature of the human condition or as the decisive truth and hence to assert the absolute validity of his fundamental conviction. This does not mean, of course, that his fundamental conviction is sound. One reason why I doubt that it is sound is that if his authority were right, every resolute liberal hack or thug would be a civilized man, while Plato and Kant would be barbarians.

Berlin's statement seems to me to be a characteristic document of the crisis of liberalism—of a crisis due to the fact that liberalism has abandoned its absolutist basis and is trying to become entirely relativistic. Probably the majority of our academic colleagues will say that no conclusion can be drawn against relativism from the inadequacies of Berlin's statement because these inadequacies arise from his wish to find an impossible middle ground between relativism and absolutism; if he had limited himself to saying that liberalism is merely his "own subjective end," not intrinsically superior to any other subjective end, that since the belief in liberalism is based on a value judgment, no case or no conclusive case can be made for or against liberalism, in other words, if he had not rejected the nonliberal positions as "barbarian," but had admitted that there is an indefinitely large variety of notions of civilization each of which defines barbarism in its own way, in brief, if he had remained within the confines of the positivism of our time, he would never have contradicted himself. Whether withdrawal to the citadel of that positivism or of unqualified "value relativism" overcomes the crisis of liberalism or whether it merely conceals that crisis is another question.

The case for relativism has been restated recently by Arnold Brecht. He takes issue with certain arguments against relativism that I had advanced. He is not impressed by my reasoning. He deals with it chiefly under the heading of "misrepresentations." Since I know Dr. Brecht to be a polite man, I was inclined to assume that he regarded it as impolite to accuse me of mere misunderstanding: relativism is not such a deep doctrine as to be likely to be misunderstood. He blames me for having ascribed to Max Weber the view that all values are of the same rank: Weber merely asserted that "ultimate" values are "equally indemonstrable."[23] This means, however, that, as far as we know and shall ever be able to know while living on earth, or before the tribunal of human reason, the ways of life recommended by Amos or by Socrates are equal in value to the way of life of specialists without spirit or vision and voluptuaries without heart. And this assertion seems to me to be as absurd as the assertion that, as far as we know or shall ever be able to know, a man who is blind or mortally ill is as perfect regarding his body as a man free from all bodily defects.

Brecht blames me also for having seen "inconsistency in the fact that relativists cannot help using value judgments themselves."

No scientific relativist would condemn words like cruelty, civilization, prostitution, or, for that matter, crime or slums, wherever they are used within a clear frame of reference as descriptive in accordance with known standards, *as long as these standards are not themselves at issue.*[24] But, on the basis of relativism, the standards are necessarily at issue, since all value judgments are rationally questionable; the consistent relativist ought to use "value-impregnated expressions" only in quotation marks, if at all.

In the appendix to his book, in a subsection entitled "Misunderstandings,"[25] Brecht reproaches me for having asserted that, according to relativism, "civilization is not intrinsically superior to cannibalism." He says:

> Where and when has a scientific relativist ever asserted as a fact that civilization is *not* superior to cannibalism? Such apodictic negative statements would be quite contrary to the principles of Scientific Method. I merely repeat that, according to the thesis of scientific relativism, as restated by Brecht, civilization is not, as far as we *know*, and shall ever be able to *know*, superior to cannibalism, provided that each—civilization as well as cannibalism—rests on an ultimate value of its own. This is to say nothing at all here of the fact that the use of the terms "civilizations" or "cultures" by scientific anthropology presupposes the abolition of the distinction between civilization and barbarism and therewith, in particular, the abolition of the distinction between civilization and cannibalism.

"The only question," Brecht continues, "that could be raised by some pedantic relativist or for the matter of methodological argument is, What is the scientific *evidence* for the superiority of noncannibalistic civilizations?" Since the question at issue is whether reason is completely unable to distinguish between right and wrong or noble and base, one must not be afraid of being pedantic. "How about civilizations," Brecht continues, "that abhor the eating of cattle or hogs?" Here Brecht seems to say that, according to scientific relativism, the eating of human beings has the same status as the eating of cattle or hogs.

> Scientific Value Relativism . . . is at no loss to show the superiority of noncannibalism, once "superiority" is defined . . . in terms other than selfish satisfaction of personal or tribal passions and with reference to humanity . . . even if the term "superior" were used in a strictly selfish sense . . . Scientific Method would not be at the end of its resources; the long-run superiority of one pattern of behavior over another can often be demonstrated even when the question is solely that of personal satisfaction.

If scientific value relativism may be able to prove the superiority of civilization to cannibalism in terms of both selfish satisfaction and unselfish satisfaction, it would indeed seem that scientific value relativism can in principle prove the superiority of civilization to cannibalism. Or is the disjunction incomplete? Must it not be incomplete if relativism is to be maintained? Is the reference to the "definition" of superiority not tantamount to a reference to such incompleteness? Is there, then, something other than satisfaction (selfish or unselfish) that is equal in rank to satisfaction before the tribunal of human reason so that one can choose dissatisfaction (pain, suffering, anguish, failure) as one's ultimate value with the same right as satisfaction? And may not dissatisfaction justify cannibalism?[26]

Brecht concludes his argument with the remark that scientific value relativism does not deny "that there may be absolutely valid, divine standards of moral value; it merely negates that this can be shown with scientific means in a serious controversy conducted in good faith." Brecht also reproaches me for having contrasted the apparent humility with the hidden arrogance of relativism. In reply to this remark he says:

> Scientific Value Relativism may indeed be too humble to offer a *scientific* decision on a question like this: whether the captain of a marooned crew ought to be condemned if he permitted his men to eat the flesh of other men killed in battle or by accident, when this was the only alternative to starving. Religious feeling and traditional education may tell us they should rather have starved, but this is no *scientific* decision.

Why did Brecht choose this example in preference to the example of men eating human flesh while they have other food in abundance? Can his science legitimate the "condemnation" of what we may call frivolous cannibalism without making assumptions regarding "ultimate values" which that very science must regard as questionable? Besides, I gladly admit that Brecht's version of relativism is humble, since it is based on the Kantian distinction between the knowable phenomena and the unknowable thing-in-itself.[27]

According to the positivistic interpretation of relativism which prevails in present-day social science and which Brecht very feebly qualifies,[28] reason is unable to show the superiority of unselfish gratification to selfish gratification and the absurdity of any attainable ends "which imagination and idiosyncrasies lead men to pursue." From this it follows that a bachelor without kith and kin who dedicates his whole life to the amassing of the largest possible amount of money, provided he goes about this pursuit in the most efficient manner, leads, in principle, as rational a life as the greatest benefactor of his country or of mankind. The choice among attainable ends may be made *en pleine connaissance de cause*, i.e., in full clarity about the likely consequences of the choice; it cannot in itself be rational. Reason can tell us which means are conducive to which ends; it cannot tell us which attainable ends are to be preferred to other attainable ends. Reason cannot even tell us that we ought to choose attainable ends; if someone "loves him who desires the impossible," reason may tell him that he acts irrationally, but it cannot tell him that he ought to act rationally or that acting irrationally is acting badly or basely. If rational conduct consists in choosing the right means for the right end, relativism teaches in effect that rational conduct is impossible. Relativistic social science may therefore be said to be one branch of the rational study of nonrational behavior.

But in what sense is the study rational? Social science proceeds by inductive reasoning or is concerned with prediction or with the discovery of causes. Yet what is the status of the principle of causality in social science relativism? The moderate Brecht is satisfied with the assertion that as regards causality, scientific method is grounded on common sense; he himself is inclined toward what he calls the Kantian view according to which "the human mind is so structured as to be unable to think [or as he also says "to imagine"] that changes have no causes."[29] According to a more widely accepted view, the principle of causality is a mere assumption. There is no rational objection to the assumption that the universe may disappear at any moment, not only into thin air, but into absolute nothingness, and that this happening may be a vanishing, not only into nothing, but through nothing as well. What is true of the possible end of the world is true also of its beginning. Since the principle of causality is not intrinsically evident, nothing prevents us from assuming that the world has come into being out of nothing and through nothing. Not only has rationality disappeared from the behavior studied by science; the rationality of that study itself has become radically problematic. All coherence has gone. We are then entitled to say that positivistic science in general, and therefore positivistic social science in particular, is characterized by the abandonment of reason or the flight from reason. The flight from scientific reason, which has been noted with regret, is the reasonable reply to the flight of science from reason.

A Marxist writer, Georg Lukács, has written a history of nineteenth- and twentieth-century German thought under the title *Die Zerstörung der Vernunft*.[30] I believe that many of us Western social scientists must plead guilty to this accusation. For obvious reasons we must be especially interested in Lukács's critique of Max Weber's conception of social science. One may summarize that critique as follows. Weber more than any other German scholar of his generation tried to save the objectivity of social science; he believed that to do so required that social science be made "value-free" because he assumed that evaluations are transrational or irrational; but the value-free study of "facts" and their causes admittedly presupposes the selection of relevant facts; that selection is necessarily guided by reference to values; the values with reference to which the facts are to be selected must themselves be selected; and that selection, which determines in the last analysis the specific conceptual framework of the social scientist, is in principle arbitrary; hence social science is fundamentally irrational or subjectivistic.[31]

According to Lukács, an objective and evaluating social science is possible provided social science does not limit itself to the study of arbitrarily selected "facts" or segments, but understands particular social phenomena in the light of the whole social situation and ultimately in the light of the whole historical process. "Historical and dialectical materialism is that comprehensive view in which the progressiveness and the rationally knowable lawfulness of history are expressed in the highest form, and in fact the only comprehensive view that can give a consistent philosophic foundation to progressivism and reasonableness."[32]

Hegel's attempt to demonstrate the progressive and rational character of the historical process was based on the premise that that process is in principle completed; for if it were not completed, one could not know, for instance, whether the future stages would not lead to the self-destruction of reason. Yet, according to Marx, the historical process is not completed, not to say that it has not even begun. Besides, Marx does not admit trans-historical or natural ends with reference to which change can be diagnosed as progress or regress. It is therefore a question whether by turning from Western relativism to Marxism one escapes relativism. "Historical materialism," Lukács had said,

> can and must be applied to itself. Yet this application of materialist method to materialism does not lead to complete relativism; it does not lead to the consequence that historical materialism is not the right method. The substantive truths of Marxism are of the same quality as the truths of classical economics according to Marx's interpretation of those truths. They are truths within a certain order of society and production. As such, but only as such, they possess absolute validity. This does not exclude the emergence of societies in which other categories, other connections of truth, will be valid as a consequence of the essential structure of these societies.[33]

This would seem to mean that the substantive truths of Marxism are true until further notice; in principle we know already now that they will be replaced by different truths. Surely, the Marxist truths will be "preserved" in Hegel's sense of the term: "the 'objectivity' of the truth accessible on the lower planes is not destroyed: that truth merely receives a different meaning by being integrated into a more concrete, a more comprehensive totality."[34] That is to say, Marxism will reveal itself as a one-sided truth, a half-truth. Lukács compares the truth of Marxism also to the truth of the ideologies of the French Revolution. Marxism is as true today as those ideologies were in their time: both make or made intelligible a historical situation in such a way as to render visible for contemporaries the root of their difficulties and to show them the way out of those difficulties. But while the ideologists of the French Revolution saw dearly the rottenness of the *ancien régime* and the necessity of a revolution, they were utterly mistaken about the goodness of the new society that their revolution brought to birth.

The application to Marxism is obvious: even if Marxism were the last word regarding the ground of the rottenness of capitalist society and regarding the way in which that society can and will be destroyed, it cannot possibly be the last word regarding the new society that the revolutionary action of the proletariat brings to birth: the new society may be as rich in contradictions and oppressions as the old society, although its contradictions and oppressions will, of course, be entirely novel. For if Marxism is only the truth of our time or our society, the prospect of the classless society too is only the truth of our time and society; it may prove to be the delusion that gave the proletariat the power and the spirit to overthrow the capitalist system, whereas in fact the proletariat finds itself afterwards enslaved, no longer indeed by capital, but by an ironclad military bureaucracy.

Yet perhaps Marxism must not be applied to itself and thus made relative. Perhaps its fundamental verities are objective, scientific truths the validity of which cannot be understood in terms of their conditions or genesis. Marxism can then be regarded as a final truth of the same dignity as the theory of evolution. Yet since other truths of great importance will be discovered in the future, the "meaning" of Marxism will radically change.

But perhaps Marxism is the final truth, since it belongs to the absolute moment in history in which the realm of necessity can be surveyed in its entirety and therewith the outlines of the realm of freedom can come into view for the first time. The realm of necessity coincides with the division of labor. The realm of freedom emerges with the abolition of the division of labor. Yet the original form of the division of labor is "the division of labor," not in the generation of offspring, but "in the sexual act."[35] It would seem that the realm of freedom, if brought to its perfection, will be the realm of homunculi produced in test tubes by homunculi, if it will not be, as is more likely, the earth of "the last man," of the one herd without a shepherd. For, to quote Machiavelli, "as has been written by some moral philosophers, men's hands and tongue, two most noble instruments for ennobling him, would not have done their work perfectly nor would they have carried the works of men to the height to which they are seen to have been carried, if they had not been driven on by necessity": the jump from the realm of necessity into the realm of freedom will be the inglorious death of the very possibility of human excellence.

But let us return to that school which is externally the most powerful in the present-day West, to present-day positivism. That positivism is logical positivism. With some degree of truth it traces its origin to Hume. It deviates from Hume in two important respects. In the first place, deviating from Hume's teaching, it is a logical, i.e., not a psychological, teaching. The supplement added by logical positivism to the critique of reason is symbolic logic and the theory of probability; in Hume that supplement was natural belief and natural instinct. The sole or chief concern of logical positivism is the logical analysis of science. It has learned through Kant, the great critic of Hume, or through neo-Kantianism, that the question of the validity of science is radically different from the question of its psychological genesis.

The second important respect in which present-day positivism deviates from Hume is indicated by the fact that Hume was still a political philosopher. More particularly, he still taught that there are universally valid rules of justice and that those rules are not improperly called Laws of Nature. This means that "he thought and wrote before the rise of anthropology and allied sciences[36] or, more precisely stated, before "the discovery of History." Hume still viewed human things in the light of man's unchangeable nature; he did not yet conceive of man as an essentially historical being. Present-day positivism believes that it can evade the problem raised by "the discovery of History" by the same device by which it frees itself from Hume's or any other psychology: through the Kantian distinction between validity and genesis. Yet Kant was enabled to transcend psychology because he recognized an *a priori*; and an a priori does not have a genesis, at least not an empirical genesis. Logical positivism rejects the a priori. Hence it cannot avoid becoming involved in psychology, in the question of the empirical genesis of science out of what precedes science. One cannot stop at simply trying to answer the question, What is science? One cannot avoid raising the question, Why science? or What is the meaning of science? Since positivism denies that there is a "pure reason" or a "pure mind," it can answer the question, Why science? only in terms of "the human organism." It must understand science as an activity of a certain kind of organism, as an activity fulfilling an important function in the life of that kind of organism. In brief, man is an organism that cannot live, or live well, without being able to predict, and the most efficient form of prediction is science.

This way of accounting for science has become extremely questionable. In the age of thermonuclear weapons the positive relation of science to human survival has lost all the apparent evidence that it formerly may have possessed. Furthermore, the high development of science depends on highly developed industrial societies; the predominance of such societies renders ever more difficult the survival of "underdeveloped societies." Who still dares to say that the development of those societies, i.e., their radical transformation, the destruction of their traditional way of life, is a necessary condition for those peoples' living or living well? Those peoples survived and sometimes lived happily without having an inkling of the possibility of science. While it becomes necessary to trace science to the needs of organisms of a certain kind, it is impossible to do so. For to the extent to which science could be shown to be necessary for man's living or living well, one would in fact pass a rational value judgment regarding science, and we know that, according to positivism, rational value judgments are impossible.

Some positivists avoid the difficulty indicated by finding the rationale of science in democracy, without being deterred by the fact that they thus merely appeal to the dogmatic premise or the inertia of established orders and without paying attention to the complications alluded to by

Berlin, or else by conceiving of science as one of the most thrilling forms of spiritual adventure, without being able to tell us what they understand by the spiritual, how it differs in their opinion from the nonspiritual, and, in particular, how it is related to the rational. Positivism grants that science depends on conditions that science itself does not produce. They are produced by the unintended coming together of various factors that may diverge as they have converged. As long as they are together, science may progress by virtue of something that looks like an innate propensity. Yet science is not autonomous; as the saying goes, thinking does not take place in a vacuum. What renders the autonomy of science questionable is not primarily the fact that science presupposes the availability of conditions external to science. If one conceives of science as a spiritual adventure, one implies that there are other forms of spiritual adventure; one cannot exclude the possibility that, just as science influences those other forms, science itself undergoes their influence. Furthermore, one must assume that the spirit changes as a consequence of its adventures, hence that the spirit may well differ from age to age, and hence that science may depend, in the direction of its interests or of its hypotheses-forming imagination, on the spirit of the age. In other words, one cannot help raising the question of the relation between scientific progress and social progress. Given the positivistic verdict regarding value judgments, positivism can no longer speak properly, or with an easy conscience, of social progress; but it continues, even if in a more or less surreptitious manner, the older tradition that believed in the natural harmony between scientific progress and social progress.

Stated generally, by virtue of the distinction between validity and genesis, positivism tries to treat science as autonomous, but it is unable to do so; that distinction merely prevents it from giving due weight to the question of the human context out of which science arises and within which it exists. Positivism treats science in the way in which it would have to be treated if science were "the very highest power of man," the power by which man transcends the merely human; yet positivism cannot maintain this "Platonic" understanding of science. The question of the human context of science, which positivism fails and refuses to raise, is taken up by its most powerful present-day opponent in the West, radical historicism or, to use the better-known name, existentialism.

Existentialism came into being through the meeting, which first took place in Germany, of Kierkegaard's and Nietzsche's thought. While being related to these two illustrious names, existentialism is as nameless as positivism or idealism. But this is misleading. Existentialism, like many other movements, has a flabby periphery and a hard center. That hard core, or that thought to which alone existentialism owes its intellectual dignity, is the thought of Heidegger. In Heidegger's first great publication, the influence of Kierkegaard was indeed as powerful as that of Nietzsche. But with the increased clarity that Heidegger achieved afterward, it became clear that the root of existentialism must be sought in Nietzsche rather than in Kierkegaard: existentialism emerged by virtue of the "reception" of Kierkegaard on the part of a philosophic public that had begun to be molded by Nietzsche.

Nietzsche is *the* philosopher of relativism: the first thinker who faced the problem of relativism in its full extent and pointed to the way in which relativism can be overcome. Relativism came to Nietzsche's attention in the form of historicism—more precisely, in the form of a decayed Hegelianism. Hegel had reconciled "the discovery of History"—the alleged insight into the individual's being, in the most radical sense, the son or stepson of his time or into the dependence of a man's highest and purest thoughts on his time—with philosophy in the original meaning of the term by asserting that Hegel's time was the absolute moment, the end of meaningful time: the absolute religion, Christianity, had become completely reconciled with the world; it had become completely secularized, or the *saeculum* had become completely Christian in and through the postrevolutionary State; history as meaningful change had come to its end; all theoretical and practical problems had in principle been solved; hence, the historical process was demonstrably rational.

The decayed Hegelianism with which Nietzsche was confronted preserved Hegel's "optimism" after having abandoned the ground of that "optimism," i.e., the completedness of the historical process. In fact, its "optimism" was based on the expectation of infinite future progress or on the belief in the unfinishable character of history. Under this condition, as Nietzsche saw, our own principles, including the belief in progress, will become as relative as all earlier principles had shown themselves to be; not only the thought of the past but also our own thought must be understood to depend on premises which for us are inescapable, but of which we know that they are condemned to perish. History becomes a spectacle that for the superficial is exciting and for the serious is enervating. It teaches a truth that is deadly. It shows us that culture is possible only if men are fully dedicated to principles of thought and action which they do not and cannot question, which limit their horizon and thus enable them to have a character and a style. It shows us at the same time that any principles of this kind can be questioned and even rejected.

The only way out seems to be that one turn one's back on this lesson of history, that one voluntarily choose life-giving delusion instead of deadly truth, that one fabricate a myth. But this is patently impossible for men of intellectual probity. The true solution comes to sight once one realizes the essential limitation of objective history or of objective knowledge in general. Objective history suffices for destroying the delusion of the objective validity of any principles of thought and action; it does not suffice for opening up a genuine understanding of history. The objective historian cannot grasp the substance of the past because he is a mere spectator, not dedicated or committed to substantive principles of thought and action, and this is the consequence of his having realized that such principles have no objective validity. But an entirely different conclusion may and must be drawn from the realization of this objective truth. The different values respected in different epochs had no objective support, i.e., they were human creations; they owed their being to a free human project that formed the horizon within which a culture was possible. What man did in the past unconsciously and under the delusion of submitting to what is independent of his creative act, he must now do consciously. This radically new project—the revaluation of all values—entails the rejection of all earlier values, for they have become baseless by the realization of the baseless character of their claim, by which they stand or fall, to objective validity. But precisely the realization of the origin of all such principles makes possible a new creation that presupposes this realization and is in agreement with it, yet is not deducible from it; for otherwise it would not be due to a creative act performed with intellectual probity.

It is in this way that Nietzsche may be said to have transformed the deadly truth of relativism into the most life-giving truth. To state the case with all necessary vagueness, he discovered that the life-giving comprehensive truth is subjective or transtheoretical in that it cannot be grasped detachedly and that it cannot be the same for all men or for all ages. We can do no more than allude here to the difficulties in which Nietzsche became involved in trying to overcome the difficulties that afflict his solution. I have in mind his interpretation of human creativity as a special form of the universal will to power, and the question that this interpretation entails, namely, whether he did not thus again try to find a sufficient theoretical basis for a transtheoretical teaching or message. I have in mind, in other words, his hesitation as to whether the doctrine of the will to power is his subjective project to be superseded by other such projects in the future or whether it is the final truth. We limit ourselves here to saying that the movement of Nietzsche's thought can be understood as a movement from the supremacy of history towards the supremacy of nature, a movement that bypasses the supremacy of reason throughout or tries to replace the opposition between the subjective and the objective (or between the conventional and the natural) by the opposition between the superficial and the profound. Existentialism is the attempt to free Nietzsche's alleged overcoming of relativism from the consequences of his relapse into metaphysics or of his recourse to nature.

Existentialism starts where positivism leaves off. Existentialism is the reaction of serious men to their own relativism. Positivism is essentially the attempt to understand science; it acts as if it knew that science is the one thing needful or at any rate man's highest possibility. It conceives of science as essentially progressive, and hence it conceives of the future of scientific development as unpredictable *in concreto*. In fact, it conceives of science as capable of infinite progress. This character of science must, however, be traced to the character of the object of science. That object is essentially accessible to reason; otherwise there could be no science. But since it reveals itself to science only in an infinite process, one can say with at least equal right that it is radically mysterious. For he who teaches, for instance, that perpetual peace is the goal of an infinite process teaches, in fact, the perpetuity of war. Existentialism is the truth of positivism, since it teaches that being is essentially or radically mysterious and that the fundamental defect of metaphysics is the assumption upon which it is based—the assumption that being is as such intelligible.

Existentialism is, however, not merely the "pessimistic" expression of the same thing of which positivism is the "optimistic" expression. Positivism asserts that the goodness of science cannot be established by science or scientific philosophy: the choice of science, of the scientific orientation, and therewith also of the scientific "picture of the world" is not a rational choice; it is as possible and as groundless as the choice of any alternative orientation. These fundamental choices are not properly interpreted by scientific psychology, for scientific psychology explains those choices on the basis of a specific fundamental choice that is not necessary, viz., the choice of the scientific orientation. The fundamental phenomenon, the only phenomenon that is not hypothetical, is the abyss of freedom: the fact that man is compelled to choose groundlessly; the fundamental experience, i.e., an experience more fundamental than every science, is the experience of the objective groundlessness of all principles of thought and action, the experience of nothingness.

Man and ultimately everything must be understood in the light of this fundamental experience. The specific manner in which man and man alone is, is directly constituted by the fundamental nothingness. That manner of being is called *Existenz*. *Existenz* is articulated by the analysis of *Existenz*, which is the fundamental part of philosophy. *Existenz* is authentic or inauthentic: authentic when it faces the fundamental situation of man, inauthentic when it flees from it. The analytics of *Existenz* contains, then, an ethics, even if only a formal ethics: to the extent to which one understands *Existenz*, one realizes the general character of the truly human. The ethics is formal since it is based, not on the nature of man, on man's beingness, but on the human situation or, somewhat more precisely, on man's manner of being. Hence, it does not say that the good life is the life according to nature, according to the nature of man, but it does say, in effect, that the good life is the life according to the essential character of *Existenz*. It does not say this, however, according to Heidegger's own authoritative declaration. For if the analytics of *Existenz* contained an ethics, its cognitive status would be the same as that of Kant's transcendental analytics of subjectivity; it would be an objective teaching or it would supply final knowledge, infinite knowledge. Yet the analytics of *Existenz* is necessarily based on a specific ideal of *Existenz*, on a specific commitment; for only committed thought can understand commitment and hence *Existenz*. In other words, existentialist philosophy is subjective truth about the subjectivity of truth or finite knowledge of man's finiteness.

Yet how can finiteness be seen as finiteness if it is not seen in the light of the infinite? These and similar difficulties seem to have led Heidegger to a very thorough revision of his doctrine. One may doubt whether through that revision the fundamental relativism was overcome. I can allude here only to one point, to Heidegger's teaching regarding historical truth. The interpreter's understanding of a thinker is true if it understands his thought as he understood it. According to Heidegger this is altogether impossible; it is not even a reasonable goal of understanding. Nor is it possible, in his opinion, to understand a thinker better than he understood himself; true understanding of a thinker is understanding him creatively, i.e., understanding him differently from the way in which he understood himself. This understanding necessarily implies a criticism, a fundamental criticism of the thinker in question. According to Heidegger, all thinkers prior to him have been oblivious of *Sein*, i.e., of the ground of grounds. This assertion implies, in fact, the claim that Heidegger understands the great thinkers of the past in the decisive respect better than they understood themselves

NOTES

Previously published in *The Rebirth of Classical Political Rationalism: An Introduction to the Thought of Leo Strauss*, selected and introduced by Thomas L. Pangle (Chicago: University of Chicago Press, 1989), pp. 13–26.

1. Isaiah Berlin, *Two Concepts of Liberty* (Oxford: At the Clarendon Press, 1958), p. 51.
2. *Op. cit.*, pp. 9, 11, 47.
3. *Op. cit.*, pp. 15, 16.
4. *Op. cit.*, p. 19.
5. *Op. cit.*, p. 32.
6. *Op. cit.*, p. 46.
7. *Op. cit.*, p. 14 n.
8. *Op. cit.*, pp. 36, 50.
9. *Op. cit.*, pp. 13–15, 48.
10. *Op. cit.*, pp. 39n., 54, 57n.
11. *Op. cit.*, p. 54.
12. *Op. cit.*, p. 38 n.
13. *Op. cit.*, p. 54.
14. *Op. cit.*, p. 50; italics mine.
15. *Op. cit.*, p. 57.
16. *Op. cit.*, p. 50.
17. *Op. cit.*, p. 50; italics mine.
18. *Op. cit.*, pp. 51–52.
19. *Op. cit.*, p. 50.
20. *Op. cit.*, p. 13.
21. *Op. cit.*, p. 57.

22. *Op. cit.*, p. 57.
23. Arnold Brecht, *Political Theory* (Princeton, NJ: Princeton University Press, 1959), p. 263.
24. *Op. cit.*, pp. 264–265.
25. *Op. cit.*, pp. 549–550.
26. Cf. also p. 430.
27. Cf. pp. 101, 103, 125, 158, 462 ff.
28. *Op. cit.*, pp. 124–125, 130–131.
29. *Op. cit.*, pp. 78, 81.
30. Georg Lukács, *Die Zerstörung der Vernunft* (Berlin, 1954).
31. Cf. pp. 484–489.
32. *Op. cit.*, p. 456.
33. Georg Lukács, *Geschichte und Klassenbewusstsein* (Berlin, 1923), pp. 234–235.
34. *Op. cit.*, p. 206.
35. Karl Marx and F. Engels, *Die Deutsche Ideologie* (cited from a new edition, Berlin, 1953), p. 28.
36. John Dewey, *Human Nature and Conduct*, Modern Library edition, p. vii.

FIFTEEN

Strauss at 100

I

About ten years ago I had a letter from Dante Germino, asking why Strauss's students had paid so little attention to the work of Eric Voegelin. Earlier, Dante had asked me to lecture at Virginia. On that occasion he had been suddenly hospitalized. Although nothing serious had resulted, I did not see him during my visit. His students however had been models of hospitality, and in the seminars I conducted they showed themselves well trained, and highly motivated in the right directions. Dante had taught political philosophy to Lawrence McGoldrick, my son-in-law to be. Dante and his wife and daughter had attended Lawrence and Karen's wedding in the University of Virginia Chapel in 1979. Dante's daughter had been a waitress at the rehearsal dinner at the Boar's Head Inn in Charlottesville (where Lawrence had been a waiter). For all these reasons I thought it fitting to respond in as friendly a manner as possible.

I wrote, in part,

> As to the "incomprehensibility" of the neglect of Voegelin by Straussians, some of it must be put down to the blinding power of the light that emanated from Strauss himself. For it is the paradoxical truth that light can at once enable one to see and, if sufficiently intense, to blind. I have often compared my encounter with Strauss, beginning in September 1944 to the experience of Saul on the road to Damascus. When one is in that kind of exalted consciousness, it is easy to neglect or dismiss other prophets (or to assume without inquiring that they must be false prophets!).

I went on to say that it was a mistake to continue to think of "Straussians" as a single class. As illustrative of this, I sent a copy of my critique of *The*

Closing of the American Mind. Unfortunately, he took offense at my implied comparison—as he thought it—of Strauss and Jesus. But he took infinitely greater offense at what I had written about homosexuality in the Bloom review. He accused me of a lack of scholarly integrity for not taking as unqualified truth what John Boswell (of whom I had never heard!) had written in his book on Christianity and homosexuality. Boswell, as it happened, was a professor of history at Yale (he died of AIDS at the age of 47), and his book was a "revision" of all traditional morality concerning homosexuality, in the Old Testament as well as in the New. (The story of Sodom, for example, was about "inhospitality").

I later learned from one of Dante's colleagues that he had come out of the closet, divorced his wife, abandoned his family, and imported a catamite into his domestic establishment. That—and his uncompromising demand for approval—brought to an end any possibility of friendly discussion between us.

I do not think my response about how my encounter with Strauss changed my life offended Christian piety. The paradigmatic account of the phenomenon of conversion—the source for Christianity itself—is the cave in Plato's *Republic*. No one's life, I believe, was "turned around" more completely than mine by my meeting with Strauss.

My five years at Yale were not wasted. They were, in fact, probably the best non-Straussian preparation for what followed. As an English major, I read only good books. For four years I attended an informal weekly Bible reading by my favorite professor, Alex Witherspoon. In my senior year I had an independent study in Plato and Aristotle with Eugene O'Neill, Jr. The three authors who had come to mean most to me were Plato, Aristotle, and Shakespeare. I had good instincts but no guide to unlock their mysteries.

Before Strauss, my greatest ambition was to write a history of Elizabethan drama. In my mind, this was the way to discover the secret of Shakespeare, which I assumed could be achieved only by the closest study of the soil out of which Shakespeare came. I was also greatly influenced by Marxist and Freudian interpretations. I recall being impressed by an interpretation of Shakespeare, in which Ariel was said to be the apotheosis of the free wage laborer! And Ernest Jones's Freudian book on Hamlet ranked very high. In all such accounts, the high was understood in the light of the low. It was Strauss who struck off the shackles in my cave, and taught me to look in the opposite direction.

Little did I, or could I, have imagined in 1939 or 1940 that my ambition would be fulfilled—at least in part—in 1977, when I set forth the hypothesis that Shakespeare was the poet mentioned by Socrates at the end of the *Symposium*.[1] Only Strauss could have led me to see that Shakespeare's inner and ultimate motivation was Platonic.

If I had any pre-Straussian theoretical framework, it was that of the sociology of knowledge. Later, Strauss would describe his own project—

ironically—as the sociology of philosophy! From the perspective of the sociology of knowledge no distinction could be drawn between opinion and knowledge. Whatever believed itself to be true could be believed to be true only relative to the environment that "produced" it. Thus, what I later learned to be historicism (the idol of our modern cave) had permeated every atom of my mental existence. I had assumed that everything was relative except the proposition that everything was relative. The contradiction therein had not of course penetrated my consciousness before Strauss.

Strauss began *Natural Right and History* by quoting "We hold these truths to be self-evident . . ." and asking, "Does this nation in its maturity still cherish the faith in which it was conceived and raised? Does it still hold those 'truths to be self-evident'?" He not only quoted from the Declaration, but used Lincoln's words, without quotation marks, to characterize it. Strauss clearly thought that the nation no longer dwelt within the precincts of the principles of the Declaration, and his book goes a long way towards explaining why. But he never addressed directly the question of how the authority of those principles might be restored.

I claim no right to speak for Strauss in this matter. I can say however that it was a subject we discussed continuously in the late forties and early fifties. I believe that Strauss believed that my restoration of Lincoln was the most apt way to restore the aforesaid authority, and that this was the form in which the statesmanship of classical political philosophy might become authoritative in our world. While Strauss articulated the connection between Plato, biblical religion, and medieval political philosophy, to discover the presence of classical principles in the post-classical world, he propelled my articulation of the connection between Plato, biblical religion, Shakespeare, and Lincoln. And Lincoln's recovery of the Founding corresponded closely with the Maimonidean recovery of the rational origins of prophecy.

II

It is almost routine in the scholarship of greatness, whether philosophic or political, to discover fathomless complexity in its subjects. Certainly this has been true about Lincoln. Yet in the case of Lincoln, as in that of many others, the difficulty has been more in the mind of the observer rather than in the subject. Scholars who do not believe in "an abstract truth applicable to all men and all time" either do not believe that Lincoln believed it, or think of him as unsophisticated. In either case, they embark on a quest for hidden motives because they cannot see the ones that lie plainly on the surface.

The recent torrent of literature about Strauss is not unlike that about Lincoln. No one would deny Strauss's complexity. Yet great minds are often, if not always, as great in their simplicities as in their complexities. Lincoln's statesmanship can always be explained in its relationship to "a central idea from which all its minor thoughts radiate." Strauss revealed himself perhaps more directly than anywhere else in his eulogy of Churchill. "The tyrant stood at the pinnacle of his power. The contrast between the indomitable and magnanimous statesman and the insane tyrant—this spectacle in its clear simplicity was one of the greatest lessons which men can learn, at any time." To the best of my recollection, in the political science of the 1930's neither Hitler nor Stalin was referred to as a tyrant. Their regimes were called dictatorships, or totalitarian, in deference to the quest for a "value free" objectivity. Yet this "objectivity" made it impossible to understand political reality. Strauss's *On Tyranny* was written in part to restore the classical term and with it the classical understanding. The centrality of "tyranny" in all its classical dimensions to the Declaration of Independence also demonstrates the essentially classical understanding of politics in the American Revolution. The magnanimity of those who pledged their lives, fortunes, and sacred honor directly parallels the contrast between Hitler and Churchill.

Strauss understood that modern tyranny was different from the tyrannies of the ancient world. But the identification of the species, or variety, depended upon recognizing the genus. The recognition of tyranny did however not come from books. It came from experience antecedent to books. The "spectacle" which Strauss says presents us with one of the greatest of all lessons, is therefore the ground of an education upon which great books can build, but without which they cannot instruct. The *Nicomachean Ethics* is addressed only to those who have sufficient experience of the moral phenomena, and who are well brought up. The greatest political books are those that reflect an original understanding of the moral and political phenomena, unmediated by ideology or philosophy. It was the corruption of that original understanding by modern philosophy that denied to the democracies the understanding of tyranny that nearly destroyed them.

In a letter to Löwith, Strauss once remarked that he had found great difficulty in understanding what Aristotle meant by magnanimity, until he realized that Churchill was a perfect example of it. That Churchill helped Strauss understand Aristotle illuminates profoundly how political philosophy depends upon the pre-philosophic experience of political life. The lesson embodied in the "clear simplicity" of the confrontation of Churchill and Hitler is that of the reality of evil, and the primacy of the good. It is also that the conflict of good and evil lies at the foundation of human experience. To reduce that experience to a subjective "value judgment" is not merely to trivialize it, but to blind one to objective reality. In Strauss's earlier work he referred to political philosophy as a part of philosophy. In his later years, I believe, he regarded it as the foundation of philosophy. So far are the moral distinctions from being merely subjective, they are the distinctions most knowable "to us," and hence the starting points of reasoning about "the whole."

"A Summary View of the Rights of British America" is Jefferson's compendium of the American position, written a year before the onset of the Revolution, and two years before the Declaration of Independence. In it he tells the King that "The great principles of right and wrong are legible to every reader . . ." These are of course the principles we hold to be self-evident. They are the principles of a free people, the principles of good and lawful self-government, distinguished from the evil principles of tyranny or slavery. They are the principles of Churchill as opposed to Hitler.

III

Everyone knows that Strauss ended his ever memorable lectures on "Progress or Return" by asserting the categorical opposition of Reason and Revelation as ultimate principles, and the necessity to make a choice between them. I have come to have doubts however as to whether this opposition is as categorical as Strauss made it seem in that lecture. That it formed part of his peroration, and was therefore a rhetorical conclusion does not, of itself, disqualify it as a dialectical conclusion. But in his desire that classical political philosophy provide the moral foundation for constitutional government that modern philosophy had destroyed, he had particular motives for absolutising the difference of Revelation and Reason.

Modern philosophy was a rebellion against both classical rationalism and biblical religion. The skepticism that accompanied Socratic rationalism applied necessarily to the enterprise of Socratic rationalism. That is to say, Socratic rationalism had to grant the premise that supplied the ground of faith. The reason in skepticism for continuing an endless inquiry, and the reason for ending such inquiry by turning to biblical religion, was one and the same reason. Nor was there, in that very reason, any ground for preferring the one alternative to the other. For Strauss, to restore the authority of Socratic rationalism was of necessity to restore the authority of biblical faith.

The attempt to remove skepticism from philosophy had proved an utter failure. The project to infinitely enhance the power of reason over human life had culminated in the fact-value distinction, and the complete destruction of reason as a guide to human life. Both the Bible and Socratic philosophy provided a firm basis for moral choices, and the moral choices they endorsed were substantially the same. Whether the ultimate reason for choosing the moral virtues was obedient love of the living God, or the goodness of the life of autonomous reason, was less important than their agreement upon the moral order which must inform the life of decent society. From this perspective Revelation and Reason, Jerusalem and Athens, were in agreement. For this reason Strauss was committed no less to the defense of Jerusalem than of Athens. For this reason, it would have been imprudent of him to allow his own preferences to weaken the case for either of these cities, or the principles they represented.

The moral and political harmony of Revelation and Reason is reflected in the Declaration of Independence, in which rational moral truths, the truths of "the laws of nature and of nature's God," are enshrined within the order of Creation. Strauss was keenly aware, however, as were the American Founders, that those who had falsely claimed the authority either of reason or of revelation, as the basis of political authority, had done so in the interest of despotism. The absolutised claims of faith, stigmatizing opposition as heresy, supported the union of altar and throne, and the Inquisition. Modern rationalism, dismissing biblical faith as superstition, had led to the regimes of the Jacobins, the Bolsheviks, and the Nazis. Neither classical rationalism, nor genuine faith in a living God would claim political power in its own right. The true constitutional regime, shaped by the wisdom both of revelation and reason, formed the character of the citizens by the free and uncoerced dissemination of opinion.

Notwithstanding the foregoing, Strauss seems on occasion to have written to the contrary. The dialectical confrontation on page 75 of *Natural Right and History* ends with the assertion that "The mere fact that philosophy and revelation cannot refute each other would constitute the refutation of philosophy by revelation." However, in his autobiographical preface he remarks that "Jewish orthodoxy based its claim to superiority to other religions from the beginning on its superior rationality (Deut. 4:6)." In the passage in question, Moses tells the children of Israel that if they keep the laws that he has set before them, the nations which shall hear these laws will say "Surely this great nation is a wise and understanding people." In citing this, Strauss seems to impute to the Bible something like the doctrine of the Meno, that learning is recollection, and that the recognition of wisdom is a human potentiality common to all nations. The suggestion here, however slender, is that the Bible is a Platonic book, and that reason is the esoteric foundation of revelation. In the introduction to *The City and Man* (1964), however, his remarks on this theme seem to point to the priority of revelation.

> It is not sufficient for everyone to obey and to listen to the Divine message of the City of Righteousness, the Faithful City. In order to propagate that message among the heathen, nay, in order to understand it as clearly and as fully as is humanly possible, one must also consider to what extent man could discern the outlines of that City if left to himself, to the proper exercise of his own powers. But in our age it is much less urgent to show that political philosophy is the indis-

> pensable hand maid of theology than to show that political philosophy is the rightful queen of the social sciences, the sciences of man and human affairs: even the highest lawcourt in the land is more likely to defer to the contentions of social science than to the Ten Commandments as the words of the living God.

Strauss—addressing the "crisis of the West"—says that it is not sufficient to "obey and listen to the Divine message of the City of Righteousness, the Faithful City." (The capitals are Strauss's.) But what is not sufficient may nonetheless be necessary. Strauss will undertake to show "to what extent man could discern the outlines of that City if left to himself," i.e., without revelation. The purpose in so doing however is, to repeat, "to propagate that message—viz., "the Divine message of the City of Righteousness, the Faithful City"—among the heathen. I do not recall Strauss speaking elsewhere of "heathen." What is most remarkable however is that the City whose outlines are sought by man's unaided powers, and which we want to understand as clearly and fully as is humanly possible is the Faithful City. Jerusalem and Athens seem to have become one.

This appears to be confirmed by Strauss's saying that it is less urgent—but nonetheless urgent—to show that political philosophy is the indispensable handmaid of theology. The reason it is less urgent than it otherwise would be is that "even the highest lawcourt in the land is more likely to defer to the contentions of social science than to the Ten Commandments as the words of the living God." Strauss is clearly referring to Warren's opinion for the Court in *Brown v. Board of Education*, the 1954 decision declaring school segregation to be unconstitutional. In that opinion Warren abandoned any attempt to ground his reading of the equal protection clause of the fourteenth amendment on the intent of its framers and ratifiers, preferring instead what he said modern psychology told us was the effect of segregation upon the "minds and hearts" of Negro children. His authority was Kenneth Clark's doll tests, which Thurgood Marshall, the attorney for the NAACP, had brought to his attention. But the aforesaid tests did not actually prove what they were said to prove, and it is unlikely that Warren (or his fellow justices) even knew what they were. Warren seized upon them because they constituted a license to disregard the genuine meaning of the equal protection clause. The "contentions of science" were nothing but a cynical device by which the Court could emancipate itself from the restraints of the Constitution. The original meaning of the equal protection clause had been embodied in Justice Harlan's dissenting opinion in *Plessy* (1898), the case that had enshrined "separate but equal" in constitutional law. Harlan had declared that the Constitution was colorblind, and did not recognize different classes of citizens. Harlan's opinion, which should have been the opinion of the Court in *Brown*, was clearly based upon the proposition that all men are created equal. The actual alternative to the "contentions of social science" was therefore the Declaration of Independence, and the Creator and author of "the laws of nature and of nature's God." To re-establish the authority of political philosophy as the architectonic social science meant therefore to reestablish both the natural and divine foundation of American constitutionalism. Clearly the crisis of the West could not be resolved apart from its biblical foundations interpreted by the *kalam* of political philosophy.

In the essay "What Is Liberal Education?" Strauss addresses the crisis of the West from the difference between mass democracy and "democracy as originally meant." For Jefferson, democracy was intended to provide more effectually than any other form of government for "a pure selection of [the] natural *aristoi* into the offices of government." Without liberal education, the natural *aristoi* have themselves become debased. The liberal education which was the ground of the Founding was supremely expressed in the Declaration of Independence, and in the harmony of reason and revelation, in the support of the moral and political order.

Strauss concludes that essay with something that more nearly approaches a confession of faith, than anything in any other writing of which I am aware. It is an appeal to experience, the experience which accompanies the act of understanding, when we not only understand, but understand that we understand. This "*noesis noeseos*" is "so high, so pure, so noble an experience that Aristotle could ascribe it to his God." Strauss continued:

> This experience is entirely independent of whether what we understand primarily is pleasing or displeasing, fair or ugly. It leads us to realize that all evils are in a sense necessary if there is to be understanding. It enables us to accept all evils that befall us and which may well break our hearts in the spirit of good citizens of the city of God. By becoming aware of the dignity of the mind, we realize the true ground of the dignity of man and therewith of the goodness of the world, whether we understand it as created or untreated, which is the home of man because it is the home of the human mind.

We are invited, on the basis of an experience available to man as man, to become "good citizens of the city of God." The realization of the dignity of man is independent of whether we understand the world to be "created or untreated." Strauss says nothing here of the necessity to choose between these two opinions. The crisis of the West does not require us to make such a choice, and we do not know that Strauss himself ever made it. What it does require is to recognize the authority of the moral order based upon the dignity of man, supported both by reason and revelation. To secure that recognition was, I believe, the essential purpose of Leo Strauss's life and work.

NOTES

Originally published at claremont.org, May, 14, 2003.

1. See Harry V. Jaffa, "The Unity of Tragedy, Comedy, and History: An Interpretation of the Shakespearean Universe," *Shakespeare As Political Thinker*, ed. John E. Alvis and Thomas G. West (Wilmington, DE: ISI Books, 2000); "Macbeth and the Moral Universe," *Claremont Review of Books*, Volume VIII, No. 1 (Winter 2007).

SIXTEEN

Moral Order in the Western Tradition

Harry Jaffa's Grand Synthesis of Athens, Jerusalem, and Peoria

Robert P. Kraynak

Abstract: Harry V. Jaffa has inspired a generation of students in American political thought by defending the natural rights principles of the Declaration of Independence and of Abraham Lincoln. Jaffa is also a defender of Leo Strauss's idea of a "political science of natural right," which Strauss drew primarily from classical Greek political philosophy. Jaffa's efforts to defend the several strands of the Western natural right tradition led him to develop a grand synthesis of "Athens, Jerusalem, and Peoria," which I argue is a noble but untenable way of upholding the moral order of the West—and a departure from the intentions of Leo Strauss.

> The crisis of the West [requires us] to recognize the authority of the moral order based upon the dignity of man, supported both by reason and revelation. To secure that recognition was, I believe, the essential purpose of Leo Strauss's life and work.
>
> —Harry V. Jaffa, "Strauss at 100" (2003)

Harry V. Jaffa is one of the great teachers of political philosophy in our times who has inspired a generation of students in the field of American political thought. As might be expected, the students bear the stamp of the teacher, which means you can always tell a Jaffa student when you see one because he or she has a glow of moral earnestness that is impossible to ignore.

The immediate cause of the moral earnestness is easy to identify: Jaffa takes the natural rights principles of the Declaration of Independence more seriously than any other scholar I have encountered, and he has sought to revive those principles as the living creed of the American republic. As a teacher, Jaffa breathes into his students the sacred fire of the Declaration and its two great interpreters, Thomas Jefferson and Abraham Lincoln; and he instills in his followers a deep reverence for the American Founding and the Union's cause during the Civil War. Lest anyone be mistaken about his intentions, Jaffa ends his latest book, *A New Birth of Freedom*, with a battle cry for all chivalrous knights of the Lincoln brigades: "We must then take up the weapons of truth and go forth to battle once again for the cause of Father Abraham, of Union, and of Freedom, as in the olden time."[1] One can almost hear "The Battle Hymn of the Republic" sounding in the background as Jaffa moves the reader to take up a moral crusade on behalf of natural rights republicanism.

While it is easy to see why Jaffa is an inspirational teacher, it is more difficult to explain how Jaffa arrived at his moral crusade on behalf of Lincoln and the Declaration. After all, Jaffa cites Leo Strauss as the most powerful influence on his thinking—as the scholar who changed his life.[2] Yet, it is difficult to find in Strauss's writings the words and tune of the "Battle Hymn of the Republic," even though Jaffa insists that he is following the lead of Leo Strauss and fulfilling Strauss's intentions. Jaffa's relation to Strauss is, therefore, a puzzle which I shall investigate in order to shed light on Jaffa's contribution to the Straussian legacy and to the natural rights philosophy of America and the Western tradition.[3]

My principal argument is that Jaffa's intellectual career is marked by continuity and change that is both faithful and unfaithful to Leo Strauss. The element of continuity is the lifelong effort to meet the challenge of Strauss's book *Natural Right and History* by defending principles of natural right against the moral relativism or nihilism that Strauss equated with the "crisis of the West." One can see that Strauss's book gave Jaffa a mission to save the West (and possibly the world) by coming up with a philosophically defensible argument for natural right—understood as a rational standard of right and wrong that is universal and timeless because it is grounded in nature or human nature; such an argument would give Western nations an objective basis for the truth of their convictions instead of viewing them as arbitrary opinions or mere historical prescriptions. Jaffa accepted the challenge of developing a "political science of natural right" as his greatest intellectual ambition and worked on several strategies in his career.[4]

What I shall also argue is that, in the course of development, Jaffa changed strategies by moving from a defense of classical natural right—chiefly Aristotle's version—to a defense of modern natural rights—chiefly, the principles of the Declaration of Independence—and that the change led Jaffa to depart from Strauss's thought. In his first book, *Thom-*

ism and Aristotelianism, Jaffa sought to recover Aristotle's teaching as a possible solution to the nihilism of modern value-free social science. The thrust of that book was in accordance with Strauss's thought because it sought to separate the pagan Aristotle from the Christianized Aristotelianism of Thomas Aquinas—a reflection of Strauss's view of the irreducible tensions in the Western tradition between reason and revelation. But Jaffa never decisively vindicated Aristotle, mainly, one suspects, because of philosophical difficulties with Aristotelian natural right.

Jaffa's response was to shift his focus from classical natural right to the American Founding in order to develop an argument for the natural rights doctrine of the Declaration of Independence. The key to the new strategy was the claim that he did not have to abandon Aristotle or Aquinas in order to vindicate American principles because a common vision of "moral order" exists in the three main elements of the Western tradition (represented by three cities)—in classical Greek philosophy (Athens), in biblical revelation (Jerusalem), and in the modern natural rights doctrine of the American Founders as interpreted by Abraham Lincoln (Peoria). Interestingly, Jaffa also argues that the moral order of the West could be vindicated without definitively resolving ultimate theoretical questions and that this practical solution was a fulfillment of Strauss's intention. The problem, I will conclude, is that Jaffa's efforts at harmonizing the main elements of Western civilization go against Strauss's emphasis on their irreducible tensions, which means Jaffa's vision of moral order rests on a false synthesis of disparate elements that are best left in their original forms.

THE EARLY JAFFA: THOMAS VS. ARISTOTLE

Jaffa's first book, *Thomism and Aristotelianism,* was published in 1952 and bears the influence of Leo Strauss in theme and format.[5] The introduction describes the motive for the book as a concern for the lack of rational foundations for contemporary social and political science due to the influence of positivism and historicism. Jaffa's study is an early statement of Strauss's thesis in *Natural Right and History,* which criticizes modern social science for being value-free—unable to pronounce rational judgments about morality (right and wrong, good and evil, justice and injustice) because it holds that only facts are objective, values are subjective. Commenting on the danger as well as untenability of this stance, Jaffa says that we need a comprehensive review of political science, including a reconsideration of its classical formulation by Aristotle.

Jaffa further observes that Aristotle's ethics and politics are currently taken seriously as sources of truth only in the natural law doctrines of the Roman Catholic Church. Catholic natural law is the last serious source of Aristotelian philosophy because Catholicism holds St. Thomas Aquinas as the greatest doctor of the Church and, of course, "Thomas is the disciple of Aristotle and recognizes his authority as paramount" (6). Therefore, Thomism and neo-Thomism are the primary means for a living encounter with Aristotelian political science and for investigating the possibility that it might be the true teaching, once and for all times. If it were the true teaching, then a rational response to the value-free nihilism of modern social science could be found in Aristotle.

One wonders why Jaffa did not simply undertake a direct study of Aristotle's texts to determine their truth or falsity, since Jaffa states that "our primary concern is with Aristotle, and our concern with Thomas is due to his great prestige as an interpreter of Aristotle" (161). Following this indirect approach, Jaffa poses the central question of his study: Is Thomas Aquinas an accurate and impartial interpreter of Aristotle, or does Thomas give us an Aristotle that has been altered or distorted by Christian faith? This question drives Jaffa's book: "We must face the responsibility of determining to what extent the moral and political, as well as the theoretical philosophies of Aristotle and Thomas are in fact the same, and to what extent they are different. And if . . . different, it is necessary to discover the principles underlying those divergences" (7–8). Jaffa is aware that this question is not original to him or to Strauss. In a postscript, he commends the Jesuit scholar Frederick Copleston for offering a similar analysis of Thomas Aquinas in *A History of Philosophy* that includes a critical evaluation of the "latent tensions in the Thomist synthesis."[6]

Nevertheless, Jaffa takes an original approach that highlights the difficulty of synthesizing Greek philosophy and biblical revelation. He has learned from Strauss the meticulous art of close textual analysis and has chosen Thomas Aquinas's Commentary on Aristotle's *Nichomachean Ethics* and Commentary on Aristotle's *Politics* as the primary means for developing his thesis rather than the usual work, the *Summa Theologiae*. This approach is demanding but rewarding because it allows Jaffa to untangle the original, pagan Aristotle from the Christianized Aristotle of Thomas. At the risk of oversimplifying Jaffa's subtle argument, I will summarize its main findings in three points.

The first point concerns Aristotle's method. Jaffa argues that Aquinas seeks to give a faithful summary of Aristotle's *Ethics* but actually gives the book an order or structure that is more rigid and more theoretical than the original Aristotle. According to Jaffa, Aristotle's argument develops by ascending from lower to higher rungs on the ladder of perfection—as seen, for example, in the overall movement in the text from the moral virtues to the intellectual virtues (an ascent from lower to higher ends); in the movement within the eleven moral virtues from courage, the lowest, to justice, the highest virtue; and in Aristotle's revision of his views on such topics as the relation of pleasure to happiness. In other words, Jaffa views Aristotle's method of reasoning as dialectical—as an ongoing argument that revises prior judgments as it proceeds from lower to higher ends—and he criticizes Thomas for obscuring this crucial feature of Aristotle's method: "Thomas's conception of the 'design' of the *Ethics* is rather of an architectural structure than an organism . . . [I]t does not imply any notion of growth or ascent in the elaboration of Aristotle's moral doctrine" (48–49).

Although Jaffa does not fully elaborate the significance of his criticism, he seems to think that Aquinas does not give full credit to Aristotle for writing a work of practical science. Thomas turns Aristotle's *Ethics* into a work of theoretical science by failing to acknowledge that Aristotle derives his ethical judgments from a dialectical analysis of what is commonly praised and blamed or what is called noble and base by discerning people in order to discover "the common element of truth in all common opinions or . . . in the most authoritative [opinions]" (90). Thomas also sees Aristotle deducing morality from theoretical notions about the human species—for example, that man is a rational animal—that are derived from metaphysics and physics rather than from common opinions (24–25, 79). According to Jaffa, Thomas is led thereby to a more exact and categorical view of moral virtue than Aristotle. Thomas demands virtuous behavior even in extreme situations, where the rules of morality might be suspended or extenuated out of necessity by most people: "Aristotle clearly indicates that it is impossible to say, in the abstract, whether a man ought or ought not to be pardoned for doing the basest deeds to save his family . . . in his view, no simply true general statement can be made on this question. [But] Thomas says unequivocally of the brave man that he will obey the dictates of reason in the face of any terror, however great" (109). Jaffa's conclusion is that while Aristotle stays within the horizon of practical experience, Thomas "presupposes knowledge of the virtues through a natural habit of understanding loosely called conscience or more exactly synderesis . . . [and Thomas] unjustifiably imputes to Aristotle his own view" (114–115). In respect to method, then, Thomas modifies Aristotle by giving the Greek philosopher a Christian "spin" (attributing a stricter approach to morality than prudence requires) that Jaffa finds unjustified.

The second major point of Jaffa's study concerns the content of virtue, especially the tension between pagan pride and Christian humility. Jaffa begins his book with an epigraph from Winston Churchill: "It is baffling to reflect that what men call honor does not always correspond to Christian ethics." Jaffa uses this thought to highlight the main challenge of incorporating Aristotelian ethics into a Christian framework. In a subtle and complex analysis, Jaffa shows that the tension between pagan pride and Christian humility drives Thomas to soften the edges of magnanimity—the virtue most concerned with honor and pride—and to diminish the difference between the horizon of morality (or of practical action) and the horizon of philosophy in Aristotle.

As Jaffa shows, the notion of what is honorable is used by Aristotle to give a rough indication of moral virtue, following the common opinions of praise and blame in political life. This culminates in Aristotle's teaching about magnanimity—the crown of the personal virtues, a kind of proper pride in which one who is truly great demands the highest honors and actually deserves them, usually for being the greatest benefactor to his country by founding the nation or by saving it during times of war and crisis. It was exemplified in England by Marlborough and Churchill and in America by Washington and Lincoln (129). How does Thomas treat magnanimity in his commentary on Aristotle, given its obvious tensions with Christian ethics?

In Jaffa's view, Thomas may have aimed at expounding Aristotle in his own terms, but Thomas also felt a need to save magnanimity from some of the harsher, unchristian features of pagan pride—such as disdain for inferiors, a tendency to be ungrateful for favors, the insistence on being the superior one, and illusions of godlike self-sufficiency. In order to soften these features, Thomas portrays the magnanimous man in more benevolent and moral terms than Aristotle does—as someone who does not choose to forget favors and as someone, in Thomas's words, whose "whole attention is taken up with the goods of the community and God."[7] According to Jaffa, Thomas portrays magnanimity as the dutiful service of a high-minded public servant rather than the glory-seeking of an obsessive egoist.

In elaborating this interpretation, however, Jaffa is led to a curious paradox. He claims that Thomas sees magnanimity as the highest form of moral behavior and tries to hide its deficiencies, whereas Aristotle describes the magnanimous man as he really is—possessing certain illusions about his own self-sufficiency that enable him to perform great deeds (31–33). Aristotle, in other words, gingerly protects the pride of the magnanimous man from the insights of philosophy that might puncture his illusions of self-sufficiency—implying a depreciation of morality in favor of philosophy and indicating that Aristotle actually has a lower view of magnanimity than Thomas does. In Jaffa's words, "Aristotle intends to portray magnanimity . . . within the moral horizon alone" (141), even though Aristotle clearly teaches at the end of the *Ethics* that "there is something greater than the virtue of the magnanimous man" (138), namely, the intellectual virtue of the philosopher. While Aristotle tries to be faithful to the moral horizon upon which men act, Thomas "repeatedly qualif[ies] Aristotle's description of the magnanimous man in order to 'save' his character in accordance with . . . a higher standard of perfection" and, in so doing, "mistakes Aristotle's intention" (141). The lesson for Jaffa is that Thomas gives us a moralistic Aristotle that fails to appreciate the nobility of pagan pride as well as the radical, amoral detachment of pagan philosophy.

The third major point of Jaffa's study concerns natural right and natural law. This issue is the culmination of the book because it demonstrates most clearly the difference between Thomas's effort to harmonize Greek philosophy with Christian revelation and Jaffa's effort to separate the two. Here again, the issue turns on a subtle analysis of Aristotle's text—the notoriously difficult passage on justice in the *Ethics* (bk. 5, sec. 7) where Aristotle says that natural right is both unchangeable and changeable. Specifically, Aristotle says, on the one hand, that "natural right is that which has the same force (*dunamin* = dynamism, potentiality) everywhere and is not affected by what men think" because "what is by nature is unchangeable (*akineton* = not moveable)" and, on the other hand, "with us [humans], there is something natural and this is changeable (*kineton* = moveable)"; for example "by nature the right hand is stronger (*kreitton* = physically stronger), although it is possible for any man to become ambidextrous" and the form of government is variable but "one form is best everywhere by nature." The obvious problem is Aristotle's seemingly contradictory claims about the unchangeability and changeability of natural right.

According to Jaffa, the ambivalence about natural right in the *Ethics* reflects Aristotle's view of the weakness of justice as a force in human affairs: justice may be a universal aspiration, and one form of government may be the best everywhere; but human nature is lacking in active agency that directs the human soul to virtue, and human beings lack an innate sense of right and wrong that gives them clear, natural knowledge of virtue (175). The relative weakness of justice reminds Jaffa of Aristotle's statement in the *Ethics* (bk.3, sec. 1) that moral virtue is a habit (something acquired by training) rather than something naturally imprinted on the human soul. Jaffa is also fond of quoting Aristotle's statement in the *Ethics* (bk. 10, sec. 9) that most people "'have not even a conception of what is noble and truly pleasant'" (177) because it reveals Aristotle's sense of the weakness of natural knowledge of justice.

While not claiming to explain fully Aristotle's complex views on natural right, Jaffa offers the following interpretation. On the one hand, Aristotle teaches that natural right is unchangeable or immutable because the best regime for all human beings (everywhere and always) is the rule of the wise and the virtuous. On the other hand, the best regime is only imperfectly realized in most cities and nations, so natural right is actually part of political right and is subject to change because "natural right enjoins obedience to any legal justice which may reasonably be said to aim at the common good . . . [hence] the mutability of natural right follows . . . the mutability of constitutions"(182).

Jaffa thinks Thomas misses the crucial point about the weakness of natural right as a force in the human soul and thereby turns Aristotelian natural right into something stronger—into Christian natural law, according to which morality is written on the human heart by a lawgiver

(God) who gives human beings "a natural habit" of moral knowledge and even a natural inclination to virtue. In Jaffa's words, "Thomas apparently takes Aristotle's statement, to the effect that what is naturally right or just does not depend on opinion, as an outright endorsement of his own doctrine that there is a natural habit of the understanding by which *we know* what is, in principle, right and wrong according to nature" (175, Jaffa's emphasis).

At the end of his book, Jaffa attributes Thomas's mistake to the Christian belief that morality is supported by "divine particular providence," "personal immortality," and "a divinely implanted 'natural' habit of moral principles"—a belief that leads Thomas to "impute non-Aristotelian principles to Aristotle" (187).[8] Jaffa concludes, then, that Thomas is an unreliable guide to Aristotle and that "[Thomas's] assumption as to the harmony of natural and revealed doctrine is entirely unwarranted" (187). In sum, Jaffa has shown that "nature elevated by grace is different from nature simply" and that "reason 'informed' by faith is different from reason simply" (200n.20).

The major disappointment for a reader of Jaffa's book is that, after separating the original Aristotle from Thomism, Jaffa makes no judgment at all as to whether Aristotle's teaching is the truth about natural right. As a result, Jaffa never answers the question he posed at the beginning of his book: whether Aristotelian political science could be resurrected as a rational alternative to the nihilism of today's value-free social science. As far as I can tell, Jaffa leaves the question open, while actually exposing two serious problems with Aristotle that he does not resolve—namely, the changeability of natural right and the relation between practical and theoretical science in Aristotle's *Ethics*. The changeability of natural right implies uncertainty about the power of justice in human affairs and raises doubts about the moral order of nature and society that Jaffa leaves unresolved. Concerning the relation of practice and theory, Jaffa seems to concede a point to Thomas Aquinas: the status of ethics as a practical science remains in doubt because the practically wise man (the phronimos) depends on the theoretically wise man (the sophos) for knowing the truth about human happiness. Practical wisdom does not stand entirely on its own ground because it glimpses the limited and secondary nature of happiness in moral and political life, while pointing toward the supreme happiness of the philosopher who contemplates the eternal things (186). Whether the moral realm is subverted by these insights is left unanswered by Jaffa, and the difficulty may well be the spur that drove him to find stronger foundations for natural right and moral order in modern doctrines.

JAFFA'S TURN TO THE DECLARATION OF INDEPENDENCE

After completing *Thomism and Aristotelianism* in 1952, Jaffa turned to the study of the Lincoln-Douglas debates and began working on the book that became his bestseller, *Crisis of the House Divided* (first published in 1959, reprinted in 1973 and 1982).[9] In the preface to the third edition, Jaffa says his study of Lincoln was motivated by Leo Strauss's challenge of finding a "political science of natural right" as an alternative to the relativism of modern social science. But Jaffa now equates natural right with the inalienable rights of the Declaration of Independence based on the "laws of nature and of nature's God" that inspired the American Founders and Lincoln. Henceforth, natural right for Jaffa means the principles of the Declaration of Independence rather than those of Aristotle's *Ethics*.

But a surprising thought accompanies the change: Aristotle does not have to be abandoned because, in some sense, Aristotle is on the same plane as Locke, Jefferson, and Lincoln. In the third preface to *Crisis*, Jaffa says explicitly that his work is inspired by Strauss's recovery of classical natural right (also called "Socratic natural right"), which includes not only natural right but also prudence and rhetoric—prudence (phronesis) in adapting general principles to particular historical circumstances and rhetoric for making those principles persuasive to people. Thus, classical Greek philosophy remains the philosophical foundation for natural right, but the content is now the Declaration's principles of inalienable natural rights and the equality of all men, expressed above all in the speeches and statesmanship of Abraham Lincoln. How could Jaffa make this shift?

I cannot say for sure what prompted Jaffa to make the change, given Strauss's teaching about the difference between ancients and moderns—the difference between classical natural right (requiring virtue and an aristocratic regime of virtuous rulers) and modern natural rights (requiring freedom and a democratic regime of equality based on the consent of the people). Strauss, of course, indicates points of continuity between ancients and moderns: both claimed reason could discover principles of justice and morality in human nature. Even as great a critic of Aristotle as Hobbes "was indebted to the tradition for a single, but momentous, idea: he accepted on trust the view that political philosophy or political science is possible or necessary."[10] But on crucial issues such as the primacy of the contemplative or theoretical life, the teleological view of nature, the priority of virtue over freedom, and the awareness of eternity in political life, Strauss presents powerful criticisms of modern political philosophy in *Natural Right and History* for rejecting classical philosophy, which led him to state explicitly that "Nothing that I have learned has shaken my inclination to prefer 'natural right,' especially in its classic form, to the reigning relativism, positivist or historicist."[11]

Given Strauss's distinction between ancients and moderns and his clear preference for the ancients over the moderns, Jaffa's turn to a synthesis of the two perspectives and Jaffa's tilt toward modern natural rights principles in the Declaration of Independence appear to be a departure from Strauss. It is a departure that Jaffa never justifies fully, leaving one to speculate about the reasons. My guess is that Jaffa was led to the synthesis partly by his authentic efforts to understand Abraham Lincoln, whose soaring ambition for honor and glory appeared to Jaffa to be an example of Aristotle's magnanimity but whose political principles were republican and American, making Lincoln a kind of classical statesman promoting a modern regime of natural rights republicanism.[12] Using hindsight to explain his new emphasis on America, Jaffa also has written that combining Aristotle and Locke was possible and necessary because the American Founding included both: "the Founding, which Lincoln inherited, was dominated by an Aristotelian Locke—or a Lockean Aristotle." Yet, Jaffa apparently seeks more than historical accuracy, because he claims that Aristotle himself would have been a Lockean natural rights philosopher if Aristotle were alive in the seventeenth and eighteenth centuries of the Christian era: "[If] Aristotle [had] been called upon, in the latter half of the seventeenth century, to write a guidebook for constitution makers, he would have written something very closely approximating Locke's *Second Treatise*." Jaffa's hypothetical suggestion is that if Aristotle had faced the tyranny of divine right kingship and the sectarian wars of Christianity, "he would have recognized those differences from his *Politics* that prudential wisdom required" and adapted his teaching to modern circumstances by advocating freedom and limited government over a regime of virtue.[13]

Here we see the new Jaffa, a Straussian scholar who begins moving away from Strauss's emphasis on the irreconcilable differences among elements of the Western tradition to becoming a scholar who seeks to synthesize (even to equate) the thinking of Plato, Aristotle, Maimonides, Aquinas, Locke, Jefferson, Lincoln, and Shakespeare as bearers of a common conception of "moral order" that not only saves the West from nihilism but elevates the Declaration and the American republic to the best regime possible.[14]

The primary argument that Jaffa develops is that a common ground for moral order can be found in the notion of human dignity—in the claim that the "essence" or "nature" of man really exists and has moral significance because man is the rational animal with a rational soul that must be respected in any just or legitimate regime. For Jaffa, the dignity of man as rational animal is an objectively true and philosophically defensible proposition that supports the moral order of classical, medieval, and modern natural right. It enables Jaffa to develop a synthesis of classical (Socratic and Aristotelian), medieval (Thomistic), and modern (Lockean, Jeffersonian, Lincolnian) principles and to find the highest expression of human dignity in the God-given natural rights of the Declaration of Independence and especially in Lincoln's 1854 Peoria speech which enunciates the "ancient faith" of the Declaration as the essential humanity of all people, equality of rights, and government by consent of the governed.

The evidence for Jaffa's turn toward a grand synthesis appears first in a short essay entitled, "In Defense of the 'Natural Law Thesis,'" published in 1957.[15] This relatively unnoticed but important article is the only sustained effort in Jaffa's corpus to offer in his own name a theoretical defense of natural right or natural law against its critics. The specific purpose of the article is to refute the skeptical attack on natural law by Felix Oppenheim, a prominent value-free social scientist of the 1950s, who adheres to the fact-value distinction and denies the rational basis for objective norms of morality, including the natural right of Plato and of Aristotle and the natural rights of the Declaration of Independence.

Jaffa contends that the fact-value distinction is untenable because it inconsistently affirms scientific knowledge of facts while denying rational knowledge of values. Yet, Jaffa claims, if facts about the world can be known, then values also can be known with some degree of certainty because both have the same premise: the real existence of the external world of nature. Jaffa's reasoning is that we assume the existence of the external world in all our actions and thoughts, even though there is no definitive way of proving theoretically that this is a fact and not an illusion. It follows that, if we cannot deny the reality of the external world, we also cannot deny the real existence of a man or human being. Arguing like a Platonic-Aristotelian philosopher, Jaffa then says that, just as we perceive the existence of "this chair" by intuiting the universal idea of "chairness," so we perceive the existence of "this man" by intuiting the universal idea of "man" or "humanity" whose distinctive feature is to be a rational animal with intelligence: "While plants and animals . . . [can] be conceived as forms that are epiphenomena of some more fundamental subhuman reality, man cannot be so conceived. Intelligence cannot be regarded as the by-product of unintelligence . . . [for] the doctrine of an unintelligent primary reality, being itself a product of man's brain, would also have to be regarded as an illusion. . . . Intelligence is [therefore] an irreducible reality" (200–201).

Following this logic, Jaffa argues that natural law or natural right is real (not an illusion) because man as a rational, intelligent being is an irreducible fact with value implications: man's rational nature implies a standard of perfection, and the perfection of our rational nature includes the idea of justice. Human nature, therefore, provides a ground for universal norms of justice, which is the premise of natural law. Interestingly, Jaffa argues like an Aristotelian against Oppenheim, concluding that Aristotle's universal norm is the happiness of the virtuous man whose perfection of reason gives him an ordered soul in which the rational part rules over the irrational part. Jaffa also says that man's nature as a rational animal supports the existence of "the laws of nature and of nature's God" proclaimed in the Declaration of Independence (190, 205 n. 2). Herein lies the metaphysical basis of natural right—the dignity of man as rational animal—that supplies the ground for moral order in Jaffa's account of the Western tradition.

With this proposition more or less settled in the late 1950s as the foundation for natural right, Jaffa moved to his grand project of vindicating the principles of the Declaration of Independence laid down by the American Founders and reinterpreted by Lincoln. Jaffa's plan in 1958 was to write two volumes: one, a historical study of the Lincoln-Douglas debates showing that they were a genuine debate about the natural rights principles of the American regime, entitled *Crisis of the House Divided*; the second volume, to be called *A New Birth of Freedom*, would be a more ambitious book in which Jaffa attempts to vindicate philosophically (as opposed to recovering historically) the natural rights principles of Jefferson and Lincoln. The two books would complement each other and have the same overarching theme: a dramatic duel between objective truth versus relativism or nihilism, following the paradigm of Strauss's *Natural Right and History* in which natural right is pitted against the relativism of value-free positivism and historicism. This paradigm remained for Jaffa the basis of his entire intellectual career—a series of writings in which all the heroes are proponents of natural right (Socrates, Aristotle, Aquinas, Locke, Jefferson, Lincoln, and Shakespeare),[16] and all the villains are relativists of one kind or another (Thrasymachus, Douglas, Calhoun, revisionist historians such as Carl Becker, and even Supreme Court Justices Rehnquist and Scalia). Let us examine Jaffa's two books to see how the battle for moral order unfolds.

In *Crisis of the House Divided*, Jaffa argues that the Lincoln-Douglas debates were expressions of statesmanship at the highest level because they focused on two principled visions of American democracy: Stephen A. Douglas's vision of "popular sovereignty" in which the people rule without being bound by a higher law of natural right versus Abraham Lincoln's vision of "republican self-government" in which the people rule in accordance with the higher law of the Declaration and its God-given natural rights.

In defending this interpretation of the Lincoln-Douglas debates, Jaffa takes on revisionist historians like Richard Hofstadter who diminish the whole debate by portraying the protagonists as nothing more than ambitious opportunists who merely paid lip service to moral principles. In the revisionist view, Douglas is a racist demagogue who exploited "popular sovereignty" to gain power by holding together the northern and southern factions of the Democratic Party; Lincoln is an ambitious politician who exploited the "myth of the self-made man" to appeal to the prejudices of the white, lower-middle classes and referred to the equality of the Declaration without believing it.[17] Jaffa also writes against the value-free social scientists who do not think that recovering a debate over first principles is important for the American republic. Against this viewpoint, Jaffa writes, "As far as I know, *Crisis of the House Divided* is the first book to take seriously the question of whether the laws of nature mentioned in the Declaration did in fact exist, and therefore whether Lincoln or Douglas was correct in asserting that his policy . . . squared with the teaching of the Declaration" (intro., 10–11; 21–26; 364). The power of Jaffa's study comes from its Straussian approach of taking seriously debates about the truth or falsity of natural right because the moral order and legitimacy of the American regime are at stake.

Following this approach, Jaffa makes the debates between Lincoln and Douglas come alive today by showing how each man sought to define the first principles of the American regime. Surprisingly, Jaffa initially creates a curious reversal of sympathies for modern readers—a reversal that perplexes people today (as I discovered when I began teaching Jaffa's book in my own college courses). Contemporary students invariably feel that Jaffa's "case for Douglas" is stronger than they expected because Douglas's principle of popular sovereignty sounds a lot like today's "multiculturalism" or "diversity": it allows local majorities in different states or regions to choose their own laws and culture without requiring one uniform set of moral principles to be imposed on the whole nation in the name of higher law. Douglas tolerates diversity among Northern, Southern, and Western regions; among industrial, agrarian, and ranching economies; and among free, slave, and mixed societies. Douglas also comes across as the noninterventionist who seeks to avoid civil war by letting people do what they want, claiming that this was what the American Founders intended when they compromised with slavery. Douglas seems opposed to the attitude of self-righteous superiority that leads to violent conflict among different visions of the good life and prefers instead to "live and let live" by fostering a loosely organized federation of states that would stretch from the Atlantic to the Pacific and even include Mexico (if it wished to join the United States) in a large, diverse, decentralized, hemispheric republic tied together by a minimal consensus about the U. S. Constitution's rules for procedural democracy (41–103). Douglas's America, Jaffa shows, is based on the appeal of moral relativism, as is today's multiculturalism, because it avoids standards of judgment according to a higher moral law and promises peaceful "nonjudgmentalism"—a policy of "don't care" that allows slavery to be voted up or down in any state, if that is what the people want. As such, Douglas's America is the ultimate expression of populist democracy.

By contrast, Lincoln believed that the true meaning of American democracy is "republican self-government" based on the higher moral law of natural right. As Jaffa shows, Lincoln was a moral absolutist who believed everyone in America finally had to accept the truth of the Declaration and its insistence on the God-given natural rights and equality of all human beings. In his famous "House Divided" speech (1858), Lincoln boldly asserts that America must become entirely slave or entirely free: there can be no compromise with regional diversity, no acceptance of the "don't care" attitude of popular sovereignty and state's rights. To be sure, Jaffa insists that Lincoln was pushed into this position by a conspiracy to nationalize slavery by the likes of Taney, Douglas, Pierce, and Buchanan—an alliance by "preconcert" of all three branches of government working together to extend slavery from the South to the West and eventually to reintroduce slavery into the free states of the North. Jaffa makes us aware that Lincoln understood the fateful consequence of saying the nation could not be divided and that all Americans eventually had to accept one abstract truth about first principles: the fateful consequence was the possibility of civil war (276–301).

According to Jaffa, Lincoln understood and was willing to accept the consequences because he had a lifelong ambition to save the American republic through a creative "re-founding" that would bring Lincoln greater glory than Washington. Using Lincoln's early Lyceum Address (1838), Jaffa argues that the young Lincoln showed signs of heroic greatness—an awareness of Aristotle's virtue of magnanimity—in his references to a towering genius of Napoleonic ambition whose passion for glory could be satisfied by either saving or destroying the Republic. Lincoln chose the constructive course of saving the Republic because he cared about the dignity of man—he believed that the American experiment was a test of "the capability of a people to govern themselves" and this, in turn, was a test of human dignity, a test of whether human beings were destined to be children, subjects, or slaves needing masters and authoritarian father figures to control them or whether they could be free, responsible, rational adults with the capacity for self-government (205–25). The success or failure of the American experiment, therefore, had universal, even cosmic, significance for Lincoln: it was "the last, best hope of earth" because the dignity of man as a rational animal was at stake. But saving the Republic meant having the natural rights principles of the Declaration recognized by the entire nation—by persuasion and consent or by force and imposition, if necessary. This was the principled prudence of Lincoln's magnanimous statesmanship: the combination of natural right and political rhetoric in a grand design that would gain recognition for the truth of the Declaration's principles, refound the Republic, and vindicate the dignity of man.

The key to the grand design was Lincoln's creative reinterpretation of the Declaration of Independence. Whereas Jefferson and the American Founders appealed to the self-evident truth of equality to justify the Revolution of 1776 but did not try to implement equality as a political program, Lincoln turned the equality principle of the American Founders into a "progressive" goal to be approximated in the future through gradual steps by the federal government (318–21). Lincoln thereby set the American nation on the future course of realizing progressively the equal dignity of all citizens of the Republic:

1. by stating publicly and repeating "an abstract truth, applicable to all men and all times," namely, that the equality stated in the Declaration applies to all human beings, including blacks and women, even if they were not freed by the Founders;
2. by focusing on the practical task of stopping the extension of slavery into the new territories as stated in the Missouri Compromise of 1820, so that new states admitted from the territories would be free states and so outnumber the slave states that slavery would be marginalized and set on the course of extinction;
3. by reacting to the Kansas-Nebraska Act of 1854, which permitted slavery in the new territories, by insisting that the nation become all slave or all free—thereby polarizing the nation and pushing it toward a crisis that would likely lead to civil war;
4. by leading the nation during the Civil War with the initial goal of saving the Union while waiting for the right time to issue an Emancipation Proclamation that would begin the process of freeing slaves;
5. by planning for reconstruction through a gradual process of changing public opinion toward equality for freed black slaves, beginning with the 13th Amendment and planning for the 14th Amendment, but never moving more than one step ahead of public opinion toward a progressive equality that would stop short of full racial mixing through intermarriage (368–381).

This grand design, which Jaffa sometimes suggests was in Lincoln's mind from the earliest years, or no later than 1854, was Lincoln's creative reinterpretation of the Declaration—the gradual recognition of the full truth of equal natural rights for future generations.

Whatever one might think of Jaffa's grand interpretation of Lincoln in *Crisis of the House Divided*, one could hardly be surprised that Jaffa aimed at an even more grandiose goal in his second volume, *A New Birth of Freedom*. In the later book, Jaffa promised not only to finish the history of Lincoln's statesmanship during the Civil War but also to vindicate the truth of Lincoln's principles philosophically. In fact, philosophical vindication is the main goal of the second volume because, as Jaffa always acknowledged, he is not a historian but a student of political philosophy in the school of Leo Strauss—meaning a defender of the truth of natural right against relativism and nihilism. As Jaffa says in *New Birth*, "The movement of this book . . . is from the debate with Douglas to the debate with Calhoun. The difficulty in characterizing [the debate] is that the premises underlying the thought of Douglas and Calhoun are the premises of historicism, positivism, relativism, and nihilism . . . that have become the conventional wisdom of our time. Lincoln's acceptance of the idiom of natural rights and natural law—above all his acceptance of the idea of nature not merely as a record of cause and effect but as a source of moral principles—has become alien to us. Hence, it was necessary to challenge the conventional wisdom of the present day to gain a hearing for Lincoln. . . . In doing so, I believe I have vindicated not only Lincoln's rejection of the Southern states's rights dogma but also the intrinsic validity of the natural rights of the Declaration of Independence" (preface, xiii–xiv).

As several scholars have pointed out, Jaffa's statement about the interpretive framework of *New Birth* makes it the most explicitly Straussian of his works.[18] It not only refers to Strauss repeatedly—"my hermeneutics are . . . those of Leo Strauss" (preface, xii)—the plan of the entire book also follows *Natural Right and History* by defending natural right against various forms of historicism, positivism, relativism, and nihilism.[19] This plan makes the later book more Straussian than the first volume: Whereas *Crisis* focuses on the clash between Lincoln and Douglas (understood as the clash between natural right and the relativism of "popular sovereignty"), *New Birth* focuses on Lincoln versus Calhoun (understood as natural right versus Calhoun's states' rights and historically based "prescriptive rights"). The surprise of Jaffa's *New Birth* is that even though it is the most explicitly Straussian of Jaffa's books, it also departs markedly from Strauss (and from Jaffa's own thesis in *Thomism and Aristotelianism*) by trying to defend the natural rights principles of the Declaration through a grandiose convergence theory of classical Greek, Christian, and modern natural rights (with new additions from Roman history).

The main argument of *New Birth* is reminiscent of Jaffa's "Defense of the 'Natural Law Thesis'" that we discussed above. Its central principle is human dignity—or the common humanity of all people—that relies on a classical version of philosophical "essentialism." One formulation that Jaffa uses in *New Birth* resonates throughout the book: "When the Declaration asserts that all men are created equal, it is asserting . . . [that] all human beings are equally human beings, in the same sense that all dogs are equally dogs, and all chairs are equally chairs. Anything denominated by a common noun partakes equally in the class characteristics referred to by that noun.... [this means] human beings as human beings are not white or black, or human beings of any other color" (120). Hence, it is possible to speak metaphysically about the essential nature of man as a distinct species in the overall hierarchy of being in the universe:

> From seeing many particulars, the mind forms the judgment that these particulars fall into different classes. It distinguishes living things from those that are not living . . . plants from animals, and . . . different kinds of plants and animals. It sees that all men are animals but not all animals are men. . . . Experience constantly revises, corrects, and improves upon the accuracy of these classifications. But no experience in re-

corded history (and certainly none since Socrates, Plato, and Aristotle) has ever revised in any fundamental way the distinction between the human, the subhuman, and the superhuman. *The distinction between man, beast, and God, as set forth in the first book of Aristotle's* Politics, *remains the framework for the thought of the Declaration of Independence, and the differences between man and beast, on the one hand, and man and God, on the other, remain self-evident and definitive.* For that reason, we know that any attempt of human beings to rule other human beings, as if the former were gods, and the latter were beasts is wrong. That is why the rule of law—ruling and being ruled in turn—is the only intrinsically just arrangement by which human beings can rule one another. This is a permanent truth, and one in no way dependent on its recognition. The truths enshrined in the Declaration are no more dependent on their recognition for the truthfulness than the truths about the relationship of the three angles of a triangle. (120–121, emphasis added)

In these passages and others like them throughout the book, Jaffa weaves together in an original way the arguments of Aristotle, Christianity, and Lincoln to vindicate the Declaration.[20] Jaffa's goal is to find a philosophically convincing rationale for Lincoln's Peoria speech (1854) in which Lincoln refers to the "ancient faith" of America as the Declaration's underlying principle "that no man is good enough to govern another, without that other's consent. . . . [T]his is the leading principle—the sheet anchor of American republicanism."[21] Jaffa emphasizes the phrase, "no man is good enough to govern another without that other's consent," as the essential meaning of equality or equal natural rights. Instead of following the strategy of modern liberalism, however (which would mean using the "state of nature" argument that John Locke used to defend equality), Jaffa constructs a quasi-Aristotelian or quasi-Thomistic metaphysical argument about the nature of human beings in the God-given hierarchy of being. According to that argument, the hierarchy of being in the divinely created natural universe is self-evidently divided into three different levels, with God and angels at the top, man in the middle, and beasts or animals at the bottom. Each of these beings has its own distinctive nature or essence, although Jaffa downplays "the rational animal" argument in *New Birth* (sensing, I suspect, the potential of this argument to uphold natural inequalities of intelligence among human beings that could justify the undemocratic rule of the wise over the unwise without their consent). Instead of referring to the essence of man as the rational animal, Jaffa merely points to the nearly universal agreement about the essential differences between God, man, and beast to establish the common humanity of all people as the basis of equality:

The great proposition of human equality, the central idea of the Gettysburg Address as of the Declaration, means at the very least that those consenting to government recognize the humanity that they and their fellow citizens share with all men everywhere. It means they recognize

> that human beings are neither beasts nor gods. It means therefore that no one has a right to govern other human beings as God may be said rightfully to govern the world or as human beings may be said rightfully to govern the beasts of the field. It means that laws are rightfully for the benefit of the governed . . . [and that] human freedom is itself an aspect of nature. (106)

For Jaffa, this is the clinching argument for the truth of natural rights in the Declaration of Independence and in Lincoln's vision of America.

Jaffa uses the clinching argument to explain why Calhoun is wrong about slavery and states' rights, although the characterization of Calhoun in *New Birth* is admittedly ambiguous and disputable. On the one hand, Calhoun is depicted as a twisted proponent of natural right—as an advocate of natural inequality who sounds like a twisted or racist Aristotelian in applying the doctrine to the white and black races. On the other hand, Calhoun is depicted as a historicist who rejects "nature" altogether for a historical view of reality that emphasizes evolutionary forces and Social Darwinism. In other words, Jaffa acknowledges that Calhoun refers to both nature and history in *A Disquisition on Government* and *A Discourse on the Constitution and Government of the United States.* Despite the references to both standards, Calhoun emerges in Jaffa's book as the arch villain because he is ultimately a historicist—someone who rejects an unchangeable view of human nature and a permanent essence of man. Jaffa defends the historicist charge by dismissing Calhoun's references in *A Disquisition* to the "law of our nature," which describes man's social nature (or natural need for society) as well as man's antisocial nature (or natural tendency to violence and domination). Jaffa writes, "In Calhoun's writings, 'laws of nature' do indeed appear; but they are laws of cause and effect. They are not prescriptive or normative, as in the political philosophy of the Declaration" (431). Hence, "with respect to the end or goal of his science, man would appear to be for Calhoun—as he is for Aristotle and Jefferson—the being in-between God and beast, partaking of both the lower and higher natures" (442). But Calhoun is really a historical materialist like Marx and Darwin: "Calhoun's account of [the Roman and British] constitutions reminds us of Darwinism. The constitutional organisms that enabled Rome and Britain to survive, prosper, conquer, and rule were the unintended results of the struggle for survival of their constituent elements. . . . Calhoun's teaching [is] one variety of Social Darwinism that dominated the later nineteenth century" (451–52).

After fitting the debate between Lincoln and Calhoun into the Straussian framework of nature versus history, Jaffa moves beyond Strauss with the claim that the principles of the Declaration and of Lincoln are supported by all major strands of the Western tradition. How is it possible for Jaffa to make this claim? The answer in general terms is that all the major strands uphold natural right against relativism. The more particular answer is that all share the "essentialist" view of man in the hierarchy of being as a species between God and the beasts, and all see the dignity of man as a rational animal supporting a basic idea of justice as equality as well as government by consent of the people. In *New Birth*, Jaffa actually describes a convergence of four separate strands of the Western tradition, all upholding the Declaration's and Lincoln's principles:

- The first (discussed above) is classical Greek philosophy, especially Aristotle's *Politics* and a version of Platonic essentialism, that is the primary source of the argument that all humans share a common nature and a common dignity as rational animals, existing as they do between gods and beasts and, therefore, deserving to rule and be ruled in turn rather than be subject to alleged superiors, such as kings or aristocrats.
- The second source is Christianity, in the form of Thomism and in the form of a newly developed, twentieth-century school of theology that affirms a necessary connection between Christianity and democracy. In a footnote to *New Birth*, Jaffa points to the similarities between Thomism and the Declaration: "The perspective of the Declaration is in agreement with Thomas Aquinas's conception of the natural law as the rational creature's participation in the eternal law, the law by which God governs the universe" (509 n. 84). Jaffa even finds affinities with Pascal (usually viewed as a great critic of natural right): "Pascal himself assumes the existence in his own mind of something like the truths of the Declaration" (104). Jaffa also supports his case by citing theological developments within Christianity: "That the equality of human souls in the sight of God ought to be translated into a political structure of equal political rights has come to be regarded as the most authentic interpretation of the Gospel itself. . . . This view was set forth with matchless eloquence in 1910 by Bourke Cockran, the leading lay spokesman for the Catholic Church in America at the turn of the century" (151–152).
- The third source of support for the Declaration's and Lincoln's principles that Jaffa cites in *New Birth* is Roman imperial history. According to Jaffa, the Roman Empire began the process of distinguishing God's realm from Caesar's realm, but it was unable to realize fully the notion of religious liberty implied in that distinction. The idea remained unfulfilled until the time of the American Founding and the proclamation of the Declaration's natural rights principles: "The solution to the problem of the relationship of emperor and pope, or of Caesar and Christ, was only discovered in the American Revolution and the American Founding in the separation of church and state. . . . Since the American Revolution, the Jeffersonian principle that it is against natural right for any government to

intervene between a man and his God has come to be widely accepted . . . as the authentic interpretation of Jesus' reply to the Pharisees" (140–141).

- The fourth source is the philosophy of Jefferson and Lincoln themselves, especially the notion that men are not ordained by God to be either kings and subjects or masters and slaves. Jaffa is fond of quoting Jefferson's saying that "the mass of mankind has not been born with saddles on their backs, nor a favored few booted and spurred, ready to ride them legitimately, by the grace of God." In Jaffa's view, Jefferson's statement denying divinely ordained hierarchies within the human species (but not among different species) is equivalent to Lincoln's statement that "no man is good enough to govern another without that other's consent"—an affirmation of the Declaration's basic human equality that is the legitimizing principle of the American republic.

In sum, Jaffa's thesis in *New Birth* is that moral order is upheld by a grand convergence of classical Greek philosophy, medieval and modern Christianity, the development of Roman imperial history, American idealism, and even Shakespearean poetry—all of which support the God-given natural rights of the Declaration of Independence and help to make them the permanent truths of mankind, which no form of relativism, nihilism, positivism, or historicism can defeat (whether it is espoused by Douglas and Calhoun or by modern historians, Supreme Court justices, and value-free social scientists).

JAFFA'S RESERVATIONS ABOUT THE GRAND CONVERGENCE

Despite the optimism expressed in *New Birth* about the grand convergence of forces upholding moral order, Jaffa indicates in other writings that this is not his final word on the matter. It appears to be a deliberately exaggerated view, emphasizing the common belief in some kind of higher law of justice or natural right among the various elements of the Western tradition, all embracing a common belief in the dignity of man as a rational animal. As such, Jaffa's arguments could be regarded as a partially true but overstated expression of a public philosophy, designed as an exoteric teaching to strengthen moral order in the West by emphasizing common ground and downplaying differences.

In other writings (mostly during his later career while still being contemporaneous with the long gestation period of *New Birth*), Jaffa offers a more nuanced view of the Western tradition. He seems to acknowledge Strauss's point about irreducible tensions between reason and revelation and, to a lesser extent, the tensions between ancient and modern political philosophy. The more refined position still finds a convergence in the different strands of the Western tradition, but it admits the fact of irreconcilable differences between reason and revelation and irresolvable debates on first principles—for example, divergences on the question of the creation or eternity of the world. From this viewpoint, Strauss's teaching about the open-mindedness of the philosopher—an openness that resembles Socratic "skepticism" or Socratic "knowledge of ignorance"—provides Jaffa with a different kind of justification for the moral order of the West and the principles of American natural rights republicanism.

In other words, Jaffa's collected writings present two different strategies for defending moral order. One is a theoretical argument about human dignity (the dignity of man as a rational animal, existing between beasts and God in the hierarchy of being) that supports equality and natural rights. This appears to be Jaffa's partly true but overstated exoteric teaching. The second is a practical argument derived from Socratic skepticism, according to which the philosophical openness required by the unsolvable debate between reason and revelation, combined with the broad agreement of classical philosophy and biblical faith about morality, supports American civil and religious liberty. Let me finish this essay by discussing the second strategy in relation to the first strategy, with some concluding thoughts about how both strategies depart from Strauss's thinking.

In a memorial essay, "Strauss at 100" (2003), Jaffa argues that Strauss's life-long aim was to restore Socratic philosophy and biblical revelation in order to overcome the dogmatic skepticism of modern philosophy, which culminated in nihilism or the loss of confidence in reason and truth. In this essay, Jaffa goes beyond *Natural Right and History* by appealing to two of Strauss's essays "Progress or Return?" and "What Is Liberal Education?" Jaffa claims that in these two essays Strauss acknowledges the irresolvable nature of the debate between reason and revelation about first principles, especially the debate about creation or eternity—whether the universe is created by God or is uncreated because it exists eternally by its own natural powers. Neither side seems to be able to refute the other: the biblical claim that the universe is the creation of an omnipotent, mysterious God is a miracle that faith alone can embrace because it is beyond reason to prove or comprehend. The philosophical claim that the universe is eternal (meaning it exists necessarily in some fashion) is the underlying assumption of any rational inquiry that aims at understanding why things are the way they are and not otherwise.

Fortunately, Jaffa argues, Strauss did not view the matter as an exclusive choice but as a "dialectical conclusion" that allowed for mutual cooperation: "Socratic rationalism had to grant the premise that supplied the ground for faith [namely, the mysterious character of the whole]. The reason . . . for continuing an endless philosophical inquiry, and the reason for ending such an inquiry by turning to biblical religion, was one and the same. . . . For Strauss, to restore the authority of Socratic rationalism was . . . to restore the authority of biblical faith. [Moreover,] both the Bible and Socratic philosophy provided a firm basis for moral choices, and the moral choices were substantially the same . . . [implying] agreement upon the moral order which must inform the life of decent society" (4). In other words, Jaffa interprets Strauss to be saying that Socratic philosophy and biblical faith share a sense of the mysterious nature of the whole universe while also agreeing about the fundamentals of moral order and the principles of a just and decent society.

After making this point about shared theoretical premises and shared practical principles, Jaffa quotes from the essay "What is Liberal Education?" in which Strauss speaks of "the dignity of the mind . . . [as] the true ground of the dignity of man and therewith the goodness of the world, whether we understand it as created or uncreated" (6). Jaffa's inference is that "Strauss says nothing here of the necessity to choose between these two opinions. The crisis of the West does not require us to make such a choice, and we do not know that Strauss himself ever made it. What it does require is to recognize the authority of the moral order based upon the dignity of man, supported by reason and revelation. To secure that recognition was, I believe, the essential purpose of Leo Strauss's life and work" (6–7). The implication is that Jaffa recognizes Strauss's view of the ultimate, theoretical incompatibility of biblical faith and Socratic philosophy about creation and eternity; but Jaffa believes that Strauss finds a common ground in both elements of the West for the moral virtues, human dignity, and a decent political order. This is a different sort of argument than the one Jaffa presents in the Lincoln books about man's place in the hierarchy of being between God and beasts because the argument about Strauss is based on Socratic skeptical wisdom rather than a rationally settled doctrine about the metaphysical nature of reality and man's dignity in the natural universe.

Taking the skeptical argument one step further in "The American Founding as the Best Regime" (2002), Jaffa shows how the tensions rather than harmonies among the elements of Western civilization support the greatness of the American regime. Jaffa's thesis is that America is the best regime because it established civil and religious liberty (albeit "under God") without forcing a decision on the theoretical debate between reason and revelation. Thus, the American Founding did not deny or inhibit the quest for human excellence through philosophical activity or moral virtue: it "limited the ends of government but not the ends of man." The American regime did not deny the highest ends of man because it was not a product of the dogmatic skepticism of the Enlightenment or modern philosophy, which culminates in the denial of reason's power and of revelation's claim to know the truth and in the value-free relativism of modern social science. American political freedom is based on the moderate and open-ended skepticism of Socratic rationalism, which does not deny the possibility of biblical faith but opens a space for faith and for a debate about reason-revelation within philosophy itself. According to Jaffa, this is an unprecedented achievement in the Western world—an achievement not found in the ancient Greek polis, the Roman Empire, Christian feudalism, or the seventeenth-century world of divine-right kingship. No regime has ever been founded on this combination of theoretical openness to the highest ultimate questions and of practical commitment to moral order through a morally virtuous conception of freedom. In Jaffa's words: "The unprecedented character of the American Founding is that it provided for the coexistence of the claims of reason and revelation in all their forms, without requiring any political decisions concerning them. It refused to make unassisted human reason the arbiter of the claims of revelation, and [to make] revelation the judge of the claims of reason. It is the first regime in Western civilization to do this, and for that reason, it is, in its principles or speech . . . the best regime. But the virtue of the American Founding rests not only upon its defusing of the tension between reason and revelation, but on their fundamental agreement on a moral code. . . . This moral code is the work of 'Nature's God'—reason—and the 'Creator'—revelation . . . making reason and revelation, for the first time, open friends and allies on the political level" (8–9). Once again, Jaffa's strategy is to use Socratic openness or nondogmatic skepticism to vindicate American patriotism and natural rights rather than using settled doctrines about nature's hierarchy of being.

CONCLUSION AND EVALUATION

The last quotation provides a convenient stepping stone for the evaluation of Jaffa's political and philosophical thought. It indicates that Jaffa is faithful and unfaithful to Strauss in very interesting ways. In his early work *Thomism and Aristotelianism,* Jaffa stressed the irreducible tensions between classical philosophy and Christian revelation; he criticized Thomas Aquinas for trying to harmonize the two and sought to recover a pure Aristotelian teaching but never fully vindicated Aristotle's doctrine of natural right. In his middle work on Lincoln, Jaffa emphasized the grand convergence of Aristotle, Christianity, Roman history, the American Founders, and Lincoln in supporting the Declaration's principles of God-given natural rights and government by consent of the people. Jaffa claimed common ground in a notion of human dignity that sees man as the being between beasts and God. In his later writings on Strauss and America, Jaffa acknowledges the theoretical differences of Socratic philosophy and biblical faith but finds common ground in the non-dogmatic skepticism of classical rationalism and in a shared commitment to moral order, which Jaffa equates with the American Founding and its unprecedented openness to theoretical and theological issues.

In assessing these writings, one can admire Jaffa for accepting the challenge posed by Leo Strauss to develop a natural right teaching that could overcome the relativism and nihilism of the modern West; and one can recognize Jaffa's original contributions in his arguments about human dignity and Socratic skepticism in the service of American natural rights republicanism. But the arguments for human dignity are driven by wishful thinking about the convergence of Athens, Jerusalem, and Peoria that leads to repeated exaggerations. Some of the attempts at convergence are so strained that they seem almost funny, like the statement that "the Bible is a Platonic book,"[22] or "Lincoln's recovery of the Founding corresponded closely with the Maimonidean recovery of the rational origins of prophecy,"[23] or Lady Macbeth "rejects the traditional moral distinction between beast, man, and God which we find in Aristotle's *Politics* as well as in Locke's *Second Treatise* and in the Declaration of Independence."[24] But the exaggerations are serious problems because they suggest that the classical and medieval philosophers would have embraced the principle of equality or equal rights underlying American republicanism as a kind of adaptation of natural right. Despite Aristotle's view of the changeability of natural right, he held as immutable the view that "one form of government is best everywhere by nature" and the best form is based on natural inequality and implies an aristocracy of the wise and virtuous, compared to which a polity is a decent second choice and a democracy a third choice. Insofar as Strauss himself embraced the teachings of classical natural right, he offered a more prudent—and a decidedly cooler and more detached—view of America than the moral idealism and ardent patriotism of Jaffa and his students would permit.

Similarly, Jaffa's use of Socratic skepticism on behalf of American greatness seems like an ingenious but fanciful way of reconciling reason, revelation, and American patriotism; and it is a reconciliation that Strauss never proposed and that the American Founders, as far as I can tell, never embraced. Jaffa exaggerates the Socratic openness of the American Founding on theological issues, including the Declaration of Independence, which clearly mentions God as the source of natural rights, implying a settled doctrinal decision in favor of the creation of the natural universe by an eternal God who endows human beings with their inherent rights—a religious feature of the Declaration that Jaffa sets aside in most of his discussions about Socratic America.

My conclusion, therefore, is that Jaffa goes beyond Strauss in his passion for moral order in the Western tradition and in American political life. Strauss, of course, took very seriously the question of moral order, but he always left arguments open to ambiguity and to a version of Socratic doubt that did not endorse any nation or regime because philosophy ultimately transcends the realm of politics altogether for the detached contemplation of eternal things. Jaffa also departs from Strauss in his enthusiasm for reconciling all the elements of the Western tradition out of an apparent unwillingness to live with the tension of exclusive choices that Strauss celebrated as the secret of the vitality of the West. Jaffa's journey from Athens and Jerusalem to Peoria has obviously inspired many people to follow in his footsteps, but it also encourages people to oversimplify the path to moral order and to understate the radical nature of the philosophical and spiritual life.

NOTES

The sections of this chapter were first published in *The Review of Politics*, Vol. 71, Issue 2 (Spring 2009).

1. Harry V. Jaffa, *A New Birth of Freedom: Abraham Lincoln and the Coming of the Civil War* (Lanham, MD: Rowman and Littlefield, 2000), 471.
2. See Harry V. Jaffa, "Strauss at 100." Posted on May 14, 2003, The Claremont Institute, www.claremont.org/writings/030118jaffa.html
3. Leo Strauss's legacy is a topic of endless fascination in recent years, and many books have been written to clarify the controversial issues. Among the best are Thomas L. Pangle, *Leo Strauss: An Introduction to His Thought and Intellectual Legacy* (Baltimore: Johns Hopkins University Press, 2006); Catherine Zuckert and Michael Zuckert, *The Truth about Leo Strauss: Political Philosophy and American Democracy* (Chicago: University of Chicago Press, 2006); and Steven B. Smith, *Reading Leo Strauss: Politics, Philosophy, Judaism* (Chicago: University of Chicago Press, 2006). I have benefitted greatly from the account of Jaffa and his contribution to "West Coast" Straussianism in Zuckert and Zuckert, *Truth about Leo Strauss*, 217–227, 239–252.
4. Harry V. Jaffa, *Crisis of the House Divided: An Interpretation of the Lincoln-Douglas Debates* (Chicago: University of Chicago Press, 1982), preface, vi.
5. Harry V. Jaffa, *Thomism and Aristotelianism: A Study of the Commentary by Thomas Aquinas on the Nicomachean Ethics* (Chicago: University of Chicago Press, 1952). All page references are to this edition.
6. See Frederick Copelston, *A History of Philosophy*, vol. 2, *Mediaeval Philosophy from Augustine to Scotus* (London: Burns, Oates, and Washbourne, Ltd., 1950), 302–434.
7. *St. Thomas Aquinas, Commentary on Aristotle's Nicomachean Ethics*, trans. C.I. Litzinger, forward Ralph McInerny (Notre Dame, IN: Dumb Ox Books, 1993), 779. Jaffa does not use this quotation, which I found in Thomas's commentary and I cite to support Jaffa's case. However, I also found evidence that contradicts Jaffa. For example, Thomas cites Julius Caesar's habit of forgetting injuries done to him as a mark of Caesar's strength—clearly an example of pagan pride which Thomas does not hesitate to mention, indicating that Thomas does not always try to soften or Christianize pagan pride.
8. See Mary M. Keys, *Aquinas, Aristotle, and The Promise of the Common Good* (Cambridge: Cambridge University Press, 2006), 165–169. Keys offers an alternative to Jaffa's view by arguing that Aquinas was deliberately improving upon Aristotle rather than attributing or imputing Christian views to Aristotle.
9. Harry V. Jaffa, *Crisis of the House Divided: An Interpretation of the Lincoln-Douglas Debates* (Seattle and London: University of Washington Press, 1959 and 1973; and with a new preface, Chicago: University of Chicago Press, 1982). The page numbers are the same in all editions and are indicated in parentheses.
10. Leo Strauss, *Natural Right and History* (Chicago: University of Chicago Press, 1953), 167.
11. Ibid., vii, emphasis added. I also corrected what appears to be a clear typographical error in the 1971 preface, which says, "to the reigning relativism, politivist [sic] or historicist." Politivist is clearly meant to be positivist.

12. I have taken the phrase "natural rights republicanism" from Michael P. Zuckert's book, *The Natural Rights Republic: Studies in the Foundation of the American Political Tradition* (Notre Dame, IN: University of Notre Dame Press, 1996).

13. Harry V. Jaffa, "Aristotle and Locke in the American Founding," 1–2. Posted February 10, 2001, The Claremont Institute, www.claremont.org/publications/crb/id.1130/article_detail.asp

14. To see how far Jaffa traveled in his career, one should compare his two tributes to Leo Strauss—the early tribute on the occasion of Strauss's death, "Leo Strauss: 1899–1973" (written and published in 1973), and the later tribute, "Strauss at 100" (written and published in 2003).

In the early tribute, Jaffa follows Strauss in separating the elements of the Western tradition, emphasizing "the difference between ancients and moderns" and the impossibility of a "synthesis of reason and revelation" as well as the lowness of modernity for being Machiavellian-inspired and for "getting rid of the wise man as the judge of the moral man." Reprinted in Harry V. Jaffa, *The Conditions of Freedom: Essays in Political Philosophy* (Baltimore: Johns Hopkins University Press, 1975) 3–8. In the later tribute, Jaffa is the grand synthesizer, invoking Strauss's blessing for his scholarship on Lincoln as the restorer of classical statesmanship in the modern age. Jaffa even claims that Strauss "propelled my articulation of the connection between Plato, biblical religion, Shakespeare, and Lincoln. And Lincoln's recovery of the Founding corresponded closely with the Maimonidean recovery of the rational origins of prophecy."

Obviously, Jaffa's evolution from a separator to a synthesizer of the elements of the Western tradition was gradual, but the two tributes to Leo Strauss document clearly the change from being an "orthodox" Straussian to a "Jaffaite" Straussian.

15. Originally published in *The American Political Science Review* (March 1957) and reprinted in Harry V. Jaffa, *Equality and Liberty: Theory and Practice in American Politics* (New York: Oxford University Press, 1965), 190–208. Page references are to the reprinted edition.

16. The inclusion of Shakespeare in this list is justified by Jaffa's essay, "Macbeth and the Moral Universe," a lecture given in 1974 and published by The Claremont Institute in February 2008, www.claremont.org/publications/crb/id.1510/article_detail.asp

Jaffa argues that Shakespeare's play displays a clear "moral order" in the universe, unlike Camus's and Dostoevsky's novels. *Macbeth* is punished for his excessive manliness and ambition because they violate the moral order of natural right, and he is goaded by Lady Macbeth who "invokes, and rejects, the traditional distinction between beast, man, and God, which we find in Aristotle's *Politics* as well as in Locke's *Second Treatise* and in the Declaration of Independence." And, of course, "Abraham Lincoln's *Second Inaugural Address* reaffirms the same power of morality as *Macbeth*" (8, 11). In other words, Aristotle, Locke, Jefferson, Lincoln, and Shakespeare all share a common view of moral order in the universe.

17. See Richard Hofstadter, *The American Political Tradition and the Men Who Made It* (New York: Vintage Books, 1989; originally published by Knopf, 1948), chap. 5, "Abraham Lincoln and the Self-Made Myth."

18. See Thomas G. West, "Jaffa's Lincolnian Defense of the Founding: A Review of 'A New Birth of Freedom,' by Harry Jaffa," *Interpretation* (Spring 2001) and posted on The Claremont Institute website, www.claremont.org/writings/011031west.html. See also Edward J. Erler, "Philosophy, History, and Jaffa's Universe," review of Harry V. Jaffa, *A New Birth of Freedom*, *Interpretation* 28 (Spring 2001): 245–257.

19. For other references to Strauss, see *New Birth*, the epigraph to chapter 2 (73–74), three footnotes (500n.2, 505nn.17, 20), and in specific polemical setting of chapters 1 and 2.

20. See *New Birth*, 106, 120, 155, 370, 408, 442, and 509n.84.

21. Abraham Lincoln, *The Portable Abraham Lincoln*, ed. Andrew Delbanco (New York: Penguin Books, 1992), "Speech on the Kansas-Nebraska Act at Peoria, Illinois, Oct. 16, 1854," 63.

22. "Strauss at 100," 5.
23. Ibid., 3.
24. "Macbeth and the Moral Universe," 8.

SEVENTEEN

Too Good to be True?

A Reply to Robert Kraynak's "Moral Order in the Western Tradition: Harry Jaffa's Grand Synthesis of Athens, Jerusalem, and Peoria"

I am indebted to Professor Kraynak for the generous things he says about my career as teacher and scholar. I have had vague hopes for some such recognition in a distant future, but not in my lifetime. Leo Strauss, who had virtually no recognition in his lifetime except from the circle he created around himself, is having a veritable renaissance, some thirty or more years after his death. I believe that, in the last several years, there may have been more new books about Strauss than about Lincoln (the most written about of all time!).

At a banquet on Lincoln's birthday about ten years ago, Justice Clarence Thomas celebrated the prudence of the Founding Fathers. The prudence Thomas celebrated had particular reference to the compromises in the Constitution concerning slavery. Today, most justices, and most scholars, deplore the guarantees given slavery in the 1787 Constitution. This apparently immoral acceptance of slavery tells against a jurisprudence of the "original intent" of the framers and ratifiers of the Constitution. It has accordingly given impetus to an alternative jurisprudence, of a "living Constitution," one that claims to have "evolved" to a higher level of moral consciousness than that of the eighteenth-century intellectuals who framed and ratified the Constitution celebrated in *The Federalist*. Such a "higher level," we are told, liberates the justices from a reactionary past. The greatest example of this liberated jurisprudence is *Roe v. Wade*.

Justice Thomas, in his speech, praised the Framers of the Constitution for the very thing for which others have blamed them. Following the argument and example of Abraham Lincoln, Justice Thomas noted the unvarying condemnation of slavery by the generation of the Founders, not only in the Declaration of Independence, but elsewhere in their writings.[1] But it was a political necessity in 1787 that slavery receive certain guarantees, if the Constitution was to be ratified. This was not a circumstance over which the framers had any control. They knew, however, that the failure to ratify the Constitution would leave slavery in a more powerful position, with a far greater possibility for growth and perpetuity. The concessions to slavery were made to a necessary evil. The failure to make these concessions would have assured a greater evil. The essence of prudence, or practical wisdom, is in any given case always to choose the lesser of two evils, or the greater of two goods. It is of course often difficult, sometimes even impossible, to know with any certainty which of two evils is the lesser and which of two goods is the greater. But the distinction between good and evil, however difficult it sometimes is to apply, is, nonetheless, the sovereign principle of human practical reason. Lincoln reduced slavery to "You work; I'll eat." How can there be an obligation by a rational being to consent to an uncompensated taking from his mouth of the bread that his own hand has earned? Yielding to superior force is not consent. In his speech Justice Thomas followed Lincoln precisely, and very generously mentioned my writings on Lincoln as one source of his inspiration. He concluded this Lincoln's birthday banquet by calling for a toast, "to Abraham Lincoln and Harry Jaffa." A Supreme Court Justice offering a toast on Lincoln's birthday to me and Abraham Lincoln together! I thought I had died and gone to heaven. Perhaps, then, Professor Kraynak is not altogether wrong concerning my supposed influence.

Turning to Kraynak's critique, he begins with my first book, *Thomism and Aristotelianism: A Study of the Commentary on the Nicomachean Ethics* (henceforward known as *T&A*). He correctly observes that this book marks the beginning of a lifelong quest for a rational and moral foundation for civic life (political and personal), one that is consistent with reason and immune to the corruption of the relativism and nihilism of a "value free" social science that claims the authority of modern natural science. He observes that I sought in Thomas Aquinas an interpreter of Aristotle who might confirm the ground in reason of Aristotle's *Ethics*. He says I found instead a Christianized Aristotle, deferring to principles of revelation that could not be so confirmed. Kraynak's review of *T&A* is noteworthy for its sensitivity and accuracy, but it fails to account for a change in the author's perspective from a book written nearly sixty years ago.

I recently wrote a new introduction to the reprinting of *T&A*, in which I said that, when I wrote it, I thought it was Thomas's intention to make

Aristotle safe for Christianity. I now think it was his intention to make Christianity safe for Aristotle. I have reason to believe that in time Leo Strauss had the same change of opinion concerning Thomas. The interpretation of Thomas in *Natural Right and History*, like that in *T&A*, reflects an earlier perspective. Strauss later came to a deeper appreciation of the complex subtleties of the mighty monk.

I have illustrated what I meant by making Christianity safe for Aristotle in a lecture I gave recently at Princeton and at Notre Dame. In it I took the Jefferson of the Virginia Statute of Religious Liberty to represent Aristotelian prudence.[2] ("Thomas Aquinas Meets Thomas Jefferson" was published in *Interpretation*, Spring 2006). I pointed to Thomas's doctrine of natural law—that it represented the rational creature's participation in the eternal law, the eternal law being the law of God's government of the universe. By this doctrine Homo sapiens could by his reason (that is to say, by the perfection of his reason) participate in God's government. In this, there is no necessary participation of positive divine law. According to Jefferson's statute, a man's civil rights have no more dependence upon his religious opinions, than his opinions in physics or geometry. It seems shocking to suggest that Thomas Aquinas had similar views. Yet the possibility of the direct participation of human beings, possessed of reason (but not necessarily Christian faith) in the divine government of the universe, would certainly seem to entitle them to an equal possibility to participate in civil government. This would mean, for example, that Jews or Infidels, no less than Christians, had that right. This perfectly correct Jeffersonian inference from Thomas's premises is one that Thomas did not make and would no doubt have denied. He would have denied it for the same reason that Lincoln in 1858 denied any intention to make voters or jurors of Negroes or of permitting them to marry whites. An intention to follow the dictates of a color blind Constitution would also be a perfectly correct inference from Lincoln's explicit commitment in the Peoria speech to the principles of the Declaration of Independence. These principles led him to conclude: "Allow ALL the governed an equal voice in the government, and that, and that only is self-government" (emphasis by Lincoln). However, to have explicitly endorsed direct participation by Negroes in government in Illinois in 1858, to a public with overpowering racial prejudice, a public very imperfectly committed to the principles of the Declaration, would have destroyed Lincoln as a leader of the free soil movement. Lincoln's proximate goal was arresting the spread of slavery into the territories. To have advocated voting rights for Negroes in Illinois before the Civil War would only have divided those who were united in their opposition to the extension of slavery. Lincoln made it clear that in his mind stopping the spread of slavery was only the first step on the road to its ultimate extinction. He did not in 1858 address the question of what might become prudent when the end of that road was in sight. Similarly, Thomas was engaged in a great effort to bring reason (as distinct from unreasoning prejudice) into Christian doctrine. The benefits that might eventually accrue to Jews or Infidels from that effort were not something that he could prudently bring to the attention of inquisitors hunting for heretics to burn. This comparison illuminates the fact that at different times and places religious prejudice and racial prejudice are among the most powerful obstacles to reason that prudence must circumvent. Prudence counsels caution and indirection in the face of such obstacles, but compromises do not of themselves imply a lack of principle.

No better commentary on the meaning of prudence has ever been written than Churchill's essay on "Consistency in Politics."[3]

> [A] Statesman in contact with the moving current of events and anxious to keep the ship on an even keel and steer a steady course may lean all his weight now on one side and now on the other. His argument in each case when contrasted can be shown to be not only very different in character, but contradictory in spirit and opposite in direction: yet his object will throughout have remained the same. His resolves, his wishes, his outlook may have been unchanged; his methods may be verbally irreconcilable. We cannot call this inconsistency. It may in fact be claimed to be the truest consistency. The only way a man can remain consistent amid changing circumstances is to change with them while preserving the same dominating purpose.

In what follows, Churchill takes Edmund Burke as an unsurpassed example of inconsistency in the service of consistency.

> His *Thoughts on the Present Discontents,* his writings and speeches on conciliation with America, form the main body and lasting armory of Liberal opinion throughout the English speaking world. His *Letters on a Regicide Peace,* and *Reflections on the French Revolution,* will continue to furnish Conservatives for all time with the most formidable array of opposing weapons. . . . History easily discerns the reasons and forces which actuated him, and the immense changes in the problems he was facing which evoked from the same profound mind and sincere spirit these entirely contrary manifestations. His soul revolted against tyranny, whether it appeared in the aspect of a domineering Monarch and a corrupt Court and Parliamentary system, or whether, mouthing the watch-words of a non-existent liberty it towered up against him in the dictation of a brutal mob and wicked sect.[4]

However, what Churchill says, "History easily discerns," may not always be so easily discerned, as the vast literature of controversy on Burke himself attests. It may, however, be easy when history speaks through the rare and compelling genius of Winston Churchill. What Churchill sees, but what others do not see, is the perspective that unites Thomas Aquinas, Thomas Jefferson, Abraham Lincoln, Edmund Burke, and Winston Churchill himself. Contemporary scholarship, under the domination of historicism, regards differences of time and place as fundamental, while regarding assertions of principle, especially universal principles of right and wrong, just and unjust, as not meaning what they say, but merely reflecting the interests of the persons expressing them. It was Leo Strauss's mission to persuade us (or at least some of us) that there was a realm of principle that had no time or place, within which political philosophy had its being, and from which there was a view of the human condition which embraced all times and all places. From this view it was and is possible to judge the relative merits of the moral and political judgments of time and place-bound partisans. From this same perspective it is also possible to see the notable intrusions within time and place of those great thinkers and actors who have illuminated the human condition by insights from beyond the veil of mortality.

Professor Kraynak writes:

> What I shall . . . argue is that in the course of development Jaffa changed strategies by moving from a defense of classical natural right—chiefly Aristotle's version—to a defense of modern natural rights—chiefly the principles of the Declaration of Independence—and that the change led Jaffa to depart from Strauss's thought. (182–183)

In reply I shall argue that classical natural right and the natural rights of the Declaration of Independence, properly understood, do not differ in the sense assumed by Professor Kraynak. Correctly understood, the principles of the Declaration represent the principles of classical natural right in the most perfect form possible in a political world dominated by Christian monotheism. I shall also argue that far from departing from Strauss's thought, this interpretation of the American Founding represents the fulfillment of Strauss's intention to find a means whereby classical natural right might remedy the defects of present-day constitutional thought, thought that is based upon a radical rejection of the Socratic tradition of political philosophy. The core of Strauss's rejection of doctrinal modernity was the degeneracy of that modernity into moral relativism, legal positivism, and finally, into nihilism.[5] In the currently dominant version of modernity, individual rights become individual preferences. These in turn are called "value judgments" and are said to be rooted in our passions, which reason is said to be unable to validate or invalidate. Stephen A. Douglas was in perfect agreement with a majority of today's social scientists and legal scholars, in saying that he cared not whether slavery was voted up or voted down. However, in saying that he did care for the "sacred right" of the people to decide, he did recognize a right having a status akin to the one he denied. In this he differed from the "pure" value neutral theorists who rule the present scene.

Strauss saw no such separation of classical natural right from the American Founding as Kraynak assumes. Strauss's essay "On Classical Political Philosophy" was first published in 1945 and was reprinted in 1959 in *What Is Political Philosophy?*[6] There is no more profound or authoritative record of Strauss's understanding of and commitment to classical political philosophy. Its writing and publication happened to correspond with the first year I studied with Strauss, and I was certainly exposed—before publication—to its argument, both in his classes and in my visits to his home in Riverdale. The close connection between classical political philosophy and pre-philosophic political opinion articulated in this essay was decisive in shaping my scholarship. In this essay we find the most emphatic articulation of Strauss's thesis that classical political philosophy was grounded directly in the distinctions intrinsic to prephilosophic political life. This is the point of his break with Heidegger. In his quest for the roots of Western philosophy, Heidegger went behind Socratic to pre-Socratic philosophy, where the moral cosmos is dissolved into the chaos out of which our world—whether created or uncreated—emerged. According to Aristotle and Strauss, we must begin our reasoning with what is known to us, prior to philosophy. The political philosopher thus comes to light presiding over the conflicts that arise in prephilosophic political life. The philosophic resolution of these conflicts preserves the prephilosophic distinctions, but preserves them in a form emancipated from the contradictions that caused the conflicts. But the continuity between the prephilosophic and the philosophic understanding is the notable difference between classical political science and today's version, which attempts to understand politics scientifically, that is, in a vernacular alien to political life itself. I never reread this essay of Strauss without seeing *Crisis of the House Divided* springing from its pages. Although Lincoln is a political partisan in the Lincoln-Douglas debates, he brings into his analysis of the chief question dividing them—the morality of slavery—a perspective which is nothing less than that of political philosophy. When Lincoln said that a black woman had the same right as he himself, or Judge Douglas, or any other man, to put into her mouth the bread that her own hand had earned, he was invoking natural right—and the principle of natural equality—in their purest form. In doing so, he was appealing to distinctions rooted in the human condition, that transcend ancients and moderns, and that required no recasting by modern science. In 1946, when I discovered the Lincoln-Douglas debates, at a time when I was reading Plato's *Republic* with Strauss, I was struck by the resemblance, nay identity, of the issue between Socrates and Thrasymachus, and that between Lincoln and Douglas. Thrasymachus had defined justice as the interest of the stronger. In a democracy that meant that whatever the people—or a majority of the people—decided was in their interest, was for that reason just. Whoever had the power—whether the people or a tyrant—had the right. According to Douglas, if the people of a territory, or a state, decided that slavery was in their interest, they had the right to make it lawful. Or they might reverse themselves and by their votes cause it to become unlawful.[7] Lincoln on the other hand, like Socrates, did not believe the people (any more than tyrants) made the moral law, but rather that the moral law made them a people, as distinct from a gang of thieves. Lincoln did not believe there was such a thing as a right to vote for what was wrong, any more than that there was a right to do wrong. In thus drawing the issue between himself and Douglas, Lincoln demonstrated the relevance of Socratic political philosophy in the postclassical world, exactly as Strauss intended.

The central theme of classical political philosophy, according to Strauss, is the question of the best regime. The discussion of this question is in the exact center of the essay.[8] Strauss's summary rendition of the classics' understanding of the best regime follows:

> The groups, or types, whose claims to rule were considered by the classical philosophers were "the good" (men of merit), the rich, the noble, and the multitude, or the poor citizens; in the foreground of the political scene in the Greek cities, as well as in other places, was the struggle between the rich and the poor. The claim to rule which is based on merit, on human excellence, on "virtue," appeared to be the least controversial: courageous and skillful generals, incorruptible and equitable judges, wise and unselfish magistrates, are generally preferred. Thus "aristocracy" (rule of the best) presented itself as the natural answer of all good men to the natural question of the best political order. As Thomas Jefferson put it, "That form of government is the best, which provides the most effectually for a pure selection of [the] natural *aristoi* into the offices of government." (*What is Political Philosophy?*, 83–84)

Surely it is remarkable that Strauss chose the author of the Declaration of Independence to express his own most profound insight into classical political philosophy. Nor could he for a moment have supposed that Jefferson had contradicted—or forgotten—what he had written in the Declaration. Our insight into Jefferson, Strauss, and the American Founding will be greater if we read the larger passage from which Strauss took his quotation. It is from a letter to John Adams of October 28, 1813.

> For I agree with you that there is a natural aristocracy among men. The grounds of this are virtue and talents. . . . There is also an artificial aristocracy, founded on wealth and birth, without either virtue or talents; for with these it would belong to the first class. The natural aristocracy I consider as the most precious gift of nature, for the instruction, the trusts, and government of society. And indeed it would have been inconsistent in creation to have formed man for the social state, and not have provided virtue and wisdom enough to manage the concerns of the society. May we not even say, that that form of government is the best which provides the most effectually for a pure selection of these natural *aristoi* into the offices of government? The artificial aristocracy is a mischievous ingredient in government, and provision should be made to prevent its ascendancy.

Notice that Strauss has turned a somewhat less emphatic rhetorical question into a simple declaration. Strauss becomes even more Jeffersonian than Jefferson! More important, however, is the pure classicism of the whole passage. In saying that creation, or nature, had formed man for the social state, Jefferson rejects one of the main contentions of Hobbes's anti-Aristotelian individualism, which asserts the nature of man to be asocial, or anti-social. In some respects this passage is more Platonic than Aristotelian, as when Jefferson speaks of human beings belonging by nature to one class or another. Calling the natural aristocracy the most precious gift of nature for the government of mankind locates Jefferson's political thought—and the political thought that informed the Declaration of Independence—wholly and irretrievably within classical boundaries.

We see moreover that in Jefferson's mind—as in Strauss's—there is no impediment to the rule of the *aristoi* arising from the equality proclaimed in the Declaration of Independence. On the contrary, it is the consent of the governed, arising from original equality, which becomes the means whereby the people may distinguish the pseudo-*aristoi* from the real ones. The non-*aristoi*, who in the Jeffersonian republic will have full participation in the electoral process, will have the same interest in choosing real aristocrats to govern, as the layman has in choosing real doctors rather than quacks. For Jefferson, as for Strauss, the means for preventing quacks from taking over the government was by education.

When Strauss wrote "What Is Liberal Education?" he was thinking of how liberal education might rescue us from the evils that had come upon us in the name of democracy. What is now called democracy has drifted far from anything wished for by Thomas Jefferson. It is in fact democracy drugged by relativism and nihilism, and demoralized by a "value free" social science. Here is what Strauss wrote in 1959:

> Liberal education is the counter-poison to mass culture, to the corroding effects of mass culture, to its inherent tendency to produce nothing but 'specialists without spirit or vision and voluptuaries without heart.' Liberal education is the ladder by which we try to ascend from mass democracy to democracy as originally meant. Liberal education is the necessary endeavor to found an aristocracy within democratic mass society. ("What Is Liberal Education?")

We see here agreement between Strauss and Jefferson, both as to the desirability and possibility of aristocracy within democracy. If "democracy as originally meant" had prevailed, no counter-poison would now be required. But the relevance of classical political philosophy, as Jefferson expressed it, is endorsed by Strauss, and creates a presumption in favor of the Founding as an attempt to create a classical republic, so far as possible, within a postclassical world.

It follows that the problem of government is twofold: First to discover and empower the genuine *aristoi*, and then prevent the ascendancy of the spurious. Jefferson's reputation as anti-aristocratic stems from his ceaseless denunciation of the pseudo-aristocracies of the ancient regimes of eighteenth-century Europe. The rule of kings and priests, whose claims were without merit, aroused Jefferson's greatest indignation. Divine right monarchy, supporting and supported by a class system of inherited wealth and birth, constituted the negation of aristocracy, as understood by classical political philosophy no less than by Jefferson. But the true *aristoi*—the guardians of the republic provided by nature—still required the education that would turn their potential for rule into actual qualifications for rule. It is good to remember that the third of the three things by which Jefferson wished most to be remembered was "Father of the University of Virginia." The success of the Jeffersonian vision—the vision by and large of all the Founding Fathers—depended upon an essentially classical education. This education would assist the people in a democracy to recognize their true representatives, and defeat the plots of the scoundrels posing as aristocrats.

However, how do we reconcile the commitment to the rule of the natural *aristoi* with the equality proclaimed in the Declaration of Independence? Before addressing that question directly, let us consider how differently the prudence or practical wisdom (*phronesis*) of political philosophy operates in the environment of the city of classical antiquity, compared to that of the state of the modern centuries. The idea of law in the ancient city is expressed by Aristotle, in the *Nicomachean Ethics*, when he says that "whatever the law does not command, it forbids." There is no action which is neither commanded nor forbidden. There is no personal freedom apart from the law. What we call personal freedom is no part of the law of the ancient city. We can instantly recognize the agreement here with the law in the Books of Moses. It would also fit the ancient cities described in Fustel de Coulanges's *The Ancient City*, a book praised extravagantly by Leo Strauss. But the ancient polity was one that evolved from the family to the clan to the tribe, and was essentially a collection of tribes—as it was in ancient Israel. The morality of ancient law resulted from a syncretistic process, whereby the gods of the different families and tribes elided, and thus became the gods of the city. In their origin, however, the gods of the cities were family gods, and an inward looking ethnocentric patriarchalism governed the outlook of the citizens, who scarcely recognized the humanity of noncitizens. Consider the fate of the Melians at the hands of the Athenians, and of the Canaanites at the hands of the Israelites. This patriarchalism was also reproduced in the Senates of ancient cities, which were constituted by the elders of the elder families, who were considered to be closer to the gods than were later comers. In the *Antigone* we see a conflict arising between the gods of the city and the gods of the family. The law of the family appears as the older and more authoritative, but it is anarchistic in its harm to the ability of the city to defend itself. Freedom in the ancient city is entirely preoccupied with the independence of the city itself, and it has nothing to do with the rights of individuals apart from the city or within the city. To be conquered or captured in war meant being separated from the gods of one's city, the defeat of one's city and its gods being more or less the same. There was little or no respect for the life of someone captured in war, and a captured warrior, or any citizen of a defeated city, was subject to being killed or enslaved, unless he or she had the good fortune of being adopted into a family of the victorious city.[9] Citizenship was understood as partnership in the worship of the families of the tribes that made up the city. "Whoring after strange gods" meant treason. The accusation against Socrates for not believing in the gods of the city, and of teaching his unbelief to the young men of Athens, corresponds closely to the anti-communism of the late Senator McCarthy.

The books of Moses chronicle the never-ending struggle between a jealous God and an inconstant people. A detached observer (not that such is possible) might wonder whether God needed Israel more than Israel needed God. It is clear, however, that the identities of Israel and of God were inextricably linked. God strives tirelessly (and it sometimes seems vainly) to secure the fidelity of His people, like a husband trying to domesticate a straying but yet beloved wife. The husband (God) is monogamous, but the wife (Israel) is not! It has been well said, and often said, that it was easier for Moses to get the Jews out of Egypt than to get Egypt out of the Jews. The episode of the golden calf illuminates this most essential difference between law in the ancient city and in constitutional government as we understand it. The first table of the Ten Commandments is almost entirely devoted to disciplining Israel in the exclusive worship of the One God. The making of graven images or, indeed, of any images, is prohibited because God knows that any sensible image of a sensible object, and in particular of an animal, is likely to become an object of worship. God had staked everything upon the fact that, as an invisible God, whose name could not be pronounced, he differed from every other deity. And God knew the propensities that the Israelites shared with other ancient peoples, and in particular with the Egyptians, among whom they had dwelt for so long. This was proved the moment Moses was absent upon the mountain. In the worship of the golden calf we see the crisis of the regime in its starkest form. It is difficult for us today to understand the profundity of this political crisis, which concerns something we would regard as essentially and constitutionally private. No one could tell Moses, or God, that the Israelites were exercising their natural right to the free exercise of religion. Only the discipline of God's law could turn a ragged and demoralized band of runaway slaves into the fighting force that would invade Canaan. To imagine ancient Israel, imagine a whole people subject to the same discipline as the United States Marine Corps, with the individual completely absorbed into the mission whose aim and purpose is found only in the Law. And it is difficult, if not impossible, to tell any difference between the Law as means and the Law as end. "The reward of the commandment is the commandment." Indeed, the idea of religion, or the idea of a church as distinct from a state, was unknown to the ancient world. The words "Congress shall make no law respecting an establishment of religion" are inconceivable in the law of an ancient people. Nothing better illustrates the difference between constitutionalism—ancient and modern—or better illustrates the different role of prudence with respect to these differences.

The separation of what we would call religious worship from political loyalty or obedience to lawful government is perhaps the most momentous step in the political history of mankind. When Jesus answered the Pharisee that we should "render unto Caesar the things that are Caesar's, and to God the things that are God's," he drew a distinction between civil and religious authority which I believe was unprecedented. Consider that, under David and Solomon, when Israel was an independent polity, Jesus could never have made such a statement. The law of Israel came from God. There was no distinction between what Israelites might owe to God and what they might owe to lawful authority. Jesus' response to the Pharisee was the first giant step on the long, long road to our First Amendment, to limited constitutional government, and to a prudence that affirms (contrary to the words but not to the intentions of Aristotle and Moses) that "what the law does not forbid it permits."

The Israel Jesus knew was a province of the Roman Empire. Caesar's conquest of the world of classical antiquity left only one sovereign government in that world, the government of Rome. As the cities of the ancient world were conquered by Rome, so were their gods. By the logic of the ancient city, if there could be only one city, there could be only one god. The transformation of the ancient world from polytheism to monotheism, however long and complicated, seems nonetheless to have been in some sense predestined by the conquests of Caesar. Dante, in *On Monarchy*, thought the role of Caesar no less providential than that of Christ. The Gospel could not have been preached beyond the borders of Israel in cities that had not lost their gods to Rome.

However, the establishment of Christian monotheism ruptured the connection between God and law that characterized the ancient city. The Christian God, as the one and only God, would not be the author of the different municipal laws of the different peoples. The Christian God could not be to Christians what the God of Israel was to Israelites: the immediate author of their laws and of their identity as a people. While the Christian God was not seen as a legislating God, he was, nonetheless, seen as the source of legitimate political authority. Lincoln, however, saw the divine right of kings as a justification of slavery. While Lincoln may have oversimplified the history of political theories, he accurately pinpointed the prevalence for more than a millennium of the legitimation of political authority from God to rulers, from the top down. During this millennial time, the political history of the Christian West was dominated by contests as to who held the mandate to rule from God: popes against emperors, popes against kings, king against kings, and, finally, kings against peoples. In all these contests, it was never doubted that a legitimate ruler was in some way or manner anointed by God. Who was authorized to do the anointing and who was entitled to receive it were matters of the fiercest dispute, but not the requirement itself. Shakespeare's *Henry V* presents the classic formulation of this dilemma of Christian statesmanship. Before the battle of Agincourt, Henry calls on God to forget his father's crime in usurping the crown of an anointed king. Henry does not doubt that such usurpation was a crime, and that his was a tainted inheritance. Like Hamlet's uncle, however, Henry is not willing to abandon the fruits of his father's sin. His attachment to the crown is not less than that of Lady Macbeth. Henry solves his problem by attributing his victory at Agincourt to God. His forces were outnumbered by more than ten to one, so that the victory might reasonably be thought miraculous. We might reasonably attribute the victory to Henry's leadership, but it was very much in his interest to think, and to have others think, that God had given him the victory, and that this providential fact repaired the defect in Henry's title to divine right. Henry gives orders to his army that all the credit for victory must be given to God. He forbids any rejoicing or any of the looting customary in the wake of victory. We are reminded of Henry's speech before Harfleur, when he demands the surrender of the town, and warns the governor that if his troops have to take the town by storm, he will not be able to control them in the aftermath. He is very specific about the plundering and raping, in particular the raping of virgins that will ensue. Yet in the aftermath of Agincourt, he exercises precisely the control that he had before said that he would not possess. Yet that control is now precisely in the service of deploying God to bestow upon him the divine right of kings. The unfortunate Bardolph (the old companion of Falstaff) is caught in the act of plunder and is promptly hanged. That God's approval was required for government to be legitimate seems never to have been doubted within the horizon of Shakespeare's English histories. That approval, moreover, seems to have been an indispensable element of political power and influence. As we shall see, the Declaration of Independence, in submitting itself to the "supreme judge of the world," fits squarely in this mold. It was only because the signers of the Declaration were confident that the approval of the aforesaid judge was now on the side of the people, not on the side of kings, that they relied upon the protection of divine providence.

The long transition from the age of inequality to government based upon the equality of man and the rights of individuals is visible within the Declaration of Independence itself. After saying that "governments derive their just powers from the consent of the governed," the Declaration continues:

> [T]hat whenever any form of government becomes destructive of these ends, it is the right of the people to alter or abolish it and to institute new government, laying its foundation on such principles and organizing its powers in such form as to them shall seem most likely to effect their safety and happiness.

We notice that the rights with which each human being is endowed by his creator, and which are undiminished in the state of nature, are transformed into the ends of government. These are the joint possessions of fellow citizens, who are now under the authority of a common government. And those ends are safety and happiness, which are the ends—the alpha and omega—of the political community in Aristotle's *Politics*. The reference to ends in the sense of final causes is eminently Aristotelian. This transformation of rights into ends corresponds with the movement of individuals from the state of nature into the state of civil society. The right of the people "to alter or abolish . . . and to institute new government" is a collective right. In the state of nature, no one could act on behalf of anyone else. Now the many can act as one, as they must in dissolving an old government and forming a new one.

This movement from the manyness of the state of nature to the oneness of political government is accomplished by a social contract or compact. In the writings of James Madison we find repeated, again and again, that all free government rests upon compact. We take this to be an axiomatic premise of the American Revolution and Founding. It is as well the prudent form of political philosophy in the circumstances faced by the Founders and Lincoln, in their postclassical, post-Reformation world. Today, the ideas of a state of nature and of a social contract are looked upon as unhistorical, the relics of eighteenth-century thought. Yet they are intrinsic to the constitutional thought of the Founding. All intelligent scholarship on this topic stands upon the foundation of Leo Strauss's refutation of historicism. The state of nature and the social contract are more immediately intelligible, however, if we understand them as necessary inferences from that most fundamental of all propositions, "that all men are created equal." It follows that if no human being is by nature the ruler of any other human being—as any human being is by nature the ruler of any horse or dog—then legitimate political authority can arise only from consent. By this we mean that there is no rational ground of obligation other than consent. By consent we mean a rational calculation that obedience to the laws to which one is consenting is in the interest of the one consenting, and is not mere acquiescence to force or fraud. In the first *Federalist*, Hamilton opines that the success of the Constitution will determine "whether societies of men are really capable or not, of establishing good government from reflection and choice, or whether they are forever destined to depend for their political constitutions, on accident and force." This messianic view of the role of America in world history runs throughout the Founding, and finds its supreme expression in the Gettysburg Address.

The condition of human beings, prior to the social contract, is what is meant by the state of nature. That there should be such a state is, to repeat, a logical necessity inherent in the proposition that all men are created equal. Whether in any given case the contract envisaged is prior in time to an existing political community, it is always prior in thought. In any legitimate polity the citizens are aware that their unalienable rights originate in a state in which there is no dominion, no lawful authority, of one human being over another. They know that their obedience to the laws depends upon their enlightened consent to replace the state of nature with that of civil society. The commitment to original equality is enshrined in both the Declaration of Independence and the Gettysburg Address. The undeniable truth of this original equality is impressed upon our minds each time we compare the origin of the authority of humans over the lower animals, with the authority of humans over humans. The transition from the state of nature to that of civil society by a social contract is, again, a logical necessity. It is also a voluntary action, and civil society is a voluntary association. It may be thought that this contradicts Aristotle's assertion that the *polis* is natural to man's humanity, and that it "grows" out of family and the tribe as much as the oak tree grows out of the acorn. Aristotle says, however, that although the impulse to form a political community is in all men by nature, nonetheless "the man who first united people in such a partnership was the greatest of benefactors." The origins of the political community depend upon a voluntary action by a being whose nature is, above all, marked by reason, and who must, therefore, have exercised reason in fulfilling those requirements of his nature that go beyond the nature he shares with the lower animals.

The social contract theory espoused by Madison, and implicit in the Declaration of Independence, considers that human beings "created equal" with respect to the rights with which they have been endowed by their creator, assemble to form a political community. They do so recognizing that the absence of legitimate political authority means that there is nothing to defend their natural and God-given rights, other than their individual natural force. Their original natural freedom from any authority other than their own is perfect. Their insecurity is equally perfect. In the formation of a civil society, they bring into being a government in which the power of all can defend each. But the government possesses such power only because each contracting member has agreed to join with his fellow citizens in forming that power.

Let us reflect on this first and most fundamental element of the social contract. First, we must see that this agreement is unanimous. Whoever does not join is no part of the community. Whoever does join is entitled to the same protection as every other contracting member who is now a fellow citizen. Here is the origin of the seminal doctrine of the equal protection of the laws. No one, on this basis, can assert that his life or liberty or property is more deserving of protection than anyone else's. Nor can anyone assert that his obligation to join in the common defense is less than anyone else's. The very formation of the political community makes everyone a member of its militia. And no one's property is less liable to support the common defense than anyone else's. That is to say, the obligation to pay taxes for the common defense is equal to the obligation to bear arms in the common defense. These are the broad general conclusions to be drawn from the fundamental proposition that all human beings are equally endowed by their creator with unalienable rights, and that they enter into a unanimous agreement for the mutual protection of those rights. The aforesaid agreement, however, is barren until implemented by the formation of government. In making the decisions leading to the formation of government, and in the operation of the government, unanimity is impossible. The nearest practicable approach to unanimity is majority rule. Let us understand, however, that the aforesaid unanimity limits and defines the legitimate scope of majority rule. We must understand that its purpose is to implement the equal protection of the rights of individual human beings, rights which are antecedent to the political community. There can be no lawful decision by the majority to benefit the majority at the expense of the minority. The rule of the majority is, therefore, understood to be in behalf of the minority no less than of the majority. The minority may differ from the majority on the question of means, but not of ends. Strictly speaking, there are no majority rights or minority rights; there are only the rights with which each human being is endowed by his creator. In the forefront of the deliberations leading to the majority is the question of the common good. The political health of the community, like the physical health of the citizens, is not served equally by anyone, but by those whose character, intelligence, experience, and education best qualifies them for the offices. In principle, the political process is that by which a democracy is transformed into an aristocracy.

Next let us consider briefly the relationship of the rights of fellow citizens to those of human beings outside the political community. The government of fellow citizens has an equal obligation to protect the rights of each, but it has no such obligation to those outside the community. But we must remember that prior to the social contract, each one of the now fellow citizens recognized himself and every other human being everywhere to be created equal. The American cause in the American Revolution was first articulated for the nation by the Continental Congress on July 6, 1775, in the Declaration of the Causes and Necessity of Taking up Arms. The Congress declares that it is impossible for men "who exercise their reason to believe that the divine Author of our existence intended a part of the human race to hold an absolute property in, and an unbounded power over others . . . as the objects of a legal domination never rightfully resistible, however severe and oppressive." A year before the Declaration of Independence, and more explicitly than in the Declaration itself, the Congress denounces the very idea of the possibility of human beings, being created equal, having property in each other. Moral obligation, apart from political obligation, extends to all members of the human race. Participation in the human race belongs to all who "exercise their reason." The fact that slavery and unjust inequality, in many forms, have long characterized the human condition only means that reason has failed hitherto to govern mankind. As I have written before, and often, the United States was (so far as I know) the first nation in the world to claim a right to independence not because of any virtue peculiar to itself, but on the basis of rights that it shared with all men everywhere. Contrast this with the Athenian belief in autochthony, reproduced by Plato as one of the noble lies of the *Republic*, and the biblical belief in a right to a land because it was promised to them by their God. In both cases, the right claimed, whether by Athenians or Israelites, entitled them to kill or enslave anyone who stood in the way of their possession of the land they claimed.

The transformation from the law of the ancient city to that of the constitutionalism inherent in the Declaration of Independence took place because of the social contract. Before such a contract could be envisaged, the polytheism of the classical world had to be replaced by the monotheism of Christianity. Christianity transformed the covenant of God with Abraham, a patriarchal covenant with a particular people, into a covenant with all mankind, or atleast to anyone of all mankind who accepted the covenant. The invisible community of believers did not constitute a polity in this world. But it had a decisive, or rather catastrophic, effect on the polities of this world. Kings thought it their responsibility as God's anointed representatives to shepherd their subjects through the gates of salvation, while protecting them from contamination by false prophets. That belief involved their subjects in domestic or civil wars against heretics and foreign wars against infidels. These wars dominated European politics in the centuries before the American Founding. The minds of the Founders were governed by the determination to create a politics free from sectarian religious passions. Such a politics was absolutely necessary if there was to be constitutional government. Constitutional government, flowing from human equality and the social contract, requires majority rule as its instrument. But the majority can have no lawful power that entitles a majority of Catholics to determine the religion of Protestants, or Protestants of Catholics, or Christians of Jews, or Jews of Muslims, or those of any religious persuasion to determine the faiths of others. We have already noted that the first impulse to remove our relationship with God from political government came from Jesus' reply to the Pharisee. A more proximate source would be Locke's *Letter on Toleration*.

Madison's *Memorial and Remonstrance*, followed by Jefferson's *Statute of Virginia for Religious Freedom*, was a by-product of Locke's *Letters*. The essential unity of Locke's political thought and Aristotle's, across the broad spectrum of the ancient and modern worlds, may be seen here. The problem of reconciling religious freedom with political freedom did not exist in the world of Aristotle's *polis*. Each city had its own gods, and accepting or professing to accept one's own city's god, was no more sectarian than reciting the oath of allegiance. Certainly no one was burned at the stake for heresy, or for not worshipping in the prescribed manner. The peaceful coexistence of the different faiths, as well as different ethnicities, became possible only as the acceptance of human equality—that all men are created equal—brought human rationality into the formation of government. The rationality of this solution is what makes it prudent, and what makes it prudent makes it no less Aristotelian than Lockean. I would add that it makes it no less Straussian. I conclude with one of Strauss's familiar sayings, that Socrates had more in common with any intelligent American than he had with any stupid Athenian. The principles of political philosophy relate to a human condition that, like the human soul itself, is not located in time or place.

NOTES

1. He might have mentioned the first sentence of the "Declaration of the Causes and Necessity of Taking up Arms" by the Continental Congress, July 5, 1775. These were the first words addressed officially by the American people to the world. They constitute an uncompromising denunciation of the very idea that there can be any such thing as a right of property of some human beings in other human beings.

2. Jefferson, in the famous Lee letter, listed among the sources of the Declaration "the elementary books of public right, as Aristotle, Cicero, Locke, Sydney." Aristotle is at the headwaters of the tradition.

3. *Amid These Storms: Thoughts and Adventures* (New York: Scribner's Sons, 1932), 39–47.

4. Ibid.

5. "The contemporary rejection of natural right leads to nihilism—nay, it is identical with nihilism" (Leo Strauss, *Natural Right and History* [Chicago: University of Chicago Press, 1953], 5).

6. Strauss, *What is Political Philosophy?* Aml Other Studies (Chicago: University of Chicago Press, 1959).

7. "Once you adopt democratic theory . . . you accept the proposition [that] if the people . . . want abortion the state should permit abortion. If the people do not want it, the state should be able to prohibit it" (Justice Antonin Scalia in Harry V. Jaffa, *Storm Over the Constitution* [Lanham, MD: Lexington Books, 1999], 115).

8. According to Colleen Sheehan, of Villanova University, the passage in question actually occupies the mathematical center of the essay.

9. In World War II, the brutality of the Japanese towards POWs was notorious. It has been explained that the Japanese regarded anyone who allowed himself to be captured alive as beneath contempt. The Geneva Convention concerning the treatment of POWs would have been as incomprehensible in the ancient world as it apparently

was to the Japanese. The enslavement of defeated peoples is perfectly intelligible from this point of view and helps explain why there was no antislavery movement in the ancient world.

EIGHTEEN

Jaffa's *New Birth*

Harry Jaffa at Ninety

Michael P. Zuckert

Abstract: With the publication of Harry Jaffa's *New Birth of Freedom*, it is possible to see the overall trajectory of his thinking and to come to some assessment of it. *New Birth* redeems a forty-year-old promise for a sequel to *Crisis of the House Divided*. One problem, however, is that the sequel contradicts many of the claims in *Crisis*. These differences provide an ingress for reconsidering Jaffa's overall project and, in particular, his relation with his teacher, Leo Strauss.

Harry Jaffa has now far surpassed his biblically allotted three score and ten years, and has even gone beyond the nation's four score and seven when Lincoln delivered the Gettysburg Address. Although we hope that he has many years and much writing left in him, we may still take his arrival at ninety as a moment to look back over his aims and accomplishments as a student and teacher of political philosophy.

It is only since the year 2000 that it is possible to attempt such a recapitulation of his career, for it was only then that he redeemed his very longstanding promise to follow up his classic study of the Lincoln-Douglas debates, *Crisis of the House Divided*, with a sequel on Lincoln called *A New Birth of Freedom*. So long as that promise remained unfulfilled, getting a full sense of the overall trajectory of Jaffa's thinking was not possible. Of course, when it takes forty and more years to write a promised sequel, one suspects that some sort of hitch appeared in the intervening years, a hitch that stood in the way of a more timely completion. When one notices that *A New Birth of Freedom* contradicts many of the central points of *Crisis of the House Divided*, one is justified in concluding that the *New Birth* that appeared in 2000 is not the same book Jaffa promised and projected in 1958. And yet, Jaffa still presents *New Birth* as the promised sequel.[1] Therefore, despite our sense of great change, we must take seriously his implicit claim that there is some sort of deep continuity between his two studies.

Although Jaffa wrote on many other topics—Aristotle and Thomas Aquinas, Shakespeare, and Mark Twain, the errant ways of the Supreme Court and the errant ways of his fellow students of Leo Strauss—nonetheless Lincoln, read capaciously and against the background of the entire western tradition, has clearly been the centerpiece of Jaffa's intellectual efforts. And an impressive centerpiece it has been. *Crisis of the House Divided* propelled Lincoln scholarship in altogether new directions and set an agenda for the study of American politics and American political thought for a whole generation or more of scholars. He has been a giant in the field of political philosophy and a teacher with rare impact on his students. He has also been a controversial and contentious figure, a polemicist of great talent and vigor, impartially attacking friend and foe alike. He has been a figure to reckon with. To establish just what the reckoning ought to include is my purpose in this essay.

SOME PREFATORY QUESTIONS

The preface to *New Birth* is striking for the amount of information it conveys and for the questions toward which it points the serious reader. Jaffa identifies *New Birth* as the sequel to *Crisis*. He excuses the long delay by observing that Plato's *Laws* was separated by roughly the same length of time from Plato's *Republic*. *Republic*, according to Jaffa's teacher Leo Strauss, is a work without practical intent, but rather a work of theory: it attempts to bring out the nature and limits of the political as such. *Laws*, however, is identified by Strauss as Plato's only genuine work of political philosophy; it is more practical in intention than *Republic*. Jaffa suggests that a similar relationship exists between *Crisis* and *New Birth*. That suggestion is perhaps confirmed by the title of the central substantive section of *Crisis*, "The Political Philosophy of a Young Whig," indicating the philosophical or theoretical character of the central argument in *Crisis*. In a somewhat parallel way, the central chapter of *New Birth* is titled, "The Mind of Lincoln's Inaugural and the Argument and Action of the Debate that Shaped It." That title ties *New Birth* back to Plato's *Laws*, or more precisely to Strauss's reading of Plato's *Laws*, for Strauss's book-length interpretation was called *The Argument and Action of Plato's Laws*.

Jaffa tells us in his preface that *New Birth* is conceived as a commentary on the Gettysburg Address, an extremely odd claim, for the book contains extensive commentary on several of Lincoln's speeches, but has no sustained analysis of the Gettysburg Address.[2] Likewise, chapter 2 is titled, "The Declaration of Independence, the Gettysburg Address and the Historians," but contains only about two pages directly about the Gettysburg Address itself. Jaffa perhaps explains his odd characterization of the book when he tells us that "a commentary on the Gettysburg Address is necessarily, and above all, a commentary on what is meant by dedication to 'the proposition that all men are created equal.'"[3] Does the reverse hold then? Is a commentary on "the proposition that all men are created equal" "necessarily" a commentary on the Gettysburg Address? If so, then we have here a clear indication of the main substantive theme of this sprawling, often apparently unfocused book: it intends to bring out what dedication to that proposition about equality means.

If explication of the proposition about equality is the matter of the book, then, Jaffa makes clear, its "form" is a "commentary." The commentary, he informs us, is one of Thomas Aquinas's "characteristic forms," an interesting observation in light of Jaffa's further divulgence that *Crisis* "imitated the disputed question of the Scholastics," the form, Jaffa implies, of Aquinas's *Summa*.[4] The subject of Jaffa's books is human equality, an apparently modern theme; their form, however, follows the decidedly unmodern Aquinas.

Yet Jaffa goes out of his way to emphasize that "this commentary obviously must be different from that of Thomas on the *Nichomachean Ethics* . . . because a text of Aristotle's is virtually a self-contained work with its meaning altogether within that of the speech by which it is conveyed."[5] Apart from the fact we have already noticed that *New Birth* is not in any conventional sense a commentary on the Gettysburg Address (since it does not address the Address directly), Jaffa also emphasizes that one needs to look at the Gettysburg Address "as part of a drama"—the larger historical drama of the Founding and then unraveling of America in the crisis of the Civil War. Jaffa means to apply in his commentary the interpretive methods not of Aquinas, but of his teacher Leo Strauss.[6] "According to Leo Strauss, great books are works of art, and as such they are governed by what he . . . called logographic necessity." Everything, including the smallest details that go counter to the apparent drift of the whole, including likewise the "silences," must find a place in such a reading.[7] Jaffa intends to read the drama of history according to the principles Strauss applied to the most artfully written books. Jaffa anticipates the commonsense reaction:

> It may be objected that history is not poetry and that I have confused them. To this I would reply . . . that the place of necessity in great poetry imposed by the art of the poet may be occupied by a providential order in history.[8]

Jaffa attributes this view of history to Lincoln himself. But does not Lincoln's great Second Inaugural Address say the opposite? "The Almighty has his own purposes." In saying that, does not Lincoln mean to correct both North and South who thought they understood the divine purpose in history, for one cannot, to paraphrase a well-known saying of Strauss's, "understand its Author as the Author understood Himself."

Neither Lincoln nor Strauss nor Aquinas appears to be a model for Jaffa's practice. Of the three figures that he mentions in this context, he is closest to Aquinas, because he more unambiguously and consistently affirmed divine, particular providence of a robustness that could begin to support Jaffa's idea of history as a text constructed with logographic necessity. Strauss most definitely never saw history in that way, and Lincoln either fails to identify history with providence (most of the time) or, as in the Second Inaugural, identifies history with an unfathomable providence.

The premise, or rather assumption, for it surely is not proved, of Jaffa's study is the providential guidance of history. This observation brings *New Birth* close once again to Plato's *Laws*. In the one reference outside the "Preface" to that work, Jaffa calls attention to the opening of the *Laws* where Kleinias the Cretan affirms that the laws of both Crete and Sparta are said to derive from gods, a thesis that the philosophic spokesman, the Athenian Stranger, retains in much modified form in his presentation of a natural theology toward the end of the *Laws*. A deeper connection between *New Birth* and *Laws* thus comes to sight: *New Birth* represents the sort of theologization of politics that Plato presents in *Laws*.

Lurking above or within all the themes Jaffa's pregnant preface raises is the question of the relation of Jaffa's thought to that of his teacher, Leo Strauss. Throughout his career, Jaffa professed loyalty to Strauss's thought. That loyalty is visible in such aspects of *New Birth* as the chief opponents against whom he takes up arms: "[H]istoricism, positivism, relativism, nihilism." These four horsemen of the modern apocalypse were, of course, targets of Strauss's work as well. Yet Jaffa also clearly breaks with central features of Strauss's thinking. The character of Jaffa's modification of Strauss probably best comes to view if we note that Strauss was a thinker of dualities—ancients and moderns, Jerusalem and Athens, philosophy and poetry, the city and man. Jaffa, on the contrary, is a thinker of unities: he collapses Athens and Jerusalem, poetry and philosophy, and goes a long way toward assimilating Strauss's ancients and moderns, for example, when he argues that John Locke, a preeminent modern according to Strauss, is presenting what Aristotle would have said had he lived at Locke's time. What Strauss has put asunder Jaffa attempts to join together.

We might collect some of the themes or puzzles posed in the preface under the following heads:

1. How, despite so many apparent discontinuities between *Crisis* and *New Birth,* is the latter properly a sequel rather than, say, a correction of *Crisis*?
2. How is *New Birth* the more practical book, like Plato's *Laws,* and *Crisis* the more theoretical book, like the *Republic*?
3. What does *New Birth* in particular tell us about "dedication to the proposition that all men are created equal"?
4. What are we to make of Jaffa's "theologization" of history? Is this a serious doctrine for which he has some sort of proof?
5. What are we to make of Jaffa's repeated and insistent efforts to hold together the dualities Strauss constantly pushed apart? How does Jaffa relate to Strauss?

THE CRISIS OF *CRISIS*

The most efficient way to see the differences between *Crisis* and *New Birth* is to notice what Jaffa has to say about the American Founders, and about Lincoln's relation to them. The most prominent feature of *Crisis* was the claim that Lincoln went beyond and corrected the work and political understanding of the Founders. Indeed, Lincoln as refounder, Lincoln as the statesman-poet-philosopher who put the nation on a sounder footing than the Founders had left it, was the dominant theme of that book. But in the later *New Birth,* Jaffa no longer presents Lincoln as critic and corrective to the Founders. He argues that Lincoln continues and confirms the Founders' political deeds and political understanding. The later Jaffa thus appears to be a real critic of the earlier Jaffa. Jaffa's critique and reformulation takes its point of departure from his Strauss-inspired identification in *Crisis* of the Founders as Lockeans, all of whom "read the Declaration [of Independence] as an expression of the sentiments of Locke's *Second Treatise of Civil Government.*"[9] As Lockeans, the Founders affirmed two doctrines that Jaffa believes Lincoln did not accept: they understood the proposition that "all men are created equal" as equivalent to the Lockean doctrine of the state of nature, and they understood natural rights in the Hobbesean-Lockean manner as "an indefeasible desire or passion."[10] In Lockean theory, the state of nature is a state of equality because it is a condition where no person rightly can claim authority over any other.[11] Lockean-Jeffersonian equality is thus the beginning point; the movement into civil society is a movement away from it, indeed is an abrogation of it, for the coming of government is the coming of legitimate authority of some over others. For Lincoln, however, according to Jaffa, equality is not that from which we move but that to which a just society moves. As Lincoln said in the Gettysburg Address, the nation is "dedicated to the proposition that all men are created equal." That dedication is forward looking, not merely a status to be left behind; equality is an attainment, or what Jaffa calls a "transcendental goal."[12]

The early Jaffa also modifies the Founders' Hobbesean theory of rights. As Jaffa sees it, rights, as understood by the Founders, are indefeasible passions. Because human beings are constituted in such a way that the strongest moving forces in them, their passions, drive them to preserve themselves, they cannot be blamed for doing what they cannot help doing. It is right, at least in the sense that it is not wrong, that they do what they must. Rights of this sort impose no obligations on others, however, for they merely pronounce morally blameless the agent who pursues his preservation.[13] Such a doctrine of rights lacks all nobility, Jaffa objects; it does not even secure the equality and right it aims to secure, for it contains no genuinely moral restraint. If one can get away with enslaving another group, then this Hobbesean doctrine has very little to say against it.

The solution to which Jaffa appeals in *Crisis* was an Aristotelianization of the regime. Lincoln's greatness resided not merely in his reaffirmation of the principle of equality in such a form as to stand unequivocally against slavery and in favor of government by consent—government of, by, and for the people. More than that, Lincoln reconceived the good of equality in Aristotelian terms. Those terms involved affirming the deeper truth of human inequality: some human beings belong to "the tribe of the eagle" and are indeed "better" and deserve to rule. Such, in effect, was Aristotle's argument in book 3 of his *Politics*. But the greatness of a man is moral greatness, superiority in virtue. The peak of moral virtue, as Jaffa presents the Aristotelian-Lincolnian position, is magnanimity: the great-souled man who, in his greatness and virtue, is beyond concern for honor and power. The great-souled man is truly superior, but has no interest in asserting his superiority. The theoretical truth, then, is inequality because of the differential achievement of virtue or excellence, but the practical or political truth is equality, for the truly excellent man will not raise claims to honor and rule, and those who do raise such claims are not truly excellent. "Like Aristotle's great souled man . . . he alone is worthy of the highest honor who holds honor itself in contempt."[14]

Forty years later, in *New Birth*, Jaffa has transformed many elements of his story. Lincoln is no longer presented as quiet critic and improver of the Founders; he and they agree on a (basically) Aristotelian doctrine of human equality and right. Lincoln, Jefferson, and behind them Locke emphasized doctrines that seem very different from Aristotle's, but Jaffa expends considerable energy establishing how, on Aristotelian grounds, they might arrive at such doctrines as are affirmed in the Declaration of Independence. The aim of this account is very similar to the earlier account in *Crisis*: to show that on Aristotelian grounds the American regime aimed at the rationally noble and just, that is, at virtue as understood by Aristotle. Jaffa's modification of the doctrine of *Crisis* probably has many causes, but the most apparent cause is the crisis in our understanding of Lincoln that Jaffa's account in *Crisis* produced.[15] In his effort to enlist Lincoln in a Strauss-inspired reformulation or refounding of America, Jaffa unwittingly fell into a serious self-contradiction. A central part of Lincoln's refounding or reformation of the regime was the effort to instill a reverence for the laws and the source of the laws, the fathers, and the principles on which they based their legislation. But one cannot carry out this Lincolnian project by, in effect, discrediting the Founders as Jaffa did. *Crisis of the House Divided* was itself a book divided. It tells us: follow Lincoln, the higher path, because the Founding was modern, and, therefore, imperfect and inadequate. Yet Lincoln tells us: follow the Founders. We are to follow the imperfect Founders as the solution to the imperfections of the Founders. That is the crisis into which *Crisis of the House Divided* fell.

Nonetheless, *Crisis* was a book that fit comfortably into what Jaffa had learned from Strauss. The problematically modern origin of the regime required improvement via a "return to the ancients," effected through Jaffa's Aristotelianizing Lincoln. But so far as this solution made Lincoln unintelligible and also served to undermine the very reverence Lincoln sought to instill by revealing the original foundation of American law to be low and ignoble, it left much to be desired. Nonetheless, it is possible to see the thread of deep continuity between *Crisis* and *New Birth* despite Jaffa's change of mind or rhetoric about the Founding and the nature of Lockean modernity. That continuity consists in the ongoing effort to reinterpret the regime in Aristotelian terms and thus to elevate it. Although that project of redescription is consistent with the kind of political science of modern liberal democracy that Strauss had called for,[16] nonetheless, Jaffa's approach to that redescription drove him ever farther from Strauss as a more detailed look at *New Birth* makes clear.

JAFFA'S *NEW BIRTH*

In many ways Strauss is a much more obtrusive presence in *New Birth* than he was in *Crisis*. For example, Strauss's name appears only twice in the earlier book, once in the acknowledgments section, once in the footnotes.[17] Strauss appears many more times in *New Birth*: in the preface, as the source for Jaffa's hermeneutic, once in a quotation that serves as one of four epigraphs to chapter 2, another time quoted in chapter 2, and three places in the footnotes.[18] More significantly, the polemical setting for *New Birth* very noticeably echoes Strauss. Jaffa frequently inveighs against positivism, historicism, relativism, and nihilism, all well-known targets of Strauss's work. Moreover, as Tom West, a close student of Jaffa, points out, "the first two chapters of *New Birth* are devoted, respectively to natural right and history," the title topics of Strauss's best-known book.[19] West concludes from that and other observations that "Jaffa's achievement [in *New Birth*] was made possible by the work of his teacher, the political philosopher Leo Strauss."[20] Another close student of Jaffa, Edward Erler, goes even further in drawing the link: "I believe that Harry V. Jaffa's *A New Birth of Freedom* is the book (or nearly the book) that Leo Strauss would have written had his principal concern been the crisis of America rather than the crisis of the West."[21]

There are, however, a number of strong counter-currents to those obtrusively Straussian elements of *New Birth*. In the one place in the text of *New Birth* where Jaffa quotes and then discusses a passage by Strauss, Jaffa disagrees with him. Jaffa quotes Strauss on the triumph of German historicism in post–World War II America, and then comments: "This victory of historicism and relativism, culminating in nihilism . . . actually occurred long before the date assigned it here by Strauss."[22] Moreover, as we have noticed, Jaffa identifies himself as an heir of Thomas Aquinas in his two Lincoln books.[23] Strauss most definitely did not consider himself an heir of Aquinas; indeed, he is well known for arguing that the kind of synthesis of reason and revelation that Aquinas attempted to construct was impossible to achieve, perhaps even misguided to attempt. Jaffa's relations to Strauss are somehow central to understanding the trajectory of his own thinking, but *New Birth*, at least on the surface, is decidedly ambiguous about that relation. The implication is that we must probe beneath the surface. Except for the preface and the echoes of the titles of Strauss's book on Plato's *Laws* in the titles of Jaffa's chapters 4 and 5, all other explicit references to Strauss appear in chapter 2, "The Declaration of Independence, the Gettysburg Address, and the Historians." In addition to being the one place in *New Birth* where the Gettysburg Address is highlighted at least to the degree that it appears in the chapter title, chapter 2 is also the concentrated locus of Strauss's presence in the book.

Chapter 2 of *New Birth* is in many ways an odd chapter. It is surely the most wide ranging in the book, concerning among other things, the Western political and philosophic experience from antiquity into the twentieth century. On the surface, the chapter is a critique of Becker's historicizing account of the Declaration; Jaffa uses the confrontation with Carl Becker to present his own non-historicizing account and defense of the truth of the Declaration's central proposition (as he, Jaffa, understands it): "[T]hat all men are created equal." So far as Jaffa's book is a rumination on the central claim of the Gettysburg Address, chapter 2 is the place where that occurs. Yet the scope of the chapter is epic. Jaffa's obtrusively odd organization of the chapter is provided by the four epigraphs Becker attached to his book. Indeed, a discussion of the epigraphs replaces a detailed discussion of Becker's book itself. Jaffa defends his odd procedure as follows:

> Becker prefaces his book on the Declaration with four epigraphs that declare in advance his disbelief in the truth of the document to which he has given such devoted labor. These epigraphs define, perhaps better than his text, the climate of opinions, within which his mind moved and within which American historiography has moved ever since.[24]

Two of Becker's epigraphs are drawn from Pascal's *Pensées*, one of which expresses doubt about nature, the other about the rationality of law; the two together about natural law (or natural right). The third is by Thomas Burnett, who speaks of the various changes in the English polity in the seventeenth and eighteenth centuries and implies that changes in political opinion, especially opinions about the grounds of legitimacy, occur in response to changes in the political facts "on the ground" and serve as rationalizations for those facts, or, at best, as "ideologies."

The fourth epigraph, which proves to be most important for the argument of Jaffa's chapter, is taken from Joseph de Maistre, the French counter-revolutionary. De Maistre, rejecting the universalism of the French revolutionaries, famously said, "I have seen, in my time, Frenchmen, Italians, Russians, etc . . . but as for Man, I declare I never met him in my life; if he exists, it is without my knowledge." There is no existing entity "man," to which the proposition "all men are created equal" could apply. All four epigraphs certainly have as their central tendency exactly what Jaffa says: a denial of the truth of the claim raised in the Declaration of Independence.

What makes Jaffa's use of Becker's epigraphs so striking is the fact that he prefaces his chapter with four epigraphs, all of which, like Becker's four, bear on the question of the truth of the claims raised in the Declaration.[25] Taking a page from Jaffa's own book, I propose to discuss Jaffa's chapter 2, and therewith the question of the relation between his late thought and that of Strauss, as well as the other topics we saw him raising in the preface via focusing on his four epigraphs.

The first of Jaffa's four epigraphs is by Lincoln, the next by Becker; the third is by Adolf Hitler, and the fourth by Strauss. All four concern, directly or indirectly, the "self-evident truths" affirmed in the Declaration of Independence. The quotation from Lincoln praises Thomas Jefferson for including in the Declaration, a document produced for a single people at a single moment in their national history, "an abstract truth, applicable to all men and all times." Lincoln identified as true the claims raised in the Declaration, whereas Becker, in the second epigraph, avers that it is "essentially a meaningless question" to ask if these claims are true. To say that the question is "meaningless" presumably means that the question cannot be given a yes or no answer; claims of that sort are mere values, neither true nor false.

The third epigraph is, perhaps surprisingly, taken from Hitler, who is quoted as saying, in effect, that it has been all down-hill for America since the South lost the Civil War. The civilization of the South, "based on the principle of slavery and inequality" contained "the embryo of a fundamentally great America." The Southern slavocracy principle of "slavery and inequality" is superior to, because presumably true, Jefferson and Lincoln's "all men are created equal." So Hitler shares with Becker a rejection of Lincoln's view that the Declaration presented "abstract truth" but on an entirely different ground. He does not find the propositions in the Declaration to be meaningless, but false.

The interesting question, however, is how Strauss relates to these various orientations towards the critical propositions in the Declaration. As opposed to Hitler, who saw America's greatness and prosperity stunted by the rejection of the system of slavery and inequality, Strauss attributes America's great power and prosperity, at least in part, to its dedication to the propositions of the Declaration. More significant in the context of Jaffa's book, however, is the way the quotation from Strauss relates to the quotation from Lincoln. Where Lincoln in his own voice had unequivocally declared those propositions to be an "abstract truth," Strauss refers to them as "the faith in which [America] was conceived and raised." Strauss pointedly does not call them truths. Their power, in Strauss's rendition, does not derive from their truth, but from their being "held." Strauss does not endorse the Lincolnian view: what he says could but need not be compatible with it. The quotation is taken from Strauss's *Natural Right and History*, the book Jaffa's first two chapters are so clearly echoing. Elsewhere in Strauss's book, in elucidating the thought of the ancients to whom he thought we must return, Strauss gave his judgment on the issue raised by Jaffa's four epigraphs: "Since men are then unequal in regard to human perfection, i.e., in the decisive respect, equal rights for all appeared to the classics as most unjust. They contend that some men are by nature superior to others and therefore, according to natural right, the rulers of others."[26] Strauss is closer to those who deny the truth of the propositions in the Declaration than he is to those like Becker who consider them meaningless, or to those like Jefferson and Lincoln, who hold them to be true.

If, as seems evident, the two guiding stars in Jaffa's firmament are Strauss and Lincoln, then here at the opening of chapter 2 of *New Birth* Jaffa makes clear the problem with which he is grappling: his two authorities are at odds with each other. In this disagreement, he sides with Lincoln and against Strauss.

The core of the chapter must be, then, an argument on behalf of the Lincolnian over the Straussian position. At the same time, that argument in favor of the proposition that "all men are created equal" is the commentary on the Gettysburg Address that Jaffa has promised. The examination of de Maistre's claim to know "Frenchmen, Italians, Russians, etc.," but not to know man provides context for Jaffa's effort to prove the truth that all men are created equal. Jaffa is very emphatic in endorsing the Lincolnian position: "[T]he equality proposition in the Declaration and Gettysburg Address is not merely a truth but a truism."[27] It is "a permanent truth," that is, not historically relative in any sense.

The argument Jaffa gives is not at all the same argument as he gave in *Crisis*, where he, in effect, distinguished between the abstract or theoretical truth of inequality (we now see, in agreement with Strauss) and the practical truth of equality. *New Birth* is more intransigently egalitarian, but it is still rooted in an Aristotelian argument. *New Birth*'s argument for equality is based on "the human capacity to abstract or separate what is intelligible from what is sensible." Equality is, therefore, "self-evident." It is not a mere matter of faith or belief. Indeed, its truth is "in no way dependent upon its recognition."[28]

The theory of the Declaration, Jaffa now argues, rests on "metaphysical freedom," that is, on "the freedom by which human minds perceive the universal in the particulars by which they denominate anything denominated by a common noun."[29] The mind is free because it can "abstract from all sensible qualities," from all matter in order to "think the universal." "Sensible reality can become intelligible reality."[30] This power allows us to identify the "whatness" of any being; to use Jaffa's example, to perceive a dog as a dog, rather than a mere collection of sensible qualities. The universal, "the idea of the dog," is "an abstraction from every possible dog," but essential to the perception of any dog.[31]

Metaphysical freedom allows us to perceive nature, and is the ground of "all the other freedoms that we . . . hold dear."[32] It is also the foundation of the equality claim:

> When the Declaration [of Independence] asserts that all men are created equal, it is asserting what is in one sense not merely a truth but a truism. All human beings are equally human beings, in the same sense that all dogs are equally dogs, and all chairs are equally chairs. Anything denominated by any common noun partakes equally in the class characteristics referred to by that noun.[33]

That equal participation has, Jaffa insists, direct political relevance. It dissolves, for example, the professed racial basis for slavery and discrimination:

> If we say then that the Constitution, being based upon the principles of the Declaration, is color blind, we say what must be true because the idea of man is color blind. It is color blind because every common noun is lacking color or any other sensible quality. Dogs and chairs, as dogs and chairs, are not white dogs and chairs or black dogs and chairs. And human beings, as human beings, are not white or black human beings, or humans of any other color.[34]

The mind forms these classes by induction, not deduction. These truths of class character are not deduced or derivative from other truths—they are "self-evident."[35] The classifications made or discovered by the mind have an order to them, the order of genus, species, and variety.[36] The largest politically relevant classification appears to be into the classes of God-man-beast.

> The distinction between man, beast, and God, as set forth in the first book of Aristotle's *Politics*, remains the framework of the thought of the Declaration of Independence, and the difference between man and beast, on the one hand, and man and god on the other, remains self-evident and definitive.[37]

By "definitive" he seems to mean "definitional," identifying the truly essential differences.

From the threefold classification of God-man-beast, Jaffa derives a more precise notion of what the equality of human beings qua human beings means or implies. From the differences among the three,

> we know that any attempt of human beings to rule other human beings, as if the former were gods, and the latter beasts, is wrong. That is why the rule of law—ruling and being ruled in turn—is the only intrinsically just arrangement by which human beings can rule one another. This is a permanent truth, and one in no way dependent upon its recognition.[38]

Slavery or anything other than democratic rule is wrong because it involves, Jaffa implies, a kind of "class-jumping"—it involves raising claims to godliness by some and a reduction to beastliness for others. If that kind of class-jumping is ruled out by nature or being itself, then the mandate that "all men are created equal" follows.

This argument supplies not only Jaffa's vindication of Jefferson and Lincoln, but also his refutation of Strauss. The argument undoubtedly has elegance and a certain simplicity, but is it true? Do we not require a good deal more in order to draw the political conclusions Jaffa wishes to draw? What about the classical position to which Strauss adverted? All men may be equally men but some men have virtue to a higher degree than others and thus derive a claim to rule. Does the argument about species character really rule this out? All chairs are chairs, but are not some chairs better chairs than others? Sturdier perhaps? Or more comfortable? All wolves are wolves, but are there not leaders, even natural leaders of the pack?

Jaffa does not even pause to consider the kinds of moral/political critiques of essentialist argument raised by postmodern critics like Jacques Derrida. If each being is what it is by virtue of a species-defining quality, then that quality provides grounds for hierarchical ordering or ranking of the members of the class. If man is defined as the rational animal, the traditional definition that Jaffa appears to accept, then it certainly appears that some human beings are, indeed, more human than others to the degree that their rational faculties are more developed and rule the whole man to a greater degree. This is precisely the idea that Aristotle himself endorsed and Strauss was explicating in his observation that the classics rejected human equality as "most unjust." Jaffa's way of construing the being of the beings leaves no room for the central Aristotelian categories of actual and potential and thus ignores the inegalitarian implications or possibilities of classical metaphysical realism.

Jaffa's account of equality in *New Birth* is more theoretical than the argument in *Crisis*. Like the argument in *Crisis*, it looks to Aristotle and Aristotelian themes for support. Instead of looking to Aristotle on the human things, however, it looks to Aristotelian ontology, another major break with Strauss's way of reading the ancients. In *New Birth*, Jaffa reminds us more than a little of Dante, who, in his *De Monarchia*, presented an argument for universal monarchy on the basis of Aristotelian metaphysics, not his political science.[39]

Jaffa's *New Birth* represents a turn not only in the substance of what he concludes about the American Founders and Lincoln's relation to them, but more deeply in the type of reasoning that Jaffa deploys. His new account of the truth of equality (and rights?) allows him to escape some of the tangles and troubles that beset him in *Crisis*, but it brings its own set of difficulties. Probably the greatest of these should be apparent from the earlier quotation from *Natural Right and History*: the classics, including Aristotle, "contend that some men are by nature superior to others and therefore, according to natural right the rulers of others." From their common ontological premises, Aristotle himself draws the very opposite conclusion from the one Jaffa draws.

Jaffa recognizes the problem when he asks, how is it "that in the long experience of mankind, the self-evident truths of the Declaration of Independence had never, before 1776, been the basis of the experiment of popular self-government?"[40] Prior to 1776 the trichotomy of God, man, and beast led not to political life based on equality, but to divine rights of kings, or to the classical doctrine of human inequality, as in Plato's "myth of the metals."[41] "Thus one sees that the inequality between man, beast, and God has been the source of two diametrically different doctrines of the proper relationship between man and his government: the doctrine that human government requires inequality as its principle, and the doctrine that it requires equality." Jaffa embarks on the enterprise "to discover the cause or causes of this difference."[42] This inquiry must, at the same time, be the quest for the differences between Jaffa and his teacher Strauss.

Jaffa presents a long and quite interesting account of how Christianity grew up within the Roman Empire, and of how its first fruit was divine right of kings rather than the Declaration's equality doctrine. The details of Jaffa's story are not needed here, but several observations about his account are necessary. The structure of his broader argument would seem to require that he give an explanation of why Plato and especially Aristotle (and Strauss) did not see the political implications of species equality as Jefferson and Lincoln allegedly do, but he does not address this question. Instead, he begins his account with the advent of the Roman Empire and the growth of Christianity within it. In passing, he concedes that the ancient world (pre-Roman Empire) was "a world of inequality" that was transformed into a world of equality by the leveling and universalizing effects of the Roman conquest. That is, the account does not even begin to explain what most requires explaining. Although Christianity did not realize the equality principle right away, the ground for it was laid in the Gospels. "Through Jesus, God's promise to Abraham became promises for all mankind. In respect to these promises, it can now be said 'that all men are created equal.'"[43] Most significantly, Jaffa concludes his long discussion with the following very telling admission: "Whether the doctrine of equality in the Gospels was knowable by unassisted human reason as a doctrine of the natural law, apart from divine revelation, is not a question that needs to be decided here."[44] Jaffa speaks of "the doctrine of equality of the Gospels"; he does not tell us if this is the same as the doctrine of human equality he has derived from the nature of species and the trichotomy of God, man, and beast, or something different. If the same, then Jaffa's dodging of the question of whether reason alone could establish it seems out of place, for he has just professed to do just that, insisting while doing so that the claim of equality is a "truism" and "self-evident." If Gospel equality and species equality are different from each other, then we are forced to wonder how they relate to each other and to the "all men are created equal" assertion of Jefferson and Lincoln. Can it be that Jaffa's deeper view is that the equality claim of the Declaration requires an amalgamation of both species equality and Gospel equality, the latter of which apparently cannot be established rationally, or at least has not been established rationally by Jaffa? Is Jaffa's point that, despite his many claims about reason's power, politics in America must be theologized in order to find its ground?

In any case, the statement about Gospel equality and unassisted human reason occurs long after Jaffa has provided what seemed to be his rational proof for the equality proposition in his argument for species equality and the trichotomy of God, man, beast. Jaffa's late admission can mean only that he does not consider that he has as yet established the "doctrine of equality . . . by unassisted human reason." This is a telling admission, for it coheres with the impression that the arguments he has forwarded for equality are not very solid. That all men are men, that is, participate in the universal man, says nothing whatever about whether there is a natural principle of authority within the species.

By the time Jaffa comes to the end of his narration of the supplanting of divine right of kings by divine right of the people (i.e., by the doctrine of the original equality and the doctrine of rights), he has quietly but clearly withdrawn his earlier claim that the equality proposition can be rationally established on the basis of the arguments he has produced. The equality proposition is a result of Christianity, not reason, and Christianity, he very strongly suggests, is the (necessary?) result of purely secular developments, that is, of the overcoming of the ancient city by the Roman Empire. "After Rome conquered the ancient world and Caesar conquered Rome, there was but one city, and there could be but one paramount law and, with equal reason, but one God."[45] The condition of the world under Rome required the rule of the one God. "Only a transcendent God whose rule of the universe was unchallengeable, since he was the only God, corresponded with Rome's supposedly unchallengeable rule of the human world."[46]

Jaffa's analysis sounds like a naturalistic account of the coming of Christianity, reminiscent of Machiavelli, Gibbon, Hegel, or Tocqueville. That analysis leaves us with a series of puzzles about Jaffa's position, however. It would appear that the equality principle is not rationally true (at least not on any grounds Jaffa presents), but has become persuasive to mankind because of a certain history. Equality is not a truism, nor a self-evident truth; it is a contingent belief, a matter of faith, persuasive for reasons Jaffa thinks he can explain. But as Jaffa quite forcefully points out, "what is persuasive is not the same as what is true."[47] It is in that very context that Jaffa reminds us that the "limits of action are not the limits of thought, [but] the limits of action may . . . impose limits upon the manner in which the thought that directs action is expressed."[48] The immediate subject of this sentence is Dante, but it is difficult not to apply Jaffa's observation to himself. As Jaffa says,

> Sometimes the best argument is the least persuasive, and the most persuasive is far from being the best. That those who dissemble often do so in the cause of injustice does not mean that those who dissemble may not do so in the interest of justice.[49]

The various lines of the argument converge in the suggestion that Jaffa is himself the one who dissembles in the interest of justice. His dissembling takes the form of distorting the thought of the American Founders by assimilating them into the classics and Christianity to a much greater degree than is warranted. It takes the form also of apparently endorsing the equality proposition and apparently endorsing arguments like ontological realism and the trichotomy of beings as supports for the equality proposition. Perhaps most revealingly, his dissembling takes the form of obtrusively endorsing Strauss, while only slightly less obtrusively breaking with Strauss. In the deepest bowels of his argument, however, Jaffa appears to return to the surface of his claims—he remains with Strauss, but dissembles greatly in order to do so. At the end of the day, Jaffa seems to endorse a position rather like Strauss's: belief in the propositions of the Declaration is a matter of ancient faith. They may be useful beliefs but, he implies, it is not evident that they are true beliefs.

We can make sense of Jaffa's peregrinations along the following lines. He started with Strauss, but Strauss had a tension-filled and nearly contradictory position on America. He saw America in a dual light—as a product and partaker (in large part) in modernity, but also as the "last best hope on earth" for all that is politically valuable in the world today. For all his reservations about modernity, Strauss was, nonetheless, a friend and partisan (so far as his philosophic temperament allowed partisanship) of America.[50] But he necessarily came across as a lukewarm friend of America. Not only did some of Strauss's students and friends understand him thus, but so did many, indeed most, of his enemies—and his enemies are many. His suspect political loyalties remain one of the sources of enmity to him. He sought to support America in the modern world as part of reviving the political philosophy of the ancients. But reviving the ancients stood in tension with supporting America. Jaffa, in effect, attempts to domesticate Strauss, to make a warmer defense of America that at the same time remains loyal to the broader causes Strauss championed—political philosophy as opposed to positivism and historicism (two targets of *New Birth*), and the ancients as opposed to the moderns. Jaffa has had to modify Straussian orthodoxy substantially, in the expression of his thought if not in his understanding of things, in order to effectuate the deeper rapprochement between Strauss and America that he seeks. In a great act of loyalty, Jaffa became disloyal to Strauss. By his own testimony that is perfectly legitimate. If I am correct in my attempt to reconstruct the levels of Jaffa's project, it should come as no great surprise that many of his historical arguments are less than persuasive, and that some of his philosophic arguments are inadequate.

Let me close by paraphrasing a passage quoted already from a review of *New Birth* by Edward Erler. *New Birth* is definitely not a book Leo Strauss would have written, but it is a book that Jaffa thinks Strauss should have written if he (Strauss) took as seriously as he should have the great importance of America in the modern world. So far as America is the political hope for a solution to the crisis of modernity, both modernity and America, Jaffa thinks, require a different presentation than Strauss gave them.

NOTES

1. Harry Jaffa, *A New Birth of Freedom* (Lanham, MD: Rowman and Littlefield, 2000), xi.
2. Ibid.
3. Ibid., xii.
4. Ibid., xi.
5. Ibid.
6. Ibid., xii.
7. Ibid.

8. Ibid., xi–xii.
9. Harry V. Jaffa, *Crisis of the House Divided: An Interpretation of the Issues in the Lincoln-Douglas Debates* (Garden City, NY: Doubleday, 1959), 314.
10. Ibid., 319, 329.
11. Second Treatise, §§8, 54.
12. *Crisis*, 318.
13. Ibid., 323–324.
14. *Crisis*, 218.
15. For a fuller account see Catherine Zuckert and Michael Zuckert, *The Truth about Leo Strauss* (Chicago: University of Chicago Press, 2006), 240–243.
16. See *Truth*, 198–202.
17. *Crisis*, 4, 435n.21.
18. *New Birth*, xii, 73–74, 83–84, 500n.2, 505nn.17, 20.
19. Tom West, "Jaffa's Lincolnian Defense of the Founding," *Interpretation* 28 (Spring 2001): 279–296.
20. Ibid., 279.
21. Edward Erler, "Philosophy, History, and Jaffa's Universe," *Interpretation* 28 (Spring 2001): 245.
22. Jaffa, *New Birth*, 84.
23. Ibid., xi.
24. Ibid., 102.
25. Ibid., 73.
26. Leo Strauss, *Natural Right and History* (Chicago: University of Chicago Press, 1954), 134–135.
27. *New Birth*, 120.
28. Ibid., 117–121.
29. Ibid., 119.
30. Ibid.
31. Ibid., 120.
32. Ibid., 120.
33. *New Birth*, 120.
34. Ibid.
35. Ibid.
36. Ibid.
37. Ibid.
38. Ibid., 120–121.
39. *New Birth*, 146–149.
40. Ibid., 121.
41. Ibid., 124.
42. Ibid., 124.
43. Ibid., 150.
44. Ibid., 152.
45. Ibid., 142.
46. Ibid., 140.
47. Ibid., 148.
48. Ibid.
49. Ibid., 124.
50. See *Truth about Leo Strauss*, 74–79.

NINETEEN

A Reply to Michael Zuckert's "Jaffa's New Birth: Harry Jaffa at Ninety"

I am grateful to Michael Zuckert for his kindness in remembering my birthday—something that I am trying hard to forget—but I am still more grateful for the seriousness and competence with which he has subjected my work to analysis and scrutiny.

The main theme of Zuckert's critique is the difference between my thought and that of Leo Strauss, notwithstanding my professions of loyalty and fidelity to Strauss's teaching.

> The character of Jaffa's modification of Strauss probably best comes to view if we note that Strauss was a thinker of dualities—ancients and moderns, Jerusalem and Athens, poetry and philosophy, the city and man. Jaffa, on the contrary is a thinker of unities: he collapses Athens and Jerusalem, poetry and philosophy, and goes a long way toward assimilating Strauss's ancients and moderns, for example, when he argues that John Locke, a preeminent modern according to Strauss, is presenting what Aristotle would have said had he lived at Locke's time. What Strauss has put asunder Jaffa attempts to join together.

I would here, first of all, remind the reader of Churchill's essay on "Consistency in Politics," which I quoted at length in my reply to Kraynak. Zuckert says, correctly, that Strauss was a thinker of dualities. But there are few if any of the great dualities, with respect to which one cannot find contrary assertions in Strauss's writings. As in the case of Edmund Burke, cited by Churchill, there is, however, always a singular purpose that is consistently served by the apparent dualities. In my essay on "Strauss at One Hundred," I said that in all his work, Strauss's intention was to address the crisis of the West. At the heart of Western civilization were the principles of reason and revelation, whose symbolic homes were, respectively, Athens and Jerusalem. Neither of these principles could refute the other, but their dynamic interplay was the life-giving source of the greatness of our great tradition. Athens and Jerusalem may have disagreed on what they believed to be the "one thing needful." They nonetheless agreed, almost entirely, on the moral foundations of civilized existence. In Strauss's world of dualities, there is always compensating unity. The crisis of the West, to which Strauss addressed himself, is precisely the decline of both reason and revelation, as sources of the meaning and purpose of life. Historicism and relativism, culminating in nihilism, have corroded not only our understanding but our belief that there is anything to understand in the great works and deeds which constitute the glory of the West. Whether any particular work looked ultimately to Athens or to Jerusalem, Strauss examined it relentlessly and passionately and with unsurpassed keenness of intellect.

He sought in the art informing each a reflection of that greater creativity that informs the mystery of the cosmos. He often praised the surpassing greatness of the art of Shakespeare, but he would always add that there was something greater than Shakespeare's art, in the nature that made Shakespeare possible. One could not read a truly great book with Strauss, without believing, at the end, that the author, whether right or wrong, had served the purpose for which he had been created. There is accordingly always a singular end underlying Strauss's exoteric dualities.

A great deal of Strauss's writing is devoted to refuting those who have ridiculed the Bible, as well as those who have ridiculed Plato or Aristotle or Xenophon. In the one case he appeared as a defender of revelation, in the others as a defender of reason. But his intention was always to defend the civilization that was built upon both. Strauss also believed that, notwithstanding the theoretical differences between reason and revelation, there was, as we have said, substantial agreement on morality. The dialogue on the differences of the two great principles need not, Strauss thought, disturb the harmony of moral reasoning. In exploring this harmony, I have, I believe, been faithful to Strauss's intention.

One ground of Strauss's opposition to any attempted synthesis of reason and revelation may be found in his opposition to modern philosophy. The great enterprise of the seventeenth century, notably in Descartes, Spinoza, and Hobbes, was to provide a geometric demonstration of the nature of the moral and political. It was the essence of the modern enterprise to leave no ground for either Socratic skepticism or biblical faith. In fact, in the world we now inhabit the aforesaid enterprise, to abolish both skepticism and faith, has succeeded remarkably. The morality recognized by both Socrates and the Bible has been utterly discredited, not only in our universities, but to a great degree in our churches as well. But modern philosophy has failed utterly to provide that account of the Whole that was to have proved its superiority and justified its authority. Instead of a superior understanding of the objects both of moral and of metaphysical knowledge, it has ended in a radical denial even of the possibility of knowing. If this was merely theoretical ignorance, as in the dilemmas in which most Socratic dialogues seem to end, it might, like the dialogues, have led to renewed and reinvigorated inquiry. That ever renewed inquiry, which pronounced the unexamined life to be not worth living, was not a commitment to any particular resolutions of the dilemmas, but to an inquiring way of life. However, the virtues of the skeptical life celebrated by the heirs of Socrates closely resembled the virtues of that other way of life, which consisted of obedience to the commandments of the living God. The modern attempt to provide a scientific account of reality has ended, not in knowledge superior to that of Jerusalem or Athens, but rather to the abandonment of any idea of knowing anything about the mystery of the universe, or of the conflict of good and evil within it. It has led to the abandonment of the morality that has sustained Western civilization. Postmodernism has proved to be an aimless wandering in a chamber of horrors. Athwart the gates of that postmodernism Leo Strauss has cried "Stop!"

Modern philosophy had undertaken to solve the differences of reason and of revelation by transcending them. The doubt that afflicted the conclusions of Socratic reason and of biblical faith could be eliminated, it was believed, and the scientific method made accessible to the common man no less than to philosophers. Thus wisdom would be accessible to all. This would point the way to democracy or, more precisely, democracy understood as the general will. This, however, has resulted, in one instance, in the belief that the general secretary of the Central Committee of the Communist Party represented the wisdom and authority of the common man. Another version claimed that the evolutionary process, as discerned by science, led to the absolute right of the white over the black race, and later to the absolute right of the Aryan race, embodied in its leader. Still another version, milder in practice but not very different in theory, believed that constitutional government could be set aside for a pure democracy of unlimited majority rule. An elected government of the common man would turn over the application of power to a highly trained bureaucracy that would bring scientific method to bear upon the problems of society. Science and democracy would march in lockstep. We can see that the distance between communism and progressivism is not great. We can also see that the obstructions to tyranny by constitutionalism are the only defenses left to us. And the only coherent defense of constitutionalism is in the legacy of Athens and Jerusalem.

Zuckert's major preoccupation is the relationship between my thought and Strauss's, particularly as found in *A New Birth of Freedom*. The reader should know, however, that that is a subject explored at greater length in *The Truth About Leo Strauss*, a book authored by him and that other very distinguished Professor Zuckert, his wife. I am grateful to both for the attention they have given my work, and my gratitude goes beyond any agreements or disagreements. I should also mention, however, that I am planning a collection of my own essays on Strauss, and I am writing an autobiographical preface to that collection, which will include a more extensive response to their critique than is possible here.

We have seen that, according to Professor Zuckert, "Strauss was a thinker of dualities"; I, on the other hand, he says, collapse Strauss's great dualities into unities. The preeminent example, according to Zuckert, is that I make "John Locke, a preeminent modern according to Strauss," represent "what Aristotle would have said had he lived at Locke's time."

I would remind the reader of what I have already written on this theme in my reply to Professor Kraynack. In Strauss's essay "On Classical Political Philosophy," a work of unsurpassed authority in the Strauss canon, Strauss finds the maxim that best expresses the meaning of the best regime—the central topic in classical political philosophy—in the words of Thomas Jefferson. This maxim is preceded by Jefferson's agreement with John Adams, an agreement with which Strauss would enthusiastically concur, "that there is a natural aristocracy among men." The maxim itself, quoted by Strauss, declares "that that form of government is the best which provides the most effectually for the pure selection of these natural *aristoi* into the offices of government." Here is the doctrine that unifies Jefferson and classical political philosophy. But it also unifies Jefferson, the American Founding "as originally intended," Locke, and Strauss. Here is *e pluribus unum* exhibited in its most uncompromising form! I do not think that anyone can suppose it was inadvertence that led Strauss to present the author of the Declaration of Independence as a preeminent authority on classical political philosophy. Nor is it possible to suppose (unless one is Garry Wills) that the influence of Locke on the Declaration is other than paramount.

"The natural aristocracy I consider the most precious gift of nature for the instruction, the trusts, and the government of society. And indeed it would have been inconsistent in creation to have formed man for the social state, and not to have provided virtue and wisdom enough to manage the concerns of the society." The foregoing Jeffersonianism is unsurpassed Aristotelianism. I do not see how one can fail to see the irrelevance of a merely chronological divide between ancients and moderns. Jefferson's Aristotelianism, like Aristotle's, is based upon resemblances and differences of man, beast, and God, resemblances and differences accessible to all human beings at all times by means of sense perception. The recognition of these differences is the ground of the proposition that all men are created equal. The opinion that some human beings are well born, while others are basely born, and many other such distinctions, assumes a distinction within the species that resembles that between species. This fallacy finds its ultimate expression in the idea of chattel slavery that found its place within the original 1787 Constitution of the United States. To put the matter as succinctly as possible, a chattel is a piece of moveable property without a rational will (a dog, a horse, a chair, a table); a person (that is, a human being) is possessed of a rational will. By the law of the antebellum Constitution, Negro slaves were at once chattels and human persons. What was legally possible, however, was logically impossible and, ultimately, morally impossible. The drama of this conflict forms the substance of American history.

On the question of the meaning of the proposition that all men are created equal, Zuckert takes note of my argument, drawn from Aristotle, that every common noun—man, no less than dog or chair—is a universal applying equally to every particular to which it applies, so that one chair, or one dog, or one human being, is no more or less a dog or chair or a human being, than another. Lincoln had praised Jefferson for incorporating in the Declaration "an abstract truth applicable to all men and all times." I had noted, on Aristotelian grounds, that every common noun is an intelligible form abstracted from a sensible form, just as every sensible form is abstracted from sensible matter. I have made this argument in many of my publications including—as noted by Zuckert—*A New Birth of Freedom*. I have also argued that it is a violation of natural right—and of the laws of nature and of nature's God—for one man to assert a right to rule another, as if his nature is superior to the others. This would be like asserting that the nature of the one human being differed from that of another as the nature of the rider differs from that of the horse he is riding. No human being differs from any other human being as any human being differs from any one of the lower animals.

To this Zuckert objects: "All men may be equally men but some men have virtue to a higher degree than others and thus derive a claim to rule. Does the argument about species character really rule this out? All chairs are chairs, but are not some chairs better chairs than others? . . . All wolves are wolves, but are there not leaders, even natural leaders of the pack?"

Here I remind the reader of Strauss's agreement with Jefferson, that there is a natural aristocracy among men, and that the best form of government is the one that provides the most effectually for the pure selection of these natural *aristoi* into the office of government. But Jefferson also reminds us that there is an artificial, or false, aristocracy that is an enemy of good government and the rights of mankind. In fact, throughout history there have been ruling classes, or royal families, asserting a superiority of birth, which amounts to a claim to being a superior species. Strauss also warns that no wise man would ever assert a right to rule based upon wisdom. The assertion of such a right is a sure sign of a lack of wisdom. Throughout history, however, mankind has been vulnerable to absurd claims of natural or divinely appointed superiority. The Declaration says that all such claims are false, and that the only valid basis of the right to rule is the consent of the governed, on the basis of the rights with which we are all equally endowed by our Creator.

I would, therefore, reply to Zuckert that the claim of a species-like superiority has in fact been the basis of the most invidious of the many false claims to rule. The idea that some human beings are either gods, or descended from gods, or descended from ancestors who had a proximity to gods, has been the basis of political authority for most of the human race during most of its history. The Declaration of Independence asserts the irrationality of all such claims. But the recognition of the equality of human beings within their species does not inhibit the recognition of those qualities—those virtues—in which human beings as members of the same species are nonetheless different and unequal. In fact it is only by first recognizing the rights with respect to which all human beings are equal that we can distinguish those qualities, or virtues, with respect to which human beings differ widely, but which the political community needs to select into the offices of government. Government requires armed forces, and these require good officers, and in particular good generals. But good generals or good judges or good economists or good doctors or good pilots cannot be selected by lot. They must be selected on the basis of training and experience. In every case, the many want to be governed by the few they believe are wise in the matters in which they are to have authority. The ancient wisdom of classical political philosophy, as expounded by Leo Strauss, is that all of us want in every instance, so far as possible, to be governed by those who know, by the wise. And this is precisely true of the community of those associated on the basis of natural equality, and who set up a government to increase the security of their natural rights, who want that government to know as much as possible how to achieve its ends. It is thus the recognition of the differences within the species—which constitute that natural aristocracy in which, as we have seen, Adams and Jefferson believed, no less than Aristotle and Leo Strauss. It is by the recognition of these differences among the fellow citizens, that the natural equality of the state of nature is transformed into government by the natural *aristoi*.[1]

To understand exactly how the claims of equality and inequality—of democracy and aristocracy—are reconciled, let us recur once more to the social contract. This is the agreement, the necessarily unanimous agreement, whereby human beings, being equally free and independent, no one having authority over another, are transformed into fellow citizens, each equally subject to a government with lawful authority over them all. The agreement by which this transformation is accomplished is one in which the exercise of the right that each individual has by nature to preserve his life is transferred to a government. The power of the entire community can now be called forth, organized, and applied by the government to the protection of each. The agreement by which this is achieved is, as we have noted, unanimous. No one is bound by it, or becomes a fellow citizen, who does not agree to it. And everyone agreeing agrees to share equally in the advantages and burdens of citizenship.

No one can, at a time of danger, say that his life is more valuable than others, and ought not, therefore, to be put at risk. No one can claim that his property ought not to be taxed to support the government he expects to protect that property. This is the basic idea underlying the meaning of the equal protection of the law.

To complete the foregoing, we recall that the rights that are originally equal are the rights with which we have been "endowed by our Creator." These rights, as the foundation of the aforesaid social contract, restore the relationship of God and law, which characterized the ancient city, before the conquests of Caesar and the subsequent ascent of Christian monotheism. No social contract was needed as long as it was believed the law was given directly by God (or a god). The Lockean social contract restores a breach in the web of argument that sustained classical political philosophy in a manner that Aristotle could only have approved. By this contract the authority of God does not come down from a prophet, but up from the people. The legislative function of each people is moreover performed with prudential regard to the circumstances of that people. But this authority is not a blank entitlement, but rather an enfranchisement to fulfill the purpose God had in making the foregoing endowment. Jefferson once remarked that the ultimate repository of the principles of the Constitution was in the people, *en masse*. They, he said, were free of everything "but moral law." If the people, whether by the majority, or even unanimously, acted outside the boundaries of the morality implied in their God-given rights, they were no longer a people within the meaning of the Declaration of Independence. This is shown, within the Declaration itself, by the appeal of the Congress to the "Supreme Judge of the World" for the rectitude of their intentions. The Congress implies that they would not have been able to rely, as they did, upon the support of divine providence, had they not been confident that they were acting within the bounds approved by that Supreme Judge. We are also reminded of that other stricture of Jefferson, in the Notes on Virginia: "And can the liberties of a nation be thought secure when we have removed their only firm basis, a conviction in the minds of the people that these liberties are of the gift of God? That they are not to be violated but with his wrath? Indeed, I tremble for my country when I reflect that God is just; that his justice cannot sleep forever." This passage, which Lincoln loved, has much, perhaps everything, of the philosophy and theology that informed Lincoln's Second Inaugural Address. We might add that it also has much in common with the convictions of John Brown.

We conclude that the function of the Lockean social contract, as understood by Jefferson and Lincoln, and by Leo Strauss in the writings we have cited, does not justify the radical individualism imputed to the social contract, as in the writings of Thomas Hobbes. We would add that the Straussian argument, which is in harmony with Jefferson and Jefferson's Locke, is the only one consistent with Strauss's overriding concern with the crisis of the West, and is, indeed, the only one consistent with its salvation. It is, therefore, classical political philosophy in a form sanctioned by the practical wisdom at the heart of classical political philosophy, in a world dominated by postclassical, Christian monotheism.

One of the most emphatic expressions of Strauss's dedication to the central and unifying purpose of his life and work is in the beginning of *The City and Man*. That book was published in 1964, but the preface is dated July 1963. The first two paragraphs are extraordinary in their apparent difference from what both Professor Zuckert and I might think of as orthodox Straussianism. For that reason, I give them in full, lest I be suspected of selective quotation.

> It is not self-forgetting and pain-loving antiquarianism nor self-forgetting and intoxicating romanticism which induces us to turn with passionate interest, with unqualified willingness to learn, towards the political thought of classical antiquity. We are impelled to do so by the crisis of our time, the crisis of the West.
>
> It is not sufficient for everyone to obey and to listen to the Divine message of the City of Righteousness, the Faithful City. In order to propagate that message among the heathen, nay, in order to understand it as clearly and as fully as is humanly possible, one must also consider to what extent man could discern the outlines of that City if left to himself, to the proper exercise of his own powers. But in our age it is much less urgent to show that political philosophy is the indispensable handmaid of theology than to show that political philosophy is the rightful queen of the social sciences, the sciences of man and of human affairs; even the highest law court in the land is more likely to defer to the contentions of social science than to the Ten Commandments as the words of the living God.[2]

A full commentary on these two short paragraphs, with comparative analyses with what Strauss has written elsewhere on these topics, could fill at least a hundred pages. We begin with a short but inadequate notice of the antiquarianism and romanticism that Strauss dismisses in the first sentence. A movement that was both romantic and antiquarian was the conservatism brought into being by the Holy Alliance that defeated Napoleon. The goal of this movement was to turn back the French Revolution, and especially Napoleon's uprooting of the class distinctions of feudalism. The Holy Alliance sought to revive the ancient regime throughout Europe, with its union of altar and crown. It meant to stand astride the tide of egalitarian liberalism and shout "Stop!" When the aforesaid conservatism crossed the Atlantic in the 1830s, the defense of the *ancien regime* was replaced by the defense of slavery. This was the origin of what became American conservatism. What in Europe became the celebration of a heroic Middle Ages[3] in America became the utopian vision of the Old South, the South of *Gone With the Wind*. Even today, the stalwart loyalists of the Old South (like the *Confederates in the Attic* of a recent best seller) are, at one and the same time, harmless eccentrics living in their own imaginary world, and eccentrics who are anything but harmless, and who can be transformed at any moment into lynch mobs.

We see that in the thought that preceded Strauss there is a thin line dividing antiquarianism from romanticism. In the Germany of Strauss's younger days, there was an almost fanatical preoccupation with classical scholarship, animated in part by the belief that Germany was destined to be the reincarnation of ancient Athens.[4] The partisans of the Old South also identified with ancient Athens, especially with the conviction that a high civilization always rested upon a foundation of slavery.[5] Strauss in his youth may have been influenced by this celebration of the classics. Now clearly it is among the causes of the crisis of the West, not part of the solution, and he does not want to be identified with it in any way.

The next sentence is among the most astonishing Strauss, or perhaps anyone else in our time, ever wrote. On the surface he appears almost as a Billy Graham, peddling his own version of "the Divine message of the City of Righteousness, the Faithful City." Notwithstanding the typographical eccentricity—all of which is Strauss's, and all of which seems to persuade us that he is speaking of Jerusalem—he never mentions it by name. In what follows, however, he invites us to consider "to what extent man could discern the outlines of that City if left . . . to the proper exercise of his own powers." We would expect that the proper exercise of man's own unaided powers would discern the outlines of Athens, not of Jerusalem. Yet this city is said to be "the Faithful City," which can hardly be Athens. Yet without doubt "that City" is one city, not two. This seems almost wantonly to negate the most fundamental of all the dualisms Zuckert attributes to Strauss, and which I am said to undermine.

The rest of this paragraph is a single sentence, although it is divided by a semicolon which ought to have been a full stop. The first part of this bifurcated sentence begins with the remarkable assertion that "in our age it is much less urgent to show that political philosophy is the indispensable handmaid of theology." Strauss implies that although now it is much less urgent than it might be at some other time, there is no time at which it is not urgent to show political philosophy as the handmaid of theology. Unqualified and not contradicted, this assertion would place Strauss squarely in the camp of Thomas Aquinas. The cause of the aforesaid diminished urgency is the necessity "to show that political philosophy is the rightful queen of the social sciences, the sciences of man and of human affairs."

Now the sovereign source of the doctrine that political philosophy is the rightful ruler of the practical sciences is the first two chapters of the *Nicomachean Ethics*. Here is the unsurpassed, unequaled, and irrefutable statement of that case. There is no room here to repeat it in full, but according to Aristotle (and Strauss), political philosophy is to the other practical sciences what architecture is to the other sciences of building.

The original meaning of the word architect is "the one who rules the workmen." The architect himself is not a mason, or plumber, or electrician, or carpenter, nor does he necessarily possess any of their skills. But to the extent that he is a good architect, it is his design of the completed building, and especially his understanding of the use that the inhabitants of the building intend—or ought to intend—to make of it, that informs his art. It is not by any compulsion but by the right of this knowledge that the architect rules his subordinates. They see that the fulfillment of their work is only possible through the fulfillment of his.

Aristotle's account of what he calls *politike* is the ground of the idea that human life has a rational end or purpose, and that it can be ruled by reason, in great matters as in lesser ones. The highest end of human action is happiness, and the political philosopher is the architect of the structure of a life culminating in happiness. The *telos* of any building is the purpose of the life to be lived within it, and how that life contributes to the larger purpose of life. Just as the plumber and carpenter are workmen ruled by the architect, the architect is himself a plumber or carpenter in the service of that greater architect. According to Aristotle—and by the very nature of human existence—all the other arts and sciences, like that of the plumber and carpenter in relation to the architect—are inherently subject, within the polity, to the judgment of *politike*.

Strauss's rhetoric is designed to give effect to the Aristotelian doctrine of life as a rational enterprise. Consider now that happiness appears within the Declaration of Independence, first as a natural right of individuals, and then as the collective right of those same individuals joined by the social contract. We have confirmation of this in the inaugural address of George Washington, as first president of the United States, in which he declared "that the foundation of our national policy will be laid in the pure and immutable principles of private morality . . . since there is no truth more thoroughly established than that there exists in the economy and course of nature an indissoluble union between virtue and happiness." It is difficult to imagine a more succinct or pithy Aristotelianism. It is clear that for Washington and for the *aristoi* here represented, the pursuit of happiness, both privately and politically, meant the pursuit of virtue. Political philosophy is accordingly the architecture of virtue as it leads to happiness. This is what Strauss meant by calling for its recognition as the queen of the social sciences. In the unity of this argument, all dualisms would seem to dissolve. The ignorance of this argument, or its treatment as at most romantic antiquarianism, is among the profoundest symptoms of the crisis of the West.

NOTES

1. Consider the following anticipation of equality as the basis of aristocracy in Plato's *Menexenus*. It is from a report by Socrates of a funeral oration composed by Aspasia, who was also the reputed author of the celebrated funeral oration by Pericles, in Thucydides' history. "It is necessary then to demonstrate that the polity wherein our forefathers were nurtured was a noble one. . . . One man calls it 'democracy' . . . but it is in very truth an 'aristocracy.' . . . And while the most part of civic affairs are in the control of the populace they hand over the posts of government . . . to those who from time to time are deemed to be the best men . . . the one principle of selection is this: the man who is deemed wise and good rules and governs. And the cause of this our polity lies in our equality of birth."

2. Leo Strauss, *The City and Man* (Chicago: Rand McNally, 1964), 1.

3. E.g., Scott's novels, Tennyson's *Idylls of the King*, Wagner's operas.

4. See Charles Bambach, *Heidegger's Roots: Nietzsche, National Socialism, and the Greeks* (Ithaca: Cornell University Press, 2003). See especially, "Athens or Jerusalem?" p. 51–57.

5. One of the complaints of Booker T. Washington against former slaves was their passion for learning Greek and Latin, while ignoring the menial tasks that brought money. It is clear, however, that the slaves identified freedom with the classical culture most highly respected in the only world they knew, the world of their masters.

Epilogue

Leo Strauss (1899-1973) was the greatest mind in political philosophy in the twentieth century, and possibly in other centuries as well. That, I am well aware, is a judgment I share with very few, if any. His analysis of modernity, which was infinitely complex, can nonetheless be reduced to something very simple. The success of that branch of philosophy called science was so great that it consigned the rest of philosophy to the "dustbin of history." By eliminating formal and final causes from understanding the phenomena of existence, understanding itself was transformed into power. Whatever increased man's power over nature, to that extent represented the truth about nature. Increase in power over nature did not however increase power over human nature. Modern philosophy owed its success to narrowing its field so as to exclude human beings. Or, rather, to redefine man by making him into something subhuman. Only thus could one satisfy the premises of modern philosophy, and claim the rewards hitherto reserved to those who had claimed the divine right of kings. But the goodness of the fruits was not unequivocal. The power of science was indifferent to whether it fell into the hands of a Nazi or a Jew. The bulk of the "scientists" concerned with man have sought solutions to the human problem within the framework of the modern premises. Their efforts have been doomed to failure. No one other than Strauss has so mercilessly exposed the necessity of such failure or, rather, of the many failures now as numberless as the leaves of autumn. But the false premises of modernity are as deeply implanted in our culture as any articles of faith of revealed religion. Classical political philosophy, whose revival Strauss sought, and the seeds of which he planted, is now taking root in many far flung places, as his students become teachers in their own right. This renewed Reformation is our only hope of redemption from the barbarism of radical modernity into which we are falling.

Index